Soul Healing

Living beyond the pain of your past.

Tammy Smith, Ph.D.

LCCN 2006902037
ISBN 0-9777926-0-9

Unless otherwise noted, Scripture quotations are from the Holy Bible:
New International Version. Copyright 1973, 1978, 1984 by
International Bible Society.

Printed in the United States by Morris Publishing
3212 East Highway 30
Kearney, NE 68847
1-800-650-7888

FOR

Mike

Spencer

Shaeffer

Jesus

…the men who have changed me forever.

YOU ARE BEING PRAYED FOR.

A group of Christians has committed to ask God to do all that He wants through <u>Soul Healing</u> in each person who reads it.

Dear Reader, on your behalf, one of these caring people has held this book and prayed for you. They have recorded their initials on this page as a reminder that God loves you, is always working in you, and wants to reveal Himself to you.

Our prayer for you is that you will read the entire way through this book, even when you find doing so challenging. Pursue with intensity the healing and freedom you seek, trusting He will do it.

These initials testify to the belief that God delights to answer prayer – and will do so for you.

K·V.

To all who have shared your hearts with me over
the years and find a piece of your journey within the pages
of this book, rest assured that care has been taken to preserve your
identity. More importantly, I want you to know what a privilege I have
considered it to be invited to walk with you on the path of God's
movement in your heart, mind, and soul. I have treasured your
every word, learned many lessons from you, and been inspired
to greater faith because of what I've seen God do in you.
Thank you for allowing others to learn from your life.

ACKNOWLEDGEMENTS

There's no way I can put into words how grateful I am to Carol Young, Wendy McFarland, and Mike Borst. But, I am compelled to try...

Carol's dedication to God's vision for this book was unwavering. Her earnest prayer support, meticulous commitment to editorial detail, and sincere friendship blessed me over and over. Carol, you are a mentor full of wisdom, a soul friend who makes me laugh, and a true warrior for Jesus with whom I am thrilled to share this journey.

Wendy's level of personal support to this work overwhelmed me on a number of occasions. Her sacrificial effort, kind words of encouragement, and swift referencing assistance were stunning. Wendy, your loyalty, dedication, and sweet spirit were fuel to me to persevere, and your depth of belief in God's work through this book spurred me on.

Mike's strength of devotion to Christ in this endeavor and in his creative expression has impassioned me to a deeper excitement and vision about what God might want to do through this work. His level of giftedness, eye for excellence, and work ethic are unparalleled. Mike, your faithful friendship and commitment to God's purpose in me have blessed me beyond measure.

And to my husband...

Mike, you can't ever be given enough recognition for your enduring consistency, sacrificial support, and undying devotion to me, our boys, and God's best for us all. You have always championed my dreams, even when not convenient. You are a model of stability, surety, loyalty, and a man of the highest integrity. Honey, your input in my life has transformed me. You are my best teacher and my true love.

CONTENTS

INTRODUCTION

You were meant for more than you are experiencing right now. There is a life of peace and joy; an abundant life full of purpose, power, and victory that has your name on it, and no one else can live it for you. The problem is that deep hurts, unfulfilled longings, and general "What am I here for?" rumblings derail us from living life to the full. The ways in which we have been pained on this earth have taken a toll.

The issue is not *whether* we have been wounded. Emotional pain is part and parcel of life, so we can safely assume that every one of us has wounds. The issue is to discover *what* the damage from a particular hurt has been, and how it is keeping us from grasping all that God has for us in Christ Jesus. When God's intended abundant life eludes us, we are left hungry, longing for something more. Doesn't it sometimes feel like we are insatiable? All too often, even large amounts of the best things aren't enough.

People tend to fall into one of two overarching categories. They are either primarily looking to get or primarily looking to give. The first category of folks is driven by the inner void, and the attempt to satiate the emptiness. They unconsciously travel from person to event to substance to achievement in order to dull the gnawing ache. They dedicate themselves to trying to fill their barren soul. On the other hand, those who spend themselves freely, giving sacrificially from within, have come to fully grasp the Luke 9:24 concept – that in grappling to preserve one's life, it is lost; but in laying down the tight hold on one's self-centered desires for life to the full, it is mysteriously attained.

As we ask ourselves which description fits us, the answer is most certainly related to how we have negotiated the effects of our emotional wounds. The unhealed soul reacts to certain types of people, is constantly discontent in her most significant relationships, experiences pervasive dissatisfaction and restlessness no matter the circumstance, struggles with how often others disappoint him, feels lonely most of the time, rarely feels like he belongs in a crowd, compares herself with others, has an ongoing sense of inadequacy, and a whole host of other outworkings of unattended emotional wounds.

On the other hand, people walking in freedom from the cumulative effects of past hurts are the ones to whom we are attracted. What is it that draws us to these people? We can't quite put our finger on it, but we can sense their healed souls. Perhaps it's their peaceful attitudes, the way they take risks, how they navigate through their emotions, how well they listen, the level of authenticity they display, the freedom to laugh at themselves, the fact that they can endure conflict without being undone by it, or simply that they seem freed from the opinions of others. Whatever the case, they have something we want – be it freedom, power, presence, peace or any other attribute of an abundant life liver.

Life is like a coin. Picture holding one in your hand. You alone have the power to spend it any way you'd like. However, you can only spend it once. How will you spend yours? Trying to "get" or looking to give? Trapped in collateral damage from experiencing hurt, difficulty, and pain, or freed to move about in the self God created for you? There is *more* for you in Christ. The sole intention of this book is to free you that you might live out His truest purpose and deepest desire for you, resulting in your good, but ultimately for His glory.

1

The Intended Plan

There is another world, and it is in this one.
PAUL ELWARD

*For we are God's workmanship, created in Christ Jesus to do good works,
which God prepared in advance for us to do.*
EPHESIANS 2:10

Because your hands hold this book, there is a purpose in your reading it. While you might have a specific reason (someone gave it to you, you know the author, you wonder what the chair on the cover is all about), there is also a general pull to restoration for all who claim Christ. Some of you may immediately agree that your soul cries out to be brought back to its intended state. Others may not yet realize that the pervasive longing for "more," the struggle with contentment, and the desire to be special are all signs your deepest self yearns for a condition that you don't presently experience. You and I need restoration. We crave soul healing.

The phrase "soul healing" is meant to evoke the image of "He restores my soul" in Psalm 23:3, which is a picture of complete satisfaction. The message of this book is that He, God, can and will bring restoration to your inner being. A word study of "restores" from this verse captures the idea of being brought back, of refreshment, and movement back to the point of departure. Doesn't the mere idea of God taking you back to a place of pre-hurt move you? Even more hopeful, the restoration is not of circumstances or things. He restores my *soul*. A deeper look at "soul" reveals that it is most often used in Scripture to refer to one's inner self, related to one's preservation and sustenance or loss. Together, this concentrated look at Psalm 23:3 gives substance to "soul healing." God, our shepherd, will draw and refresh our inner selves, the heart of who we are, our very breath, back to Himself.

To undergird this concept, one look at the Scriptural idea of "shalom" reveals that all who claim Christ are drawn to it. While many think this Hebrew word means "peace," it more accurately conveys completeness, wholeness, health, well-being, and harmony.[1] The idea of soul healing is meant to evoke this biblical concept of peace captured in "shalom." Many Old Testament passages convey these nuances and demonstrate that the biblical vision for God's creation is completeness. We are not meant to have a life in pieces. Instead, implicit in shalom is the idea of "unimpaired relationships with others and fulfillment in one's undertakings."[2] "Unimpaired relationships?!?" Doesn't that sound refreshing? Said simply, you and I, as God's creation, are meant to experience a state of fulfillment from God's presence that results in deep peace and joy (Psalm 85:8, Numbers 6:23-27).

The chapters that follow are packed with meaty material about unraveling, understanding, and changing that which constricts us from living lives of shalom. We are going to discuss in detail some life-changing, practical, eye-opening concepts for living all out with and for Jesus. However, just as professional basketball players must shoot foul shots every day, we must begin with essential truths before we can progress to the "how" of healing. Before we can attend to the damage of our wounds, we must know God's intended state of health. We know that iodine doesn't heal a bruise and a cast doesn't fix a wart because we have a basic idea about what a healthy body is. Let us look with new and fresh eyes at the truths about our intended selves as sons and daughters of a King. We need to make sure we have a picture of what a shalom, life-to-the-full, healthful emotional state of living looks like. These are the foul shots of faith necessary for our daily lives.

A Primer on God

If you have accepted that Jesus Christ paid the penalty of your sin, and have pledged your heart's allegiance to Christ as God, to God the Father, and to God the Holy Spirit, you can be assured of many things. First and foremost, you are chosen. Yes, you have been handpicked, selected, wanted, top-of-the-list included! The opposite of terrifying playground team pickups, the Father God proclaims to all that you are first on His team. God Himself has said, "I want YOU!"

> "How great is the love the Father has lavished on us, that we should be called the children of God! And that is what we are!"
> (1 John 3:1)

He selected you, not just to be on the team, but also to be His very own son or daughter. He wants to take you home, for you to take up residence in Him and to live all of life in His presence. If it weren't overwhelming enough that He brings you into His kingdom as His very own, He also gives you access to all that He has. "Because you are His child, everything He has belongs to you" (Galatians 4:7).

I am concerned at this point that many of you are having one of two reactions to this mind-blowing truth (namely, that *you* were chosen by God Himself). Many of you are breezing through this section because "Yeah, I know this stuff." Oh, that those of us who have walked with the Lord for many years would never gloss over His amazing grace. Oh, that never would we cheer more loudly for our favorite sports team than over our Lord's lavish love. Stop and savor again, please, the inexpressibly awesome fact that One who is perfect treasures His handcrafted creation of you. Others of you, I've lost already, because something deep inside rises up and says that this isn't true for you. Yes, of course, you believe it for all of those other great people God loves, but you're not convinced He really chose you; you sense that somehow you've sneaked in or slipped through on some special clause. While I will address this more fully in chapters to come, would you simply for now assent to agree with this truth whether you feel it is true or not? You cannot move on without the cornerstone that a Father picked you for His very own.

And what of this Father? What kind of God would be so bizarre as to involve Himself intimately with humankind? One of the first characteristics that any Bible reader quickly encounters is that God is unconditionally loving (1 John 3:1, Romans 8:39, Psalm 118:1, Jeremiah 31:3). In fact, He does not exist without it: "God is love" (1 John 4:8). Just as man cannot exist without cells, God cannot exist without love. His love is infinite, eternal, unconditional, and irrevocable. "His faithful love endures forever" (Psalm 118:1). It is poured upon us continually like the Gatorade shower for the coach of a winning team (1 John 3:1). Ephesians 3:18 talks of how wide and long and high and deep is the love of Christ. For who? You! Me! His chosen, adopted kids! Donald Miller describes, "...to be in a relationship with God is to be loved purely and furiously."[3] The demonstration of God's love at the cross should end all doubt as to what type of God we have – unidirectional and sacrificial. His love for us is completely one-way, much like the care parents give a newborn without expecting anything in return. And even more incredibly, nothing, as it says in Romans 8:39, can separate us from His one-way, never-ending love. In contrast with how miffed we get when someone forgets to call us, how frustrated we become when someone fails us, or how quick we are to cover up our hearts when someone doesn't handle us just right, God's perfect love is overwhelming.

Not only is He utterly loving, God is completely faithful. His overriding promise through Christ is that we will never be left alone, and that He will never turn His back on us. "I will never leave you nor forsake you" (Hebrews 13:5). Practically, His promise to never leave us makes God always present, always available, and always involved. To bring it home, I've often thought of His faithfulness as God being "smack dab glued to our side." Of course He resides in us by His Spirit, but when we begin to quite practically picture God as standing there in our every interaction, sitting with us as we drive or meet, lying with us as we sleep, shopping with us as we spend, looking at the computer screen with us as we surf, the reality of His presence impacts us.

> "Where can I go from your Spirit? Where can I flee from your presence? If I go up to the Heavens, you are there. *If I make my bed in the depths, you are there.* Even there your hand will guide me; your right hand will hold me fast." (Psalm 139: 7, 8, 10)

Think of the places we have dragged the God who is with us. To what depths have our thoughts, our habits, and our sins taken the Faithful One? It doesn't matter if we are trying to run 100 miles an hour away from Him, if we have committed our lives to Christ, He is right there. When we sleep, smack dab right there. When we are in a compromising situation with that person whose approval we desperately want, smack dab right there. Reading this book, smack dab right here.

Such faithfulness is promised to be the case as long as we live, "for He loves us with unfailing love; the faithfulness of the Lord endures forever" (Psalm 117:2). Whatever the need of the human heart, Christ offers himself as the solution, and His answer is always "I am." He promises us daily bread (Matthew 6:11) and promises to meet all our needs according to His riches in Christ Jesus (Philippians 4:19). We can count on God for everything that's necessary for our lives: "God richly provides us with everything for our enjoyment" (1 Timothy 1:17). Such precious realities as God's unconditional love and enduring faithfulness are crucial if we are to experience real and deep healing from ones who have not loved us well or who have betrayed, abandoned, and hurt us.

As God is entirely loving and faithful, it follows then that He offers complete forgiveness in Christ. Whatever the offense, whatever the sin, He zeros it out for those who look to Christ's sacrifice. And again, while this might be so familiar to some of us that we speed-read through, the freedom purchased at great expense for us should never be glossed over. Since we are self-concerned to the core, it is nothing but unconditional love in its purest form that could provide such grace: "When you were dead in your sins, God made you alive with Christ. He forgave us all our sins" (Colossians 2:13). Similarly, Romans 5:8 says, "While we were yet sinners, Christ died for us." This is an incredible concept here. It's a life-changing one as a matter of fact. Looking at these verses, we see that He doesn't wait for us to get our acts together: *while* we were sinning, *when* we were dead. God is not bound by time. He is outside of time as we know it. He gives us this paradigm for our benefit. If we focus our minds on the Father's vantage point in all of us – think hard about His perspective – we realize that there is a sense in which Christ is hanging on the cross right now at this moment for our sins. In other words, at the very moment we are choosing self in some judgmental thought, some fleshly indulgence, some bitter interaction, even as we profane His name, Christ is bleeding to death for that very sin.

Combine the reality that God is outside of the progression of history as we know it with Psalm 103:3, "He forgives all my sins," and we have another stunning truth. God offers forgiveness for all trespasses against Himself whether they be past, present or *future*. Forgiveness for sins He knows you will commit in the future? Oh, what love is this! Charles Spurgeon's words capture God's one-way grace: "His mercy is so great that it forgives great sins to great sinners, after great lengths of time, and then gives great favours and great privileges and raises up to great enjoyments in the great heaven of the great God."[4] Some say a primary reason Christians don't experience a deep and fruitful relationship with Christ is that they do not grasp the significance of their forgiveness. Do we really believe we're forgiven for that sexual sin, that abortion, saying that wicked thing to your mother that *she* hasn't forgiven you for? That He is constantly extending forgiveness is another life-altering, life-determining reality.

Knowing these essential fundamentals of God's character is critical if we are to change, progress, or even function on this earth. While sovereign, almighty, holy, mighty, righteous, just, and to be feared, He is also tender, intimate, and full of grace and mercy (Ephesians 2:8, James 4:8, Exodus 34:6, Psalm 145: 8, John 1:14, 2 Corinthians 12:9, Isaiah 30:18). We have total acceptance because of God's abundant provision of grace given us through Jesus Christ:

>"...all who receive God's wonderful, gracious gift of
>righteousness will live in triumph over sin and death through this
>one man, Jesus Christ." (Romans 5:17)

This means we are absolutely, positively worthy to stand in God's presence without any fear of condemnation. Grace is totally undeserved – we recipients are extended the opportunity to commune with the Lord at no expense, absolutely free. "By grace you are saved through faith—and this is not from yourselves, it is the gift of God" (Ephesians 2:8).

While obedience blesses God and us, there is no list of "have to do's" in order to be saved. If you have said "yes" to Jesus, Scripture quite literally says you are the apple of his eye, that He has your name engraved on the palms of His hands, that you are always on His mind (Zechariah 2:8, Isaiah 49:16, Psalm 139:17). And, He *longs* to be gracious to you (Isaiah 30:18)! This is not a God who reluctantly lets us hang around Him, but who longs to reveal Himself to us and have us see Him (Romans 1:20).

As a result, He is constantly wooing and communicating with us. The music you love, the art that connects with you – it's Him wooing you. It's Him loving on you in that compliment she just gave you, the laugh you just had, that smile from a stranger, the excitement from reading the Bible, that sunrise, your feelings during that great praise music. The Spirit of God within us is saying continually -- that's Him, that's Him, that's Him! God is speaking to us more than we can imagine. If you are one who struggles to hear God, it's important to realize this is a skill to be developed. You don't just sit down and know how to play the piano. We can develop in our capacity to attune ourselves to the voice of God through familiarity, practice, and "time in the saddle."

While this overview of some of God's most prominent characteristics as far as mankind is concerned is brief, it is imperative we start here in any healing discussion. I've been trained by Ph.D.s of all sorts, observed clinicians in many settings for years, served in prominent Christian counseling agencies, and say unequivocally that *there is no true healing without Jesus Christ.* There are strategies, theories, exercises, behavioral adjustments, and even symptom relief, but with great passion, I reiterate that there is no full reparation of hurt and pain on this earth without the picture God offers of Himself as Abba Father (Romans 8:15-17, Galatians 4:6). God has a much bigger agenda than our hurt – than *us*, period – but by His grace we are provided the opportunity to participate in His magnificent plan. Figuring out why we struggle is important inasmuch as it keeps us from realizing God's exciting plan and purpose for us as part of His larger story.

A Primer on Us

As God's creation, and His chosen child, we have an identity beyond whatever worldly labels we can give ourselves. A first step in the process of overcoming sin, self, struggle, and hurt is that we must know who we are in Christ. For instance, you are not first and foremost a mother, boss, student, or even an elder in your church. Your *primary identity* is a child of the King of Kings. Getting this right has significant implications for our lives.

Hear this: people who love Christ are *powerful* because of our *position.* As you let that sink in, keep reading beyond any initial reaction. Remember what our primary position is? Children of God. So positional power is what comes from my primary position as a daughter loved by God. That's it. The only way He will ever relate to us is in love. That's also our sole purpose – to experience God's love and love Him in return.

My primary purpose is to "enjoy God and love Him forever"[5,] not to be the best mother I can be, the wealthiest neighbor, the neatest housekeeper, the most successful salesperson, the greatest political activist, or the best party-giver.

As His children, we are completely loved and delighted in (Jeremiah 31:3). Completely! We are also completely forgiven (Colossians 2:13). He never tires of us and our weakness, but instead loves us patiently, is longsuffering, and always longing to be gracious to us (2 Peter 3:9, Exodus 34:6, Numbers 14:18, Psalm 145:8, Isaiah 30:18). When my little child gets hurts even after doing something I warned him not to do, I don't look at his hurt and tears and say, "Well, it serves you right. That's what you get!" No, instead, I pick him up, listen to his pain, hold him and comfort him. How much more does our heavenly Father treat us with gentleness and forbearance?

In our position as specially loved children, there is no greater truth than that we each have a specific, unique purpose. Ephesians 2:10 is abundantly clear: "For we are God's workmanship created in Christ Jesus to do good works, which God prepared in advance for us to do." What is "workmanship?" Something crafted. Something that took thought, time, and energy to make exactly as the craftsman desired. This is you, child of God! And this God who fashioned you just as He desired created you to do what? *Good works.* You are not on this earth to try to make the best of it, to just get by in some sort of survival mode, or to "get while the getting's good." You are here to do good works. Isn't that exciting? Further, these good works are ones that God prepared in advance for you and only you to do. Your friend can't do what you were created to do, your Bible study leader can't, nor can your boss, your pastor or Mother Teresa. There are things that have your name on them that only you can do – no one else.

Also as God's child, you are salt and light. Matthew 5:13-16 instructs,

> "You are the salt of the earth…You are the light of the world. A city on a hill cannot be hidden. Neither do people light a lamp and put it under a bowl. Instead they put it on its stand, and it gives light to everyone in the house. In the same way, let your light shine before men, that they may see your good deeds and praise your Father in heaven."

In other words, you bring something to every situation you are in that can "flavor things up" and "brighten the room." It is not because you are so charming or particularly fantastic, but because you are God's child in whom His Spirit resides. His Spirit promises to ooze from us and work through us, and all the more as we cooperate with Him and seek to listen to the voice of that Spirit. You are a bright light because of Christ in you, even though you could argue at length about how you're not. We'll address that more in a moment.

God has also promised that He will continue working in you no matter what. Isn't it great news that who you are today will not be all that you are five or ten years from now? Philippians 1:6 promises that He will continually be molding us, His clay (Isaiah 64:8). As clay, there is never a moment for us when our Potter is not doing something with us. When the clay starts to take on a form that is not intended, His fingers are pressing into it to reshape it. His fingers are on His people all the time. From every side God presses, pushes, tugs, kneads. He never gives up. He never discards what is ruined. Like the potter, He reuses it. I often think of myself like one of those old homes that you know would be beautiful were it renovated, and then someone gets hold of it and begins to transform it room by room. I praise my God who doesn't tire of such tedious work, but instead continues to give all His resources to the project!

The bottom line of this discussion that we believers are powerful because of our position is this: *You and I are meant to have impact and influence in every situation and circumstance of which we find ourselves a part.* Positional power is the reality of everyone who gets his or her identity from Christ alone. We have power because of our position as a child of the King. I am reminded of my friend who was the moderator of the Presbytery in his area. He and his just-out-of-high-school son went on a mission trip to Africa within the same denomination. While the moderator title means one thing in our country, it has a bit of a different meaning in the other. There it seemed to be a title given much weight, honor, and respect. When my friend got too sick to speak for a crowd that had gathered to listen to him, the leaders turned to his son. The young man was shocked when they asked him to speak, thinking, "Hey! I'm just a young kid here." However, from their vantage point, he had power because of his position as the moderator's son. So it is with us – while we may be undeserving, immature "kids," *we have power solely because of who our Father is.*

Acting from our positional power is living a deep-seated awareness of the Ephesians 2:10 truth mentioned earlier: "For we are God's workmanship created in Christ Jesus to do good works which God prepared in advance for us to do." It's believing that there are things I alone, of all the humans on the earth, was created to do. Positional power involves a deep-seated trust in God's word about me – that I am a special work of His with a specific purpose only I can do.

My six-year-old son and I were talking (okay, *I* was doing the talking) about the special purpose God has for each of us and that's why He makes some of us with some talents, and others with different gifts. After ten seconds of silence (an eternity for this particular child), he said, "Mom, I know why you're not dead yet." *Who said anything about being dead?!!* As I was catching my breath, he said, "Because you have songs to sing and choirs to direct." You see, he has watched me lead our Christmas and Easter programs at church, and rightly concluded that God must have more of such activity planned for me since I am still here. He "got it" that only I can do what God created me to do. Do you get it that you're not dead yet?!

If we are operating from this powerful position as a child of God with a specific purpose, then we come at every situation from the foundation of our position as a loved child, rather than a second-guessing employee or a needy spouse or an insecure friend. You would instead realize that you <u>are</u> (not wish you were) a bright light because the Holy Spirit resides in you. You'd believe, therefore, that you are effective as you interact with people because God said you're a light for Him (Matthew 5). And catch this, these things are true *whether you <u>feel</u> like you're a light or not, whether you <u>see</u> your effectiveness or not, and whether it <u>seems</u> like you're doing any good or not.* Our power comes from living from the position of a dearly loved child with purpose, regardless of what our feelings are. It is standing firm in the unbelievable truth that "His divine power has given us everything we need for life and godliness through our knowledge of him who called us by his own glory and goodness" (2 Peter 1:3). Doesn't the very thought of being so secure stir you? This is a reality within our reach!

Have you ever stopped to wonder why the book *The Purpose-Driven Life* has had such overwhelming success?[6] People want to know they have purpose. You and I want to believe there's more to this life than just busy schedules and financial security. Everyone is longing to have purpose and to be powerful – to know we *matter*, that our presence is important to someone. The phenomenal truth in God's Word is that ours is. Psalm 139:16 says, "All the days ordained for me were written in your book before one of them came to be." When the truth of Psalm 139 is deep within me, I realize that the line of traffic I'm in, that toilet I'm cleaning, the conversation I'm in, that song I'm singing, that person I'm smiling at are not coincidences, but part of exactly why I'm still here – my purpose!! Directing a large program is not *more* my purpose than silently praying for the woman standing behind me at the post office. Power characterizes when we are living life from a position of security instead of insecurity. Apprehending this truth enables us to live life taking each next step before us in faith that He is glorifying Himself through us. Whether you're performing for thousands or silently listening to a friend talk, you can be sure God has a purpose and plan to use you for His glory in each and every situation.

The person who acts and reacts out of positional power is a person who understands that God, who is unidirectional and unconditional in His exuberant love, has a very specific purpose carved out for him or her. The child of God can experience such depth of purpose because on every page of God's word, He proclaims, "You are part of God's eternal purposes." Whether in a whisper or a shout, we can hear, "You are a vital part of something much bigger than yourself." To operate from positional power means you know you are set apart by God, for God, and can walk in the gentle confidence that results.

Why Can't I Hold On?

If purpose and power are truths for all Christ-followers, why do so many struggle with being insecure, unsure, or even weak? Perhaps you're reading this book because something inside you knows you are stuck in your ability to get to the point of living in the freedom and confidence you hear that Christ bought for you. So many people can read words like these, or listen to a similar talk, nodding and smiling, all the while believing it's for every other person and not him or her. How is this the case? What causes such a disconnect?

Unequivocally, a primary reason so many Christians struggle to live a life that is abundant – a life filled with a sense of power, purpose, and peace – is because of hellish damage done in times of hurt. Understanding how we have been wounded provides a key to how we are struggling today. The relational patterns we detest, the overreactions we have, and the insecurities that plague us have become a part of us most often by way of our woundedness. Think of your most prominent shaping experiences. For many people, these are times of great pain. While I wish it were our successes, affirmations, and loving relationships that impact us the most (and they sometimes are), often it is our wounds that have a more significant shaping effect. This is especially true of how we are relationally.

The principle of roots and fruits (John 15:5-8) applies here. If your life is characterized by love, peace, joy, self-control, and satisfaction, it is likely that your roots are deep in God's truth. However, if things such as fear, anxiety, isolation, vigilance, distrust, depression, or the feeling of being pent up describe you, your roots probably extend from your wounds and pain. I can say with 100% certainty that He is calling you to freedom, trust, comfort with your emotions, intimate communion with Him and others, joyous self-sacrifice, and a sense of being part of something much bigger than yourself. He is in the business of moving us to deeper places with Him, but that will not happen unless we realize we are not our intended selves. Purpose and power are truly ours. Chosenness, too. Complete favor in His eyes, yes. Impact. Peace. We were intended for shalom, and something has gone wrong in the process. Life on this earth is painful, and the residue from our major disappointments, betrayals, and hurts has stolen the perfect peace Christ bought for us. We are going to spend time unlocking the secrets of our pasts and uncluttering souls through intense exploration and clear explanations. However, looking at wounds for wound's sake, psychologizing about why we are who we are, and finding ways to be more positive in our self-talk will not get us there. I write with one goal in mind – the glory of God through your heart set free in Him.

2

FULL AWARENESS

*I ponder my experience and I recognize once more that the way for us
to be in the world is to focus on the spiritual life.*
HENRY NOUWEN

*The thief comes only to steal and kill and destroy.
I have come that they may have life and life to the full.*
JOHN 10:10

The first series of questions that will be asked of a person who
comes to the emergency room for treatment will include an assessment of
the surrounding context in which the injury occurred. Before an effective
healing plan can commence, information on what the person was
exposed to and what was happening at the time needs to be attained. So
it is with us. If we agree that our intended state is health (purpose,
power, peace) and that we are not fully living thus, then we must begin to
assess the nature of our damage by looking more closely at what's going
on around us.

The Larger Canvas

Scripture informs us through a variety of passages that there is a
significant, unseen yet very real assault on anything that would give God
glory. Well, what is God's plan for His glory on the earth? It's you and
me: His people. How He can be glorified through human beings like
you and me who have to do lowly things like go to the bathroom and

sleep is mind-boggling. Yet our Almighty God will do this. Isn't that amazing? God has something He wants to do so uniquely through your life that you're not dead yet. You're not with Him yet. You're still here because it's yours to do and only you can do it. It's very unique...to you. But, because you are a vessel meant for the glory of God, you are presently under attack.

There is one who is bent on our destruction (1 Peter 5:8). Scripture is very clear about this. There is a schemer who's scheming against us to wound us in ways that keep us from walking in God's purpose (Ephesians 6:11). Let's be clear here: Evil is ultimately after the glory of God, so whatever damage we have received will be used to keep God from getting glory. What is the primary way God gets glory from us on the earth? It is through our relationships. It makes sense because God is relational in His very essence. He is a Trinitarian being. He is Father, Son, and Holy Spirit. He said clearly that He is most glorified in relationships (1 John 4:11-12). In John 15:12, Christ tells us to love His people. Scripture is clear on the point that if we love Jesus, then we will pour that love out to others (1 John 4:21). His sacrificial love was given in complete freedom and victory. He is glorified in our relationships when He is the center of them. He says, "Where two or three are gathered in my name, there I am with them" (Matthew 18:20). There is something about the corporateness of us being together, whether it is two or 200, where God moves in power. He is glorified in us being together in deep love and unity (Hebrews 10:24-25).

It is not too far a leap, then, to see that the battle plan against us targets our relationships. Do damage to our relational desires and capabilities, and therefore affect the level of glory God will receive from our lives. The aim for our wounding is our relationships. Indeed,

through what have we received our most significant hurt? Other people.
Think of it -- if I'm with you and you've hurt my feelings before, and I've
got my heart walled off to you, we're going to have a fairly shallow
interaction. Most likely, we're not going to go anywhere deeper and more
authentic where the Lord would be glorified. Self-protection, distrust,
bitterness, and judgment – these are indeed opposed to God's way.
When we've been wounded, though, such things become a way of life,
and we insidiously become more committed to staying safe, than to living
God's way.

All evil is going to attempt to wound your heart to keep you
from freely loving for God's sake. Our significant hurts damage our
relationships most profoundly. Just like in the physical realm, if such
wounds are allowed to fester, rather than being accurately identified and
tended to, they can keep us in a state of disease forever. Our intended
state as healthful, free, loving, giving people can be permanently impaired
if we do not seek to heal the damage of major wounds. The diabolical
plan is to so wound us that we then become out of commission for the
great and unique purpose for which God created us. Understanding this
larger canvas upon which our lives are being played is crucial to the
healing process.

Seeing the Right Battle

If you are in doubt about this ploy, think about it. Isn't it true
that we generally desire deep connection with other people? But so often
when we feel like we get too close, we do something to sabotage it. Isn't
that maddening? We want to be in close relationship and are moving
there, but it starts to come apart, and we are a party to its demise. Why is
that? We're all longing to be in deep connection with the Lord and with
others, and yet often we do the thing to screw it up even when we say

this is not the thing I want to do. This sounds an awful lot like Romans 7, wherein Paul depicts our state as flesh and righteousness side-by-side in our being this side of Heaven. The battle over our lives has God's glory as the price, and our wounds and the effects of them are part of a diabolical scheme. This is not hyperbole for effect. The Scripture is very clear. First Peter 5:8 says, "Your enemy, the devil, prowls around like a roaring lion looking for someone to devour." Whose enemy? What's he trying to do to you? He's not trying to bother you a little. He's trying to destroy you. To this point in your life that which has wrought the most destruction in your life is probably hurt from other humans. As your heart is wounded, then you will do all sorts of things that take you out of the game – like keep your heart pent up, so that God's glory is not fully displayed in you.

Second Corinthians 2:11 says, "For we are not unaware of the devil's schemes." This is my goal, that we are not unaware of the devil's schemes. Anyone who's ever been a part of a scheme knows what it involves. Sinister waiting and watching. Patient anticipation until the very moment where an attack can spring forth with greatest surprise and effect. There is one lying in wait for you. He and his minions are watching when you're in your bedroom at night, driving the car, or in a conversation. They're waiting for when the weakness comes, to trigger that Achilles' heel, trip that emotional wound, and rush in to take you out so that at age 45, you're sitting in a counselor's office saying, "I don't know…I've just never been able to love anybody," or some similar destructive untruth.

It is imperative that we see the right battle. While many of us have definitely felt as though we were in a battle, we have often failed to see the correct source. We have to get the right battle in mind. My battle is not against my husband. My battle is not against my family. Your battle is not against your boss or neighbor or previous friend. We have to see clearly that our battle is against the evil one (Ephesians 6:12). Sometimes it's like we're at a movie, and the people in front of us start to have an intense discussion. Many of us are missing the very large screen we should be looking at because we are so caught up in the interaction right in front of our faces. We miss the larger picture because of the immediate humans in our path. What are you pinning on others which is actually a part of the larger spiritual battle ensuing over your soul?

Seeing our Real Condition

The point is that we must be wise about how we are wounded or God's manifest glory in us will be obscured. I must speak to being wise about our wounds. In Christendom, this is controversial. I feel the weight of this controversy even as I write, but know that unless we can identify that we have been hurt, we will not seek healing. In other words, unexamined pain can rule us. There are many people who have some physical ache or pain that they ignore. What happens, then, is that they simply adjust to living life differently, to avoid the spot of injury. Some won't go on a walk because of that bum knee, give a hug because of that tender rib, or carry in the groceries because of that backache. *Their lives have become different, altered, because of their choice to leave the source of pain unidentified.* Sometimes they've lived this way for so long that they don't even notice the pain or injury any more. Is this you?

The truth is that we've all been walking around on this earth and, therefore, we've been wounded. Jesus said, "In this world you will have trouble" (John 16:33). There are so many verses about comfort, casting burdens on Him, and not worrying because He knew we would need to be comforted! There is an all-too-popular version of spiritual maturity that goes something like this: "I am happy and confident all the time and don't let the things of life affect me because I'm so strong and great and that's what God means by being joyful and trusting Him." Some Christians think to pay attention to our pain is to be unspiritual. I wholeheartedly agree that introspection which results in a victim mentality is detestable, and the wrong path for believers. However, those who love Jesus want to pay attention to the many emotions we have been given to negotiate our way to further freedom and dependence on Him.

For some, if you have agreed that surveying internal damage might be necessary, you immediately minimize what you see. You think, "In comparison to others, I'm really not that bad in terms of my past. So-and-so was terribly sexually abused from the time that she was little, and my dad just sort of yelled at me sometimes. That just takes me out of this whole thing. I don't really have that bad of a background." That kind of thinking has to be counteracted with the truth that Jesus cares deeply about your "lesser" hurt and offers you His healing. Those of you who are parents know that when one of your kids comes to you with a broken arm and your second child comes crying with a cut, you don't say, "Oh, get it together, your sister has a broken arm." If we don't do this, how much more will our Heavenly Father not (Matthew 7:11)! Your Father loves you and He cares about the tiniest wounds that you have received. Remember it is He who numbers the hairs on your head (Matthew 10:30), knows your thoughts before you think them (Psalm 139:2-4), and collects every one of your tears in a bottle (Psalm 56:8). Second Corinthians 10:12 says when we compare ourselves with one another, we're not wise. The bottom line, as John Eldredge says, is that Jesus addresses us *all* as if we are brokenhearted.[1] Is that how you feel – brokenhearted? Maybe not as much as you were yesterday, but because we don't live in Eden anymore and we live in an Earth where Satan has some power, we're all brokenhearted. Psalm 147:3 says, "He heals the brokenhearted and binds up their wounds." I thank the Lord that He cares about us more than we can imagine, which includes the smallest details of our lives.

While it is challenging for some of us to attend to our internal condition, others of us can be stuck in paying too much attention to it. Our mind can be too much on the pain. Undealt with, our wounds cause us to go through all of life impaired and out of synch. Hebrews 12:13 refers to this as being "out of joint." It says to "make straight paths for your feet so that the limb which is lame may not be put out of joint but rather be healed" (New American Standard). Have you ever had anything go out of joint? When you go through a period of time with a shoulder or even a finger out of joint, you don't function fully. You don't function well. Your mind is on the pain. Your mind is on, "When's my next doctor's appointment to deal with the pain…the pain…the pain…the pain?" This is how our lives can be if we don't make straight paths, according to Hebrews 12. I endeavor to provide guidelines for making straight paths for healing. If we don't deal with the evil assault on us through our relational wounds, it can make us out of joint for life. We can be walking around limping and wounded and so focused on the pain that we're missing out on how we can run the race with endurance (Hebrews 12:1).

I have seen time and again through 13 years in an office where people open their hearts to me that our *unexamined* stuff will rule us. For instance, someone who came from a large family, both in number and stature, always felt like the little sibling and was even referred to as "little so-and-so." Does the fact that this person works out to be fit and strong, has attained high levels of education, and exerts a powerful personality in all situations have anything to do with compensating for feeling like a puny, picked-on kid? If left unexamined, our pain can become an idol. We can bow down to it; we can let it define us and we can give it all sorts of power in our lives. Perhaps you think, "I can't ever open up to anybody again because of X that happened to me." Well, that's your pain becoming your idol. "I am just a person who's depressed. I've struggled with depression for fifteen years." Is your pain an idol – something that has a measure of control over you because of your commitment to it? Unexamined pain can rule us which means *God's free reign and purposes for us cannot rule us if we have put our pain in that position.* I want to be very clear on this, because as we move forward, we are going to talk about specifics of painful things and how to heal them.

I want to be sure that any discussion of pain, past hurt, and resultant damage is seen upon the larger canvas. The only framework for such exploration is the truth that (1) there is a battle, (2) whatever has happened to you can be used for the advancement of the gospel (Philippians 1:12), and (3) this is about God's purpose for your life. I have significant personal experience with the reality that psychological babble is a waste of time. I am a big proponent of dealing with your wounds, though, solely because I do not want the devil to get a foothold. Ephesians 4:26-27 says, "Do not let the sun go down on your anger, in that it may give the devil a foothold." A foothold is as if somebody is trying to get in the door and, on the other side, we are pulling it shut. If the door is shut, and the person pushes with all force, he cannot enter. However, if he just gets his foot in the door, we are no longer as secure as we were. There is an access given, and most likely he will be able to enter, even if we are trying very hard not to let him in. A foothold is not big. It's just a tiny little place, and yet it compromises the security of the whole room. It's a stronghold also, which means there is a place that the evil one is having some power. The principle of Ephesians 4:26-27 tells us that if we do not deal with our emotional issues and reactions to hurts and difficulty, it creates a place in my heart where Satan can have a heyday.[2]

How does this foothold usually occur? If we knew it was evil at the door, we wouldn't allow entry to any part. However, many of us have given over to some manner of self-protection because of the hurts in our past. The way we most likely have given in can be discovered in Revelation 12:10: "And the accuser of the brethren has been cast down who accuses them day and night before the throne." This important verse reveals some critical aspects of the larger spiritual battle to us. The evil one here is referred to as "the accuser of the brethren." We children of God are the brethren who are being accused.

This brings up a very important question – do you know what accusation sounds like? Especially against yourself? "Oh you're so dumb." "Oh, you did it again." "You think He'll forgive you for that?" "Didn't you just ask for forgiveness for that yesterday?" "If you were a good Christian, you certainly wouldn't have done that." "You had that thought and you're leading a small group?" "If anyone ever knew about your little secrets, they'd throw you out of church." "You'll never get any better – look at how you're struggling today even after that great prayer time last night." That's accusation. This is what I love about God. His word is clear. Anytime we hear accusatory thoughts, we can know precisely where it comes from. These are not just your own thoughts! Would you really *want* to think that about yourself? Does Father God encourage you to think that about yourself? There is one bent on your destruction – looking to take you out – who knows how effective accusations are. Furthermore, these are being hurled at you day and night!

That accusations are being thrown at us day and night is an important place to pause for a moment. This very minute we are being accused. *Day and night.* Have you ever wondered why your sleep is so wacky and convoluted at times? It's the only place in our human lives where we must submit to a mandatory altered state of consciousness. Tangentially, this is why we are not to get drunk with wine. Scripture says, "Do not get drunk with wine" (Ephesians 5:18). Let's extrapolate that out. Jesus quite obviously approved of wine. He made it and liked it himself. The issue, then, is not the consumption of alcohol, but that we are not to get drunk. Why? Because it allows Satan more access. It puts us into an altered state of consciousness.

So, for all who have fallen in ways they never would have had they not been drunk, realize this is why. It's also why some of us have hellish dreams where we wake up in the middle of the night and think, "I have never thought about him or her before in a sexual way ever in my life, and what am I doing having that kind of dream?" Evil has more access to us in altered states of consciousness. Sleep is one of those. Getting drunk is another one. I have a client who I emailed just last night and said, "Whatever you do, don't drink at this outing," because he's figured out that when he drinks, he goes downhill fast. He has said, "Any progress I've made, I go down. I get drunk, and I am toast. All the ugliness and lies come in." A few weeks ago in church, I prayed with a devastated young woman who the night before had gotten drunk with friends and ended up losing the precious virginity she has held onto for so long. She described having been in much more tempting situations before, but holding true to her pledge. Drunkenness gave room for accusation, suggestion, and temptation that otherwise would not have been allowed in.

James 4:7 says, "Resist the devil and he will flee from you." He is after God's glory and he will wound us to succeed, but we are not powerless. As we resist his plan, he must depart the scene. However, it is critical to grasp the concept that *unless I know that something is coming against me, and how it is coming, I will have difficulty resisting.* The greater scheme against us is to cause us to hear and buy into some hellish accusation that is aimed right in our weak areas. The scheme is to use hurt from our relationships as fodder to fertilize lies that we unwittingly agree with, thereby allowing Satan a foothold. Awareness is key for fighting the greater battle. Psalm 51:6 says, "Surely you desire truth in the inner parts, wisdom in the inmost place." The Message says it thus: "What you're after is truth from the inside out."[3] This is why we must examine ourselves and that which has shaped us in our lifetimes. Psalm 139 says, "Search me, O God, and know my heart; test me and know my anxious thoughts." Do we say "yes" to the searching of God? We must be wise about how we are wounded in order to be transformed beyond the damage. In other words, deal with your stuff, or it *will* deal with you.

Bowing Down or Not Bowing?

Being sure to see the right battle and choosing to examine that which is within us are important to the soul healing. As you submit yourself to this process, you'll probably see ways in which you do what Beth Moore describes as "bowing down to your past."[4] Have you never really spoken out in public again because of that one thing a person said to you when you were in the third grade? Do you not really share your opinion when you're in a group because of one time in a Christian ministry group you said something and a person didn't respond to you very well? Have you been shut down ever since? Have you thought, "Because I have been so sexually abused, I will be damaged goods for the rest of my life? Fine, here I am, world. Use me." How have you been bowing down to your past?

Beth Moore provides a picture of what a person who does not bow to their past believes. She cites Paul's amazing proclamation in Philippians 1:10: "Now I want you to know, brothers, that what happened to me has really served to advance the gospel." Paul, the Paul of shipwreck, beating, imprisonment, betrayal, persecution, misunderstanding, misrepresentation, and, oh, yes, the one who had been left for dead, is telling us God used all that for the advancement of the gospel? It is a freeing truth that He will use whatever it is, if you allow Him. If you say no to protective tactics and if you say no to hellish accusation, God will take whatever you've been through and use it powerfully for your good and His glory. Is this a vision that you can say yes to in your life today? It takes faith to say, "This thing that happened to me—God could use it to further His kingdom." Let's by faith, together, today, say yes! Beth Moore says it's like we're saying to our past and all its pain, "I have bowed down to you for ten…fifteen…thirty years. No more. I'm not going to bow down to you anymore."[5]

And now, can you catch a glimpse of God turning it around and you saying, "Past, now you bow down to me for the glory of the gospel…for the glory of God!" Joseph's brothers put him in the ditch to kill him and thought he was dead. How at the end of his life was Joseph able to say, "You intended to harm me, but God intended it for good" (Genesis 50:20)? He had a vision of the greater battle and was quite aware of his wounds. He expressed great emotion over his hurt, but did not allow the pain of his past to defeat him altogether. Do you have this vision and belief that you can apply to yourself today? These are not just stories out there for these "greats" of the faith. This is your story and mine, if we'll let it be.

When we have this vision of God taking our hurt and using it for our good and His glory, it is much easier to live beyond whatever pain we have in our past. With such encouragement, we can live way beyond our stuff. Do you believe that for yourself this day? Satan's plan is to keep us stuck in past moments through our wounds. Drink in this quote by Erwin McManus from the book *Seizing Your Divine Moment*:

> If you could capture one moment of your life, which one would it be? Some particular moment in the past? A moment of regret? How many of us haven't spent many moments reflecting on moments lost? All the time unaware that moments lost in regret are exactly that. Moments that are lost. If you could take a moment, seize it, and squeeze out of it all the life available in it, shouldn't that moment be in the future, rather than in the past? What if you knew somewhere in front of you was a moment that would change your life forever? A moment rich with potential. A moment filled with endless possibilities. What if you knew that there was a moment coming, a divine moment, one where God would meet you in such a way that nothing would be made the same again? What if there was a defining moment where the choices you made determined the course and momentum of your future? How would you treat that moment? How would you prepare for it? How would you identify it?[6]

One of the reasons we're unprepared for the moment ahead of us is because we're stuck in a moment behind us.[7] I earnestly want the reading of this book to make today an "unstuck" day for you. I want it to be a no-turning-back day. An incredible life of ours is to be seen and experienced, but you and I will be tragically unaware of it if we're stuck in a bygone moment. Satan's plan is to keep us stuck in past moments through what? Access he gains through our unattended wounds.

John 10:10 states, "The thief comes only to steal, kill, and destroy." We cannot minimize the impact of this full-on assault. We must be committed to awareness, to vigilantly inspecting our own souls for agreement with hellish accusation, for festering hurt, for ignored injury. This same verse also provides the why for *why* we would expend all this effort: "I have come that they may have life and have it to the full!" Is this not the greatest news?! If we aren't willing to engage in the battle for our own hearts and souls, we will be so wounded that our eyes won't look much different than those of the lost around us. He's come to give us life to the full. God intends abundant life for us and a thief works to steal and destroy it.

Let us be instructed: "The prudent see danger and take refuge, but the simple keep going and suffer for it" (Proverbs 27:12). Implicit in this verse is the fact that we must have eyes willing to see. We need to see the right battle, to see our real condition, to see how we are bowing down to our past, and to see a hopeful picture of our future. I'm reminded of a group of young people I was with a few days ago who were deeply sharing about their lives in Christ. One young man was talking about his sister and how she had hurt the family so much. As he shared, he was obviously fighting back tears, and was actually quite startled that he was. Everyone else in the room, however, could see he was filled with pain about his own hurt, but that he kept focusing on all his other family members' pain. While I trust that this wonderful young man will come to a place where he has eyes to see, I also pray we will have eyes and boldness to see what hurt we have, how evil wants to destroy us, that God has a plan to give us abundant life, how our lives are meant for God's glory, and what accusation is being hurled against us this very moment. Let's be wise and look closely now at just exactly *how* evil has wanted to sabotage our relationships.

3

Wounds, Lies, and Consequences

No matter how closely we walk with the Lord, we cannot escape the impact of a disappointing and sometimes evil world.
LARRY CRABB

In this world you will have trouble.
JOHN 16:33

Not only will a trip to an emergency room elicit questions about the surrounding context of the injury, it will also assuredly include inquiry into exactly *how* the wound happened. For instance, did the laceration occur with a knife, a piece of glass, or a saw blade? Was it accidental or on purpose? We have to know more about exactly what caused a particular wound in order to allow for the right healing treatment. This is the same with our emotional wounds. My lack of trust could have come because I've been betrayed outright by someone I love or simply because people didn't attend to my needs. Although the hurt will look similar, how it came to be is important. In this chapter, we will look closely at the primary types of wounds and how they occur in order to allow for the most effective healing plan.

Two Types of Wounds

Walking on this earth means we will get wounded, and that damage particularly affects our relationships. The very relationships that have the powerful potential to testify of Christ's love as we "encourage one another" (Hebrews 10:24), "serve one another" (Galatians 5:13) and "forgive one another" (Ephesians 4:32) are attacked in the vile scheme to suppress God's glory. At this point, are you thinking, "How might past wounds have skewed my relationships?"

There are, in general, two types of wounds. The first one is a wound of commission. A wound of commission is an injury done to you, some act committed against or upon you. Examples of wounds of commission include cruel teasing, abuse, rape, rejection, abandonment, betrayal, being smacked in the face, or being told outright, "You'll never make it."

The second general type is a wound of omission. The injury occurs because of something omitted, absent, or lost, rather than a purposeful act. If a child simply has no milk to drink when she is young, she will be damaged. It wasn't withheld; there just wasn't any, and this resulted in injury to her. If your father looked at you and said, "I can't stand having you as my kid," that's a wound of commission. But if your dad was just never there, he didn't do anything to you on purpose, you were still hurt by it. While it wasn't intentional, it still caused damage. That's a wound of omission. If your mom dropped you off at an orphanage and you remember watching her walk away, that is a wound of commission. However, if your mom was just emotionally unavailable because she did not know her own self, and though you suffered as a result, was it on purpose? No. That is a wound of omission. Something was not done. Something just didn't happen.

Unique Damage of Wounds of Commission

What is the damage of a wound of commission? It's an injury. It's an act that damages or hurts you as a person. It's literally a "wrong or injustice done or suffered, harm or damage done or sustained, or any violation of the rights of another".[1] In my mind's eye, when an act of commission is done, I picture it as if someone has taken a knife and made a divot in my arm or some other body part. A space is created that wasn't there before. An opening has been created that didn't exist prior to being cut open. While this is just a conceptualization, I think it is valuable because we then need to think about what happens in the emotional space that's created (since we are discussing emotional wounds).

It seems that when an act of commission occurs, a lie comes rushing in to fill that space. Remember the schemer and what his scheme is like? Waiting…waiting…he is scheming against you, lying in wait, so at that very moment, when someone lashes out, hits, abuses, betrays, or spews ugly words, a lie comes rushing in to fill that "space" that was created. The scheme is unfurled, and all hell breaks lose in a split-second. The idea that a hellish untruth became a part of us at a time of hurt will transform some of us reading these words.

At the moment of the greatest pain in your life, perhaps there is some evil thought which came in that you battle with to this day. When your dad, in his humanity and his own difficulties and struggles, smacked you across the face in response to your asking if you could use the phone, at that moment a myriad of lies could have attacked and attached at the sight of the wound. What are some possible lies in that scenario: an 11-year-old kid getting hit in the face by father at the end of his wits? "He doesn't love you." "You're not worth it." "You deserved it; it was your fault." "You're not lovable." "Your needs are not important." "You'd better not ever ask for anything again." "I'll get in trouble whenever I speak up about what I want or need." They can take on all sorts of forms. Think about a teacher saying to you, "You are just not like your sister. You will never be like her." What happens at that very moment?

What does Satan wish to unleash on you? "I'm a disappointment." "I'm not as good as other people." "I'm less than everyone." "Hate your sister." All manner of wickedness can enter in at this point.

The younger a person is at the time of injury, the more difficult it is to identify and separate out the lies later in life. This is because if we don't know they're there; they grow with us over time. Have you ever seen a baby that gets a little nick on his forehead? As his face grows, the scar grows right along with his skin, getting bigger and bigger. That is what has happened emotionally to you and me. If we receive a wound when we're eleven, we fare a bit better than with one implanted at age five, because it's grown with us. If you were abused, you might not know that your deep belief is "I'm here solely to meet the needs of other people, be they sexual, emotional, or whatever. That's all I'm here for. Use me." If that were the case, then you might not understand why you serve and give and sacrifice and seem to always be the one doing for others. You might even have a reputation as the most helpful person in your church: "I'll call Sandy, because she never says no." It seems like it's just your reality because it came rushing in long ago, and has been expanding with you ever since. Clearly, this comprises part of a scheme to destroy Sandy's ability to freely love and give from a position of power and purpose.

The damage of a wound of commission is that in the divot, the space that is created at the time of the wound, a lie becomes implanted, and if we do not recognize it, it will grow with us. Have you ever talked to somebody who had an eating disorder, and she swears she is fat? You look at her in disbelief and realize she has some serious issue causing her to distort reality. Those are the times we get a picture of what lies can do, because "I am fat" is her reality, not manipulation to get you to make her feel better. It's heart breaking to see someone who weighs ninety-eight pounds say, "I look in the mirror and I see fat." Such a stark picture shows us how deep our lies can go and what a hold they can maintain.

I once saw a client who was positively gorgeous, vivacious, had so much to offer, and was abundantly talented, but lived her life from an apologetic position. Hers was a life of "I'm sorry." "I really didn't mean to hurt your feelings. I'm sorry." "I really didn't mean to do that. Did I say the wrong thing?" "I didn't see you needed a drink of water. I'm sorry." It didn't make sense. This person was life-giving. She was amazing in many people's lives. So where did that come from? It came from a father that exploded in anger whenever she was in the way. So, she has learned to flinch. She's predisposed to thinking, "I can't mess up or I'll be exploded upon." Some evil suggestion from long ago continues to fuel her present behavior.

As you read, ask the Lord to reveal the three most significant shaping events in your life. If they were woundings, think about the lies that took root at the time. If your wound was being compared to a sibling and concluding, "I'm not as lovable as her," then you've lived your life from an inferior stance of, "I'm not going to be loved." You then unconsciously approach all of your relationships predisposed to thinking, "I'm not going to be loved by them." It then degenerates into all sorts of things: "I'm not going to reach out to her, even though I know that's the Christian thing to do, because she's not going to love me, because I'm not lovable. Why would I want to do that?" Do you see how God's glory is being lessened by the lie that takes root at the time of a wound? The soul, as the repository for God's image in humanity, has been beaten and bludgeoned by a relentless assault of accusation. In the next chapter, we will spend much more time talking about how to identify these embedded falsehoods and in later chapters will discuss how to undo the damage – all for the glory of our great God.

Unique Damage from Wounds of Omission

John Townsend purports, "Nowhere is the evidence of the Fall more apparent than in the universal experience of emotional injury in childhood. Things go wrong in everyone's childhood"[2] whether it be circumstantial consequences of the fall, a lack of love in the parents, or a lack of ability in the parents. The need children have for unconditional love is a universally understood concept. Unconditional love equals admiration, affection, and acceptance given freely, without condition. A person is unconditionally loved who is delighted in for their unique personality, not because they give something in return or adhere to some code of what "acceptability" is. Unconditional love is the fundamental emotional human need. Receiving such love is necessary in all stages of one's life, but particularly crucial in the younger years. It is the soil in which all other facets of personhood develop. The deprivation of unconditional love wreaks havoc on a maturing soul. Wounds of omission often involve such deprivation.

There is a conceptualization that I have found helpful to many who don't quite understand why they are the way they are and why they do what they do. While it is difficult to find appropriate words to describe, it seems every person is created with two cavernous "spaces" inside one's self. I've come to refer to them as vats. What's a vat? A massive container. It's as if we all have two huge, empty containers within us waiting to be filled with enduring, unconditional love. The two intrinsic vats deep inside every person are essentially spaces for the deposit of unconditional love by the people primarily meant to shape and form us. The first has the title "Mommy" on it and the second "Daddy."

From inception, every person has deep cravings for connection with two specific people, which makes sense because we were all created by two people. Therefore, we desire connection with the mom and the dad who brought us into existence. Now, before you react, please stay tuned and think of the evidence: a baby doesn't even know he or she is not one and the same person as his or her mother until about six or seven months of age.[3] There's no differentiation whatsoever. So many of a baby's first interactions are about realizing "We're different! I am not the same person." This is because the child is born utterly dependent on its mother for survival in this world. The entire first year of life an infant is taking in, or internalizing, the sense of belonging and safety he or she feels. "Internalization takes thousands of experiences of the parents' being there for the infant when he needs them".[4] Small children use attachment seeking behaviors like eye contact, crying, pleading, clinging, and reaching because he or she is searching for Mommy and Daddy to be sufficiently near, responsive, and attuned. It's easy to see how fear of abandonment is the fundamental human fear, so basic and profound that we have it even before we have language to express the fear. The critical nature of these earliest years cannot be underestimated.

Further, everyone can conjure up images of the incessant cries of "Mama, Mama, Dada, Dada" of the three-year-old who just showed her parents her latest trick, merely thirty seconds after the last time she showed them. At this writing, my kids are seven and nine. For the past nine years, the refrain I have heard more than anything else has indeed been "Mommy! Mommy! Mommy! Mommy! Daddy! Daddy! Daddy! Daddy!" They've been in situations full of their friends and other people they love, but they have always sought Mike and me out for our approval. The vats are longing for fulfillment – this is a representation of every human's need for unconditional love. When we are born it is automatic that we look to our biological creators, our parents, for that love. These are called "attachment needs" by various authors.[5]

When I think of the wonderful people who have shared their hearts with me in my counseling office over the last 13 years, I've come to see the prominent position these "vats" truly do have in our formulation. The ability to give and receive unconditional love, the interchange of mutuality, the conception of personhood and personality, the perspective of relational interaction and intimacy; these are just a few of the offshoots of these initial and foundational fulfillments. As well, over the years I have been involved in a large number of intensive group sharing interactions. For many years, I've asked the question to adults of all ages, "From whom do you most want to hear 'I'm proud of you?'" No matter the age or stage of life, the answer is overwhelmingly usually either one's mother or father. Sometimes the answer is shared with joy – "I know they are proud of me and still like to hear it" – but most of the time, tears surprisingly appear for the person sharing the answer. Many express being a bit blindsided by their emotion, stating, "I didn't know how much that would really mean to me."

Assessing the Fullness

Where this becomes of practical help for us is when we attempt to think of how "full" or not full our vats seemed to be at the time, or to recall this information from our memory. Unconditional love – the type we need to develop and flourish – looks different at various ages and stages. For instance, for ages zero to five, the vats will be filled with unconditional love if we experience closeness, protection, touch, gentle communication, responsivity to our cries for help, and meeting of basic needs for food and clothing. The child who experiences an abundance of these things will feel unconditional love and can be said to have a relatively full vat. Think of new mothers with their babies. Picture moms and dads with their first child taking his or her first step. Don't so many of them seem smitten, perhaps bordering on foolish? You've seen them adore every aspect of their child from his or her first green bowel movement (celebrated and proclaimed to the masses), to the recognition of their child's pure genius because of his or her words spoken at age three which clearly puts them in the "obviously more intelligent than every other three-year-old who's ever walked the earth" category.

The labels atop the vats from ages zero to five are "Mommy" and "Daddy." This is a time for intense, sacrificial, world-revolves-around-you, one-way love. It's the love that says, "I don't care if you vomit all over me, I am so nuts about you," and "I don't care if you look at me and tell me you don't like me, I am still crazy about you." I often refer to the picture of such unidirectional, unconditional love at this stage as "stupid love" or "crazy love" because parents who are otherwise stable and rational people seem to become crazed and irrational upon meeting this new child. "When we are young, we want to be precious to someone…to be desired, to be pursued by one who loves you, to be someone's priority."[6] However, some of us remember feeling neglected or distanced in those early years, whether through personal recollection or the report of others. That which we needed in those critical ages, such as protection, hugs, safety, food, physical touch, interaction, and engagement on any level were lacking, causing a serious wound of omission.

Such attachment deficits occur when a person was not "met where he was." When we desire a loved one to be there for us, and for whatever reason, he or she is not; it results in an "injury to the *self*, an emotional or relational injury – a soul wound."[7] "Most simply, an early attachment injury results when someone we love, someone who we think should love us, like a parent, fails to provide our fundamental safety and security needs."[8] This attachment need we have is like a muscle. Unattended to, that part of our soul atrophies and withers.[9] For instance, a child who has a cool, disapproving mom and a passive or absent father has been shown to have a low self-concept and is prone to later depression. It's been shown that our need for relationship is even more powerful than our need for food.[10] As such, a baby who receives too little physical stimulation through interaction with others will become weak and die, even if he or she is well fed. This is called "marasmus" or failure to thrive.[11] Attachment deficits result in *a lack of connectedness in the person's significant relationships*, which has wide-ranging implications.[12]

The importance of assessing the emptiness or fullness of one's vats will be explained later, and is quite important to understanding ourselves and how we are not living the abundant life Jesus purchased and promised for us. For now, when you think about your Mommy vat from zero to five years, how full was yours? Some of you will sense it was way up at the top. You fondly remember bedtime stories, finger painting, her "special occasion" cookies, and learning to ride a bike. For some of you, your Daddy vat will be way down at the bottom. Perhaps he was never around. Or you've been told, "he skipped out when you were two." Or you have only vague memories of one business trip you went on with him.

As mentioned, the "Mommy" and "Daddy" vats are loosely associated with ages zero to five. At some point thereafter, two more vats come into existence. They are labeled "Mom" and "Dad." This is because from ages six to 11, while the need and longing for unconditional love does not change, *the way in which it is experienced and assimilated does.* For the school-aged and preadolescent child, safety, protection, closeness and positive affirmation are still "musts." However, at that age, the need is also for validation of children's uniqueness and engagement with them in creative play as they attempt to do many more things adults do. During these ages, unconditional love from Mom or Dad is still just as important, albeit different. It is experienced through time spent together, honest engagement with the child's questions, and a sense that he or she, while entirely different, is still very important to the adult in question.

The unspoken wishes of the boy or girl at this age longing for love sound like: "I need attention." "I need help figuring out the individual that I am. Please help me see the strengths and weaknesses that I have." "I think I'm really good at drums, and even though I really like riding my bike, I keep falling off of it. Help me see I can also ride my bike well." "I need encouragement, shaping, and a modicum of independence." "I need to know that you trust me; you believe in me enough to let me go to the counter at McDonalds with eighty-five cents and order a cheeseburger!" I was at the beach during this writing, and looked up when I heard a young obviously pubescent male voice say, "Mom! Watch!!" I looked up and saw a boy, bigger than his mom, still wanting her to acknowledge his new skills with the boogie board. Like every little outfielder, all kids want to see their parents in the stands during this stage. With this in mind, when you think about your needs from ages six to 12, how full would you make your mom vat, and how about your dad's? Were they attentive to you? Were they present? What are your fondest memories? Do you have many or few?

To make things even more complicated, a loving parent of a three-month-old infant is a lot different than the sensitive parent to a 15-

year-old high schooler. Each development stage requires a new type of unconditional love, requiring new skills and new levels of patience, and new responses to their child's stress.[13] Excellent parents adjust, and need to significantly do so to fulfill a third set of vats which comes into play around ages 12 to 18. They, too, have an entirely different manner in which they must be filled with unconditional love, although the titles on these vats are again "Mom" and "Dad." At these ages, the longing for such love is precisely the same, although many parents forget this because it is certainly not as evident as when they were babies or school-aged. For the vats to feel full, Mom and Dad must find a way to affirm the uniqueness of the adolescent as an individual, interact with him or her as holding a viable opinion, and still provide input and direction that invites respect rather than demands it. Listening, and listening closely, is a crucial aspect of this corridor of time. While these new ways of showing deep love and appreciation are necessary, it does not mean the ways in the first two stages are outmoded. Physical touch, time spent together, validation of developing abilities, approval, and assurance are all still very important in addition to the more specifically adolescent needs such as respect and independence. It is no wonder that so many parents find this phase challenging or overwhelming.

Parents who are able to provide mentor-like help will fulfill the desire for unconditional love at these ages. Attentive parents during this time are like excellent coaches. They give gentle guidance from afar, as opposed to a guidance that is upfront and involved. If these children's insides could speak, we would probably hear, "I need to know that you'll be there when I fall, but let me go so I can fly." Pondering the fullness or emptiness of the Mom and Dad vats during this phase is probably a bit easier. It seems almost everyone possesses strong memories of this critical developmental period.

Finally, as it pertains to the parental vats, there is one more set. Ages 19 and on find two more vats representing the need for unconditional love. They are labeled "Mother" and "Father" and represent a more adult-like interaction, which communicates pride and joy over who the adult child has become, what his or her life path has been, and a belief that whatever he or she does is supported by the parents. This is an adult-to-adult relationship, continuing to be formed for all of us. The longing for unconditional love, while still there, again takes a different shape in this season and is experienced in other ways. There is most likely another set of vats with "Mother" and "Father" labels that develops as the child transitions into the parent and the parent into the grandparent, but it is not pertinent to this present discussion about past wounds.

While not by any means an objective measurement, it is helpful to, in your mind's eye, try to imagine how full or empty each of these eight vats were relative to one another. Consider that each vat represents a part of your internal composition hungering to experience unconditional love from the person labeled "Mom" or "Dad" or "Mommy" or "Daddy," etc. Think through what your level of unconditional love was during the various stages. Remember, attachment issues involve how we perceived the answers to questions like "Are you there for me? Can I count on you? Do you really care about me? Am I worthy of your love and protection? What do I have to do to get your attention, your affection, your heart? When these questions of attachment aren't answered positively, our psychological, relational, and even spiritual foundations can be shaken. In general,

Attachment injuries can result when: the loved one is simply not available physically or emotionally due to his or her own emotional distress or discomfort with closeness; the loved one is willing to be available but is not able to be there; the loved one wants to be available and normally would be there, but is absent at a crucial developmental phase or during a time of crisis; the loved one is there, but instead of providing a safe haven, he or she uses insensitive, off-putting, embarrassing, or sarcastic language toward the needy child or adult; the loved one is there but is smothering and overdoes safety and protection, which doesn't allow the child the freedom to explore the world and gain confidence mastering life's skills.[14]

Assessment of our personal foundation in these areas of attachment will provide many clues to our present-day struggles to experience intimacy with God.

This is certainly not an exact science, and more of an intuitive exercise than a literal one. If you find yourself struggling with it, just try to hang with the process and concepts, asking the Holy Spirit how He wants to use this in your life. In the next section we will address some very practical ramifications of your various "vat fillings." Picture a vat for each stage, with each title, and focus in on the level of unconditional love you felt you received from that person in that stage. Try to get an idea of what your internal diagram might look like. One example of this pictorial representation is found in Diagram One.

Critical Implications

The developmental needs during the various ages of childhood, if unmet because love was conditional rather than unconditional, will determine the particular type of attention, care, and concern we long for when older. If a woman experienced a scarcity of unconditional love in her earliest years, then she will likely experience a protective, physically comforting person as very loving. If a man finds great comfort and love in a mentor-like relationship with someone who is consistent and affirming, yet who trusts his independence in decision-making, he might have experienced the least amount of unconditional love in his adolescent years. Can you see the connection?

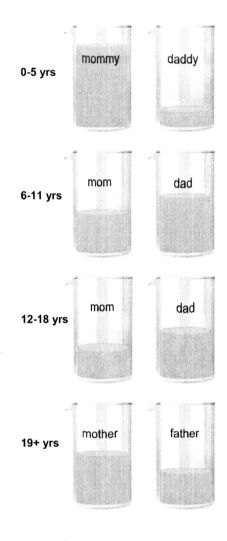

Diagram 1

As mentioned earlier, these early vats are so crucial because they occurred during our developmental years. The small cut in childhood produces a large scar in adulthood. Our past has grown with us like our skin and is part and parcel of who we are, for better and for worse. This examination is not to fixate blame or provide excuses. Instead, it is key for a depth of insight into a foundational piece of our personality. The level of unconditional love we received is fundamental to who we are.

Therefore, any empty vat or vat with a deficit affects us, but the parental vats are so crucial because we were formed in that environment.

It is a known fact that if a child was locked in a closet for the first four years of life, her physical and chemical makeup would actually be different than if she had not been. For instance, a child's developing brain is dependent on its mother's sensitive, attuned, and responsive care to the point where "our earliest relationships literally shape the chemical processes in the brain responsible for how we control our impulses, calm our strong emotions, and develop our memories of our early family life."[15] I've seen folks reared by explosive parents who now have high metabolisms, difficulty sitting still, and are prone to anxiety and panic. Our emotional environment affects even our chemical makeup.

Now to the point: ***Our emptiest vat drives much of our present-day interactions.*** In other words, we tend to unconsciously and unwittingly operate from our emptiest vat. The time and person surrounding our most significant deficit will have a large impact on much of our present-day emotional behavior. These needs were, in essence, created to throb for filling – all humans long for unconditional love – and will continue to throb in its unfulfillment. Every empty vat will cry out for unconditional love particular to the form of its primary void. In other words, if your greatest love deficit is from your Daddy in the zero to five years, while your Mommy vat was very full during that time, you might find yourself as a male extremely susceptible to nurturing women. If you are a female in the same position, you might be obsessively over-concerned with what the male in a leadership position thinks of you.

My assertion is that, essentially, many of us walk around unconsciously asking everyone we come in contact with, "Do you like me? Will you fill me up?" From catching the eyes of an attractive stranger to criticizing ourselves in front of others in the hopes that they will disagree, we take those questions to other people. And, the people to whom we are most prone to take the question of our acceptability and delightfulness are the ones whom most closely resemble the person's title atop our emptiest vat. What we "ask" others by our actions and interactions comes from our deficit: "Will you _____ me?" The blank is filled in by what your needs were at the time of highest deprivation. If you were an adolescent, it could be "Will you listen to me?" If a school-aged child, "Will you include me?" If a baby, "Will you adore me?" Identifying our greatest void will allow us to explore our relationships in depth (see Diagram two).

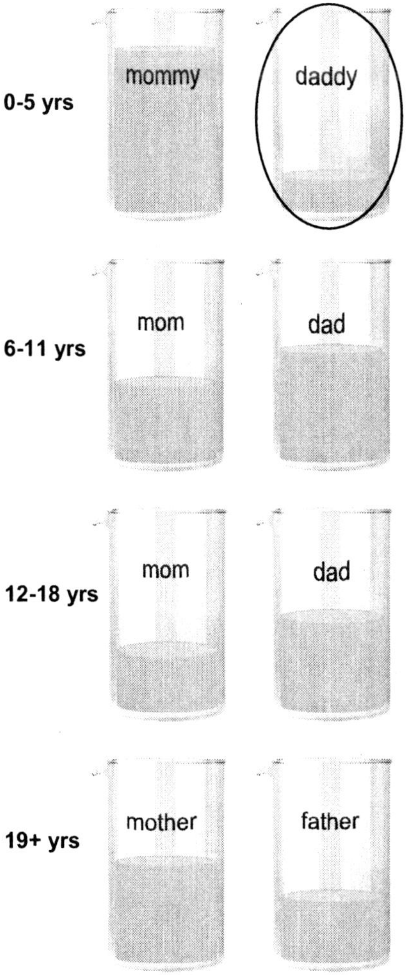

Diagram 2

If your emptiest vat was from zero to five, then you're probably going around looking for people to be crazy about you. You can't get enough touches and you can't be fawned over enough. I had a client who, I'm convinced, paid me just for the hug at the end of our sessions. How sad. What kind of deprivation took place in her life at that stage? If your emptiest vat is 12 to 18, then you're going around looking for people to acknowledge you as your own person. You probably struggle with your individuality and how you're unique and special. If it's from the Dad direction, then you'll probably have issues with the man in charge, whether he's a professor, a boss, or father-in-law. This could look like problems being under authority, significant efforts to get their attention, or high performance for recognition. Whatever form or fashion the outworkings take, they are there because it is a place of longing, and it hungers for fulfillment.

What happens is that the particular form of unconditional love called for by the morphing soul, if not provided, will shape the adult's idea of what "true love" feels like. For those with emptiest vats in the zero to five years, a woman may find herself wanting her husband to adore her and a man may crave significant physical contact of all types. The forms of unconditional love in these years are safety, protection, adoration, closeness, massive attention, overresponsivity to meet needs, being held and the like. If you constantly find yourself wanting these things, your early vats might be driving your definition of love today.

Fleshing it Out

Sally was loved well by her husband, for whom she was thankful. However, no matter what type of adult love she received through their relationship and her friendships, she was never satisfied. She saw other people who hugged in their friendships, and found that she longed for hugs, to the point where she actually obsessed about receiving them from her one nurturing friend. She would subtly place herself in situations where she would just "run into" her friend, and she was sure to share whenever she was struggling, because the comfort almost always came in the form of hugs. She became oversensitive to times when she felt others did not include her, and she was jealous when her nurturing friend made new friends. She admittedly longed for that "crazy love," because no matter how much time someone gave her, it was never enough. No matter how much affirmation she received, it was never enough. No matter how many hugs she got, they never "did the trick" to satisfy her desire. Sally still longs for that "I'm gaga about you – I will allow much of my life to center around you" type of love and attention, which comes in the first five years of life. Because both the Mommy and Daddy vats were mostly empty, she unwittingly still searches for the unconditional love she didn't receive.

If you struggle with identity and insecurity about who you are, your own likes and dislikes, and your own level of confidence to be successful at what you try, your emptiest vats might be those in the five-to-11 range. In those years, unconditional love is still communicated through closeness and attention, but takes on the added dimension of a parental attitude of "I'm going to help form you." Being taught new skills, being given feedback about strengths and weaknesses and being encouraged in vocational or hobby pursuits will likely be very meaningful to you if your deficits are from the five-to-11 year stage.

Shawn had his most significant deficit with his Mom in this period of five to 11 years. Consequently, he had become an approval junkie. He found himself searching constantly for affirmation and appreciation. He was the first on the scene to help set up for his Bible study and the last one to leave. He excelled in his collegiate work, and had the reputation as someone that could be counted on. He lived for the next: "Good job on that." "Way to set up the chairs for the ministry." "Great job getting that grade on your paper. Oh, look at what your professor wrote!" People who seem to live for the next compliment or assurance that they are doing great might be constantly going around asking for approval because of their unmet needs during the ages from five to 11. Unless we know what we're doing, our greatest unmet need can drive us for years and years without our awareness.

One day in a counseling session, Maureen and I were talking about the effects of her dad's rampant alcoholism. Because we had been working together for some time, we were actually discussing how God had shown Himself to her, and she had become adept at identifying needs she brought to others that they could never fulfill. In processing how she had looked to other people for love, especially in the fifth, sixth, and seventh grades, she burst out and said, "I just wanted my dad. I wanted someone to look to for answers, to be guided. I wanted him to tell me 'I enjoy you,' 'I love you.'" Then, more quietly, she said, "I would have given anything for him to say, 'I'll stop drinking for you. You're worth it.'" Kids in those crucial years do indeed desperately need parents' constancy, encouragement, feedback, and assurance about who they are and who they are becoming. Children from good homes often say of their parents in these years, "They were just there for me. I knew I could count on them to be there for me." Their experience of responsive and tender concern about their needs helps them believe, "My emotional needs are important, and I can count on others to help me in times of trouble."

In the 12 to 18 year period, the need for unconditional love often takes the form of wanting someone who's different from you, but who is someone you can look up to and who really likes you. A mentor-like, but not strong-handed, supportive example to look at feels quite loving to the independent-yet-dependent adolescent. Unconditional love comes through freedom and respect, but by someone who is still closely involved, not distant and unaware. Adults who gravitate towards teachers, people in authority positions, coaches, or mentors might have experienced the weakest vat filling in the 12 to 18 years.

Megan struggled with depression for most of her young life. At age 33, she began to explore why her tendency was to withdraw, to isolate, and to simply go to bed when things got tough. Through exploration, Megan realized she had a pattern of being extremely attracted to female mentors to the point where she had no friends her own age. She, not surprisingly, actually worked in an atmosphere that had many such women. It dawned on her that she was overreacted negatively to women who were what she called "gush-gush," or nurturing, but would become tearful after positive interactions with women whom she would characterize as very responsible role-model types. Her own mother left when she was a teenager, leaving her at home alone to face life. Obviously, the absence of her mother left a stark insufficiency which significantly colored her perception of the various women in her adult life.

Kelly's voids were significant at all levels, but the greatest were from her mentally ill mother, with whom she lived. She remembers visiting her dad in the summers of her adolescence, and actually feeling love through the structure and consequences he offered; she had virtually raised herself to that point. She remembers vividly getting to go to the doctor, having her first Christmas presents, and being involved in a swimming class all while at her father's. These are all evidences of a parent involved. It was so stark to Kelly because she hadn't had anything like that prior. Memories of her earlier years included having an ulcer at age nine and getting stoned and drunk in the same night at age twelve. Having given her life to Christ, today Kelly is a beautiful believer, impacting many lives through her gift of evangelism. She came to counseling because of now having her own daughter. When people who had great deficits in their childhoods have their own children, the slap-in-the-face contrast between their own love for their child and the neglect of their own life often comes crashing in.

From 18 and up, the shaping of the adult relationship between parent and child seems to best feel like unconditional love when it is as a confidant, a friend, one to whom you can always return and are accepted. Perhaps it's the feeling of "I'm home" captured in a person. The young adult who loses a parent to death early will likely feel deep affection for those professors, bosses, or neighbors who exude the wisdom and stability that only the passage of time can bring.

Jesse had truly wonderful parents. At every stage, they filled her vats with unconditional love. As an adult, Jesse was very successful on her own, with her own family, but continued to enjoy the appropriate and genuine relationship with her parents. In her late thirties, they both died suddenly, within months of each other. Of course, because they had deposited so much into her, she grieved well, and was able to negotiate the difficulty of such loss. However, a pattern she has recognized since the death of her parents is that she is deeply touched by positive, peer-like encouragement from males in her life. Her dad had played a cheerleader role for her, and while she didn't manipulate to try to get such affirmation from others, when it came, it touched her deeply, as it resonated with the form of love her dad had so consistently given.

At the time of this writing, I had an interaction with a good friend who is realizing he does not have unconditional love from his parents as an adult. We didn't speak about his past. However, at present he is coming more fully into the awareness that they are not there for him. There are multiple taboo topics that he may not broach with his mother, his parents are choosing vacations for themselves over 20-year-longstanding holiday traditions with his and his brother's families, and they never inquire as to how he is doing. He is a self-described emotionally constricted person, but described recent outbursts at his wife and kids that he's never had before. His wife agreed and added that she thought he was sad. When he asked me what I thought was going on, I said, "I think you might be grieving the loss of your parents even though they are still here." He began to cry.

Whether the vats be mostly full or empty, it is so helpful for us to assess where we personally are in all this. Everyone has something to learn from such exploration. We were all children once, and whatever elements existed in our formation live on in us now, whether to our benefit or detriment. These longings are real, and rampant! Also just yesterday afternoon, I received a phone call from a client I've had for some time. Her growth in Christ has been tremendous as we have worked together, and she has identified ways in which she manipulates others for verbal affirmation and physical touch in particular. She has admitted to swallowing pills, cutting herself, and threatening suicide in the past all in order to receive nurturing attention. As we have worked to strengthen her identity and relationship with Christ, she no longer does these things, but still must manage the inner longing that drives her so intensely. She called me to tell me that she had been placing me in a position only God could be, and that she had been attempting to use positive feedback from me to feed that longing. In an act of faith, and further understanding that no one will ever be able to undo the deficits from her mother when she was young, she told me she would tear up the few emails I had sent her and erase my voicemails from return phone calls she had saved. She realized that putting me in her empty vat wouldn't work, either. Her example serves as a befitting transition to our next major point.

What About Other People?

The prevalence of the impact of our early "vats" and their fulfillment or unfulfillment cannot be underestimated. We will work the entire way through this process, including how these deficits play into Satan's scheme by causing us to walk in insecurity and weakness, rather than purpose and power. We will look to how these are healed, and how God can use it all for His glory and your good. We will indeed move on from this point, but these are critical understandings we must possess about ourselves before we can add the other building blocks on top.

Now to the question of where others fit in this "vat formulation." For every person that is in your life and with whom you have an emotional connection, there is a vat. If you're married, there's one labeled "Spouse;" if you have a friend Jenny, there's a "Jenny" vat. There's a "Pastor John" vat and a sister-in-law "Rita" vat and a co-worker "Michael" vat. Our internal composition includes them.

Diagram three roughly depicts this concept. It is important to note that no one's vat is full clear to the top. Because we live in a sinful world, and all are encumbered with self this side of heaven, no one's vat is completely full because no one's love is completely unconditional. Sin affects everyone and everything. The closest to pure unconditional love we'll get on this earth apart from Jesus is the love of our parents, which again underscores the importance of those vats. To allow the truth that people will never love us to the fullest degree that our hearts long for because of sin is important. Such a statement is not meant to discourage, but rather to correct in the belief that clarity brings hope for real change.

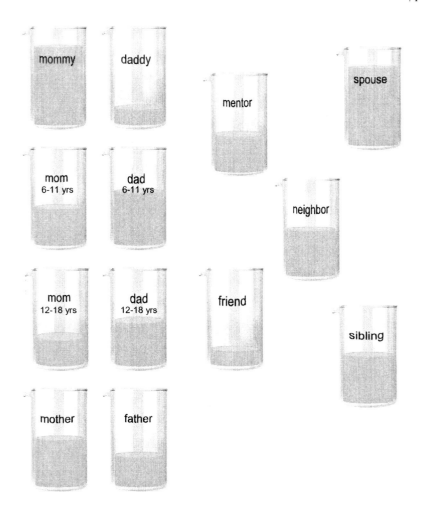

Diagram 3

Our next major understanding needs highlighted: **When we are out of touch with these formative vats of parental unconditional love in our early years, our tendency is to try to take the person whose vat is fuller in our present life and essentially shove it into the emptier vat.** Diagram four provides a pictorial representation of this concept. You have multiple vats representing relationships with co-workers, mentors, friends, and others. God has allowed them all in your life and you can give and receive His life of love in interchange with these people. Unconditional love looks different from each person, based on the nature of the relationship.

To figure out "what level of unconditional love am I feeling from so and so?" you have to evaluate those vats based upon their titles – what a good friend is like, what an appropriate pastor provides, etc. What we unwittingly do, and this is dangerous, is to take the vats that are the fullest and dump them into the ones that are the emptiest. We try to have others make restitution for that which was wrong when we were younger. So do you have a mentor who is wonderful? Do you have a friend who is really blessing your heart? Do you find though that you just can't get enough of her or him? Those are the echoes of your deficit pulling on you.

I have an amazing husband; I truly do. The level of blessing I receive from him is unable to be captured in human language. He is a great provider, a faithful friend, a loyal supporter, a consistent presence, a fun companion, a respectful leader, a wise counselor, and an incredible father. He's doing a fantastic job of meeting my needs as a spouse. Yet there are days when I think, "He just does not approve of me enough. He just does not pay enough attention to me. He just does not give me what I need. He's actually falling short on the job." And while some days, he actually is, the majority of time when I start to think such thoughts, I'm acting out of my deficit. On some days, because of my deficits, I'm looking for Mike to be gaga over me. Mike doesn't do "gaga." It's just as well, because that's not his job. That's not what a spouse is supposed to do. Some days I try to take Mike and his unconditional love and pull them into the least full vats of my past. I

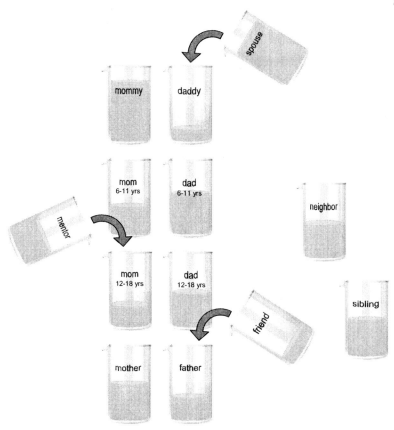

Diagram 4

want him to be nuts about me: unconditionally loving, like I could just spit up in his face, yell at him, or treat him poorly, and he would still say, "I'm crazy about you." I'm looking for zero to five Daddy.

The reason we can't go along looking for another person to fill our empty places is, simply, because they can't. Each vat is for one person, at one time. Even if our love receptacles are nearly full in every other stage, there will still be grief and some struggle if a vat in one stage was empty. Author Ann Lamott describes her own experience of trying to put a present person in a past absence. Her realization blindsided her as she sat with a boyfriend one day:

> I suddenly felt like I was dodging something, something that had a pulse and was gaining. Somehow it was tied to my romance being in trouble, with having failed once again to get my father's dog suit to fit this man. He did not want to wear it; it did not fit him any better than it had any of the other men I have loved since my daddy died…Now there were at least three major areas in which this man and I were totally incompatible. But this was not the point: the point was that the thing inside me seemed to be hurtling itself against the walls of its terrarium, and I was throwing everything I had at it to get it to lie back down. To not make trouble, because I didn't want the man to leave…The dog suit was old and had fleas. There was no way it would be comfortable to wear…
> I felt like the thing inside was conspiring to get me to *stop* – to make me stay in the extreme discomfort. I've heard it said that the Holy Spirit very rarely respects one's comfort zones…I understood that it was going to have to do once again with having tried to get a man to fill the hole that began in childhood and that my dad's death widened…[16]

There are special problems that come when we marry unaware of our propensities. Whenever I share at conferences the point that we can tend to marry out of our weakness, it often receives a significant emotional reaction from people. Perhaps it's because in the "'til death do us part" arena, we begin to realize the stakes for our unawareness of these issues could be very high. Whatever the case, the very thing that attracts us to someone then repels us. It is because at some point thereafter in the day-to-day grind, we realize that even the person we've married *can't* ever compensate. No matter how hard they tried, they *can't* fill a position that's not theirs to fill. The Eldredges explain this as it relates to the curse upon Eve: "Your desire will be for your husband, and he will rule over you" (Genesis 3:16).

There is an ache in Eve even now that she tries to get Adam to fill. There is an emptiness given to her to drive her back to God, but she takes it to Adam instead. It makes a mess of many good relationships. You know all about this. No matter how much Adam pours into your aching soul, it's never enough. He cannot fill you. Maybe he's pulled away because he senses you're asking him to fill you. Every woman has to reckon with this – this ache she tries to get her man to fill. In order to learn how to love him, you *must* first stop insisting that he fill you.[17]

It does not work. There was one person only who could fill my Daddy vat, and it could only be filled one time, until about age five. To take my 52-year-old pastor and "ask" him to love me like my daddy will never work. Certainly, we do this unconsciously. Some experts say awareness alone can be healing. Perhaps. Please continue to dialogue with the Lord, asking the Holy Spirit to speak personally to you as you read this information, that you might sense His deeper work in you, whether it be from these words, or where He takes your thoughts in reaction to them.

It is a difficult realization to see ourselves as people who are looking to get, ones who unwittingly are driven by past empty buckets, or even ones who keep trying to make right something that was terribly wrong. We attempt to develop ways of trying to get the love our hearts cry out for and to remove the ache. Our need for love and affirmation is desperate enough so we "turn to boys or to food or to romance novels; we lose ourselves in our work or at church or in some sort of service."[18] The awareness that no one can undo, refill, or correct that which is not theirs to fix, evokes sadness. However, some of us do learn, quickly, that people can't be what take the edge off our longing. Some folks actually don't look to people to make reparation for emptiness. Instead, they can take all manner of habits, patterns, and worldliness and shove it into that empty vat.

Some of us are dumping massive amounts of alcohol into an internally leaky bucket. Others are pouring your sexual purity into a vat because for at least that moment you're getting the hugs and the affirmation, and *temporarily* quieting that which is gnawing away at you. As our biggest deficit pulsates within us, it causes this internal level of hunger that will drive us unless we understand what it is. Success, food, busyness, productivity, orderliness, pornography, sports, drugs, masturbation, spending, your morning latte – you name it; we can push anything in that vat, and it will take the edge off for a moment, until it, too, leaks out because it doesn't belong there. "Most of our addictions as women flare up when we feel that we are not loved or sought after".[19] Ann Lamott adds to this discussion, providing a practical picture for us of what happens when the internal emptiness starts to "catch up" with us:

> I understood to a certain extent that these men of mine were innocent bystanders in my old family drama. But this didn't make the romantic problems hurt any less. The roar of the impending emptiness was almost dizzying. And I couldn't stop doing what I'd always done: I picked up the pace a little. We went to a lot of action movies, had another espresso, hopped back in bed, picked small fights just to get the adrenaline flowing again…It's all a way of avoiding the coming loneliness and the frightening silence inside…[20]

There are a host of other dangers associated with filling voids in these ways. It is a dangerous thing to avoid awareness, and even more precarious to avoid the pain of grief.

Exceptions

Of course this conceptual assessment of internal vats is individual for every one of us. Some readers have had the blessing of having mostly full vats. Thank God, and use the security afforded you through such love to be a strong blessing to others. Realize even still that the least full one will nonetheless pull on you for greater fulfillment. Others of you have been adopted or had a parent die and you're wondering how this all works out for you. There is no formula, but each one can prayerfully consider his or her own unique situation. Factors like the younger the age, loving parental figures in your life, and level of fulfilling relationships with other relatives all mitigate the significance of the completely empty vats, so each person's situation will be different. The principle of unfulfilled longings creating an internal cry for satisfaction applies to us all.

Jonathan

Jonathan, a successful, intellectual twenty-something, is married and has children. However, he secretly struggles with daily thoughts about other men. More specifically, Jonathan finds himself trying to catch the eyes of high school and college-aged boys. While for many years he wondered if he was having homosexual thoughts, because sexual arousal would sometimes occur, Jonathan has come to realize his desire is instead for a depth of acceptance from other males. He describes just wanting to see if they would *want him*; to catch their eye to determine if they find him attractive and worthwhile, to have them be close, if not to consume them.

Upon prayer and reflection, Jonathan has been able to piece together how overt rejection from his father has driven him to a level of deep insecurity about whether he is fundamentally okay for who he is.

The hunger to experience the "I like who you are/ I think you're neat" message are the cries of an 11-year-old boy who sat alone on one particularly haunting night, knowing his dad would have killed him and his mother, if he could have, just a few hours prior.

The reason we can determine the relationship between the unfilled vat and his present struggle is because no matter how close he has gotten to other males, it hasn't been enough attention or acceptance. He is lauded for his contributions at work, appreciated by his church leaders, and admired by his peers. But still, all types of physical, sexual, and emotional interactions with men have only left him wanting.

An interesting aspect of Jonathan's story is his attraction and draw towards younger men. Many a struggling person has admitted to me that sometimes they have this odd feeling of wanting to consume another person and therefore pull back for fear of overwhelming the desired one. If the "vat" driving this desire is close to empty, this urge will be so demanding that a person may just want to *be* another person. Jonathan expressed this, and has realized he's looking to try to put that boy or young man figuratively inside him – in his place – so that perhaps *he* (the other whom I have swallowed and now becomes me) will *finally* be accepted and declared lovable. The hunger is so severe and the resignation that one will never be accepted for him or herself is so great, that it drives many people to want to ingest (or be) another person. This results in myriad patterns – homosexual urges, extreme codependency, living a double life, manipulative charm, and on.

Jonathan additionally experiences a tremendous desire for his supervisor to approve of him. He describes attempting to get the boss to compliment him through manipulative questions about his performance and intense overproduction. Because the male authority in question is indeed encouraging and affirming, Jonathan says this makes the desire for strokes more. As presented earlier, no matter how much of what we "want" that we receive, it will never take away that emotional echo that longs for someone in the past. Only God can provide a path through such pain.

Tom

Tom grew up under the shadow of his brother, sensing that he was a mistake. He never recalls being told he was loved by his mother, even hoping against hope that this might happen on her deathbed. His hope for warmth was dashed over and over. Their last hug was typical - he reached out and squeezed her with his arms, as hers hung to the side and she made no motion towards him.

As he has moved past the half-century mark, Tom now realizes that much of his life has been shaped by minimal motherly love and affection. When he and his first wife divorced because of her extra-marital affair, he found himself in a sexual, financial, and alcoholic frenzy. He would interact with woman after woman, often seeing who he could "conquer." Although he dated and slept with multiple women, even in the same day, it was never enough. He found himself still longing. The boat, the Caribbean cruises, the sexually promiscuous environments, the success as a seminar leader - none of it met his deepest need for unconditional, nurturing love. Upon coming to the Lord after a heart attack, he began to see how much of his life had been driven by his deficits. He was constantly seeking the attention of women, and to prove to men that he was better than them.

Overview

While the stories are varied, the theme is the same: Many of us have felt profoundly disappointed in many of our key relationships over the course of our lives. Therefore, we hurt. The obvious fact is that we cannot be alive very long without being wounded. Whether through a wound of commission, or one of omission, all hell is attempting to leverage against us whatever pain we have encountered to render us handicapped from living free, open, giving, risking, and trusting lives for the cause of Jesus Christ. The specific damage of the wound of commission is the lie that takes root and grows with us if left untouched. Wounds of omission result in deficits in the types of relationships God created us to enjoy and flourish in. The longing lodged in our hearts is from Him and for His good and perfect purpose for us on this earth, especially in our relationships. Unless we recognize both the unseen world in the spiritual realm and the unseen world of our emotional selves, we will continue to be plagued by things we do not understand, or worse yet, ruled by masters we detest.

Going back to the analogy of the literal wound, we indeed must know how the wound occurred, so we know how to best treat it. Doctors will treat a puncture wound that came from a nail very differently from one that came from fiberglass. The other reason we need to know precisely how an injury occurred is so we don't have it happen again. In other words, understanding whether our lives have been impeded by remnants of wounds of commission or omission will allow us to know how to best proceed with healing. It will also permit us to avoid having further damage from an already present wound gone unattended, or even from a similar injury. These matters are addressed in the next chapter.

4

EYES TO SEE

Everybody's got a hungry heart.
BRUCE SPRINGSTEEN

*All my longings lie open before you, O Lord,
my sighing is not hidden from you.*
PSALM 38:9

Knowledge of exactly how a wound happened, what caused it, and how deep it goes allows for it to be fixed the way it is supposed to be fixed. For example, the antibiotics given my niece did not work to cure the cancer growing inside. Doctors didn't take the deeper look necessary and treated only the observable and reported symptoms. It wasn't until the cancer was identified and treated for the deeper problem it was that the other symptoms began to fade. In the same way, solving an emotional problem with a completely rational, discipline-based approach will not work. Treating a physical wound with a dose of increased Bible reading is likewise inappropriate. Approaching a spiritual issue from a behavioral perspective will also be unproductive.

It seems we are often unwise in our approaches, simply trying the same thing in larger and larger doses. My niece was given massive amounts of antibiotics to no avail. An x-ray provides a more accurate solution. This chapter will look at the depth of our issues, and provide initial healing perspectives necessary for lasting change. To continue to keep the big picture at the fore, it is important to remember that *navigating our way through effects of wounds is for the purpose of God's glory*, as we ultimately unmask and stand against the hellish plot to take us out of sacrificial, joyful living and service to the King.

Long-term Implications of Wounds of Commission

Proverbs 23:7 says, "As a man thinks in his heart, so is he." In other words, we live from our inner belief system out. What's really true inside us is what we live out. This explains why promising young people can go down a path no one would have ever predicted. What this has to do with the kingdom of God is that we were meant to "live and move and have our being" (Acts 17:28) in Him and His truth, not some filthy falsehood worn like a garment. "It is for freedom that Christ set us free" (Galatians 5:1). Yes, it is for eternal freedom and for freedom from adherence to and judgment under the law. We are also freed to move in who He created us to be, not to be bound unknowingly in the wreckage of some human blunder, or worse, abuse.

You and I have both experienced them – the people who truly seem free. They seem comfortable in their skin. They appear accepting of not only their weaknesses, but also their strengths. They have both a peace and a confidence that we intuitively can tell has nothing to do with such a shallow concept of "self-esteem." We wonder how they've done it. How are they apparently unscathed by the ever-changing opinions of others? Why do they not second-guess their every social interaction like so many of the rest of us? Most likely, these people are not blaming someone else for their problems or pain. They have also probably chosen to have their world view shaped by the Lord and His perspective and love, rather than living out of the perception of their wounds. They aren't likely bound by actions, attitudes, and behaviors that are a product of their pasts. Their perspective is dominated by something other than faulty conclusions from earlier experiences. They have learned how to be free in the present, rather than fettered by the past.

Distorted Spectacles

Upon first greeting Chandra in the waiting room, her physical beauty was impressive. When I commented on it, her reaction told me that her perception of herself did not match my perception of her. Whenever a person's opinion does not match external evidence, it is usually indicative that some previous wounding is still holding sway. In other words, *if some lie about who we are has been implanted, it then becomes a lens through which we perceive all of life.* Our interactions with others, and our circumstantial occurrences are all filtered through whatever the misperception is. It's just like what occurs whenever a person dons red colored glasses. Everything then observed is perceived as red. The same happens when some sort of lie takes root. If "I'll never amount to anything" is believed, then the experiences that characterize that paradigm are "caught" and lodge within, while other experiences are disregarded. Instances such as getting a "B" grade instead of an "A," or receiving only the standard-of-living raise instead of something higher are viewed as further "evidence" that the lie "I'll never amount to anything" is true. However, placing first in divisional sales, improving on every grade in a semester, or being invited to lead a small group at church are somehow discounted or dismissed. Why? Because they don't fit into the grid that "I'm not amounting to anything."

It cannot be overemphasized that the younger a person is at the time the filter/lens/lie is put in place, the more deeply entrenched it is. In fact, many times a person can't even comprehend that they have a terribly distorted view of themselves. It can be bewildering for those around someone with a lie in place, because they do not understand just how their friend can view him or herself that way. The young woman with the beautiful figure constantly disparaging how "fat" she is, the multi-talented man who feels a failure, and the generous woman who apologizes for everything are types of individuals with self-perception problems.

For years, I believed I was "homely" because a significant adult in my life told me so in my early elementary years. When I didn't get a boyfriend as early as Kim, or didn't seem to be as popular as Tracy, I just concluded it was because they were pretty and I was homely. Then, as a student council leader my senior year of high school, I was responsible for counting the ballots for Homecoming Court. If the lie was ever in doubt, as my hopeful young soul desired to believe, it became cemented as I opened ballot after ballot that held my girlfriends' names. Only one had mine. It was in the very distinctive (read "messy") handwriting of my boyfriend at the time, Randy. I had always believed I was popular because I had a "good personality," a cheerleader because I was "friendly," and in school plays because I was "talented." Deep inside, I knew I had to work hard in these other ways because I was not attractive. My filter had been proven correct: "Aha, only one vote for 'pretty-girls-in-the-school' court. That proves it." Because of my "I'm not pretty" lens, I ignored or missed altogether evidence to the contrary. There was plenty to prove otherwise (boyfriends, winning elections, parts in plays), but I perceived everything through a lens that kept me from concluding anything other than "I'm homely."

There are successful men and women everywhere who still believe, after recognition and reward for their contribution, that they "will never amount to anything" or "won't be as good as others." People reading even these words are filtering them through all manner of hellish distortion. "I don't deserve love," "I'll always be alone," "No one will ever understand me," "People can't be trusted," "I'll be used," "I'm not lovable," and a wide variety of other lies are part of a diabolical scheme meant to destroy us. Left unrecognized, we after time conclude, "That's just me" and don't think much beyond it.

As for Chandra, it turns out she did indeed wear an emotional pair of distortion glasses. It didn't take much discussion as we sat together before her eyes widened and she said, "I haven't thought of this in a long time." She recalled a memory of her best friend, a boy, in third grade having the opportunity to choose anyone from the class to accompany him on a special project. As her heart soared, knowing he would pick her, she proudly walked to the front of the room. When she arrived, he leaned over and said he was happy to pick her, but "if Joy were in this class, I would have picked her." Chandra identified this as the time in which the thought "you're second best" became a part of her. Upon further exploration, she realized that she believed her college boyfriend had dated her out of pity, although he had vehemently denied it. Likewise, when her husband told her she was different than everyone else he had dated, she interpreted that from her "you're second best" paradigm rather than the compliment it was intended to be. How many of us are missing bona fide evidence of the opposite of a belief we have because of our distorted perception?

Sarah didn't know she wore a pervasive lens of "I'll be rejected" into every area of her life until the Lord brought it to her attention through counseling. People will indeed mirror feedback to us about ourselves, including our lie-based spectacles, if we spend enough time with them and listen closely enough. She was overwhelmed with what she felt was overt rejection in a friendship. However, her perspective was completely assaulted when one afternoon this another friend told Sarah that she had actually felt rejected by her. Sarah just kept shaking her head in disbelief as she relayed the encounter, unable to see how this other woman was not rejecting Sarah but in fact felt just the opposite. It's not an uncommon scenario for two people to interact, each peering through their own lie-based paradigm. This is why so many times two people can have a conversation and walk away with completely different interpretations about what was said. Thinking about such interactions in our own lives can sometimes provide a revelation to us about us. A direct quote of Sandy's as we processed through this instance provides support for the lens concept: "All my life I've made decisions through that grid."

Clues to Assessing Wounds of Commission

While some of you are certain you have a lens in place that has colored your entire life, others of you are still wondering whether you fit in this category or not. Because of the Scriptural clues to the nature of the assault on us, we can be fairly certain that some manner of this plot has been unfurled upon us. How do we discover more precisely what it has been? *There will be evidence.* As alluded to above, truth-based evidence *will* emerge from around you that flies in the face of any faulty lens.

Because the Lord is in the business of making truth plain, as Romans 1 suggests, we can be sure that when we ask Him to reveal it, He will. However, we must develop eyes to see it. This is critical. An openness to "see" something outside of our own perspective and an attempt to develop the capacity to apprehend it will indeed reveal truth – whether it is truth about God, about our lives, about others, or about us. Scripture is clear on how we come to such truth: "for we fix our eyes not on what is seen but what is unseen, for what is seen is temporary, but what is unseen is eternal" (2 Corinthians 4:18). If our vision is consumed with what is tangible, earthly, and minutia-like, we will indeed be significantly impaired in our ability to see the secret things of God.

The practical take-away here is that if we are wearing some distorted lens through which we have viewed life and ourselves, there WILL BE evidence to the contrary. However, beholding that evidence will be difficult, because of our propensity to see only that which we "want to" – to see only that which fits our perspective. It reminds me of a physical pain that the orthopedic doctor sees as a joint problem, the psychologist as a psychological one, the chiropractor as an alignment issue, the homeopath as a mineral deficiency one, and the physical therapist as a muscular injury. The more convinced we are of a certain perspective, the more we see everything from that vantage point. Because of this common natural propensity, we need help to see ourselves clearly. Thank the Lord that when we're serious about taking an inside look at these things, He provides three sources of light: (1) the Spirit of God, (2) the Word of God, and (3) the people of God. Appeal to and be open to these three avenues, and we shall begin to see clearly how we have held some lie-based paradigm for viewing our lives or selves.

I am the Common Denominator

Recognition is a crucial first step to the freedom of a new perspective. As a matter of fact, without awareness, we can't go any further. If we don't know that WE are the common denominator in situation after situation that we feel validates our worst fear, we'll never make any progress. Read that sentence again. I'll talk about that more a bit later, but if we can't see that, like a faulty prescription, our lens shapes everything we perceive in distorted fashion, then we'll never be motivated to seek anything different. From the vantage point of an eyeglass wearer, the experience of a gradually deteriorating perceptual distortion is common. It takes a mini wake-up call for the individual to realize his or her prescription might be bad. A doctor's visit, an auto accident, or simply trying on a new pair of glasses could reveal that there is a problem.

To carry an analogy probably too far, these three examples are avenues by which we can become aware of our own distorted lens. These clues might move you to recognize some particular lies which have held sway. A check in with the Great Physician always provides truthful perspective, when we come admitting we might have a problem we can't see. In other words, if we come to God with a "search me and know my anxious thoughts, see if there be any offensive way in me" attitude, He will honor it (Psalm 139:23-24). The first avenue of recognizing a destructive filter is to ask the Lord to reveal it. More specifically, if we have been exposed to God's truth time and again, can spout it off easily and yet find that we still "just can't get it," this is a problem. If we find it very difficult to accept God's truth after a real desire to, then most likely we have some lens in place that is unwittingly coloring our perspective so that the freeing truth is somehow "for everyone else but me."

As mentioned, it is problematic if we keep hearing a truth over and over and know it is true, but it never "gets in." If we're hungry to hear it again, and it never becomes assimilated into us, that probably means something is keeping it out. A real stark mirror for us is to think about how we will sometimes manipulate people to hear something from them again. If Teresa said you looked great once, and you later make a comment about how ugly you feel tonight, you might be manipulating her to compliment you again. Sometimes in this scenario, we're just being manipulative. We're sinners! However, for some this could be a sign to you that the truth can't go in because some lie is wedged there instead.

A second indication that we might be subjected to a long-term faulty perspective is if we indeed do "crash," like the person whose eyeglass prescription is no longer effective. After years of "bucking up" and coping, we finally have to admit depression or burnout. A relationship we're in drastically changes, catching us off guard. Our worst fear materializes. A spouse in frustration blurts out how you're "always so _____" and in an instant holds up a mirror revealing our poor perspective which clouds everything. However it happens, a surprising or blindsiding situation can also reveal that we have unattended to residue from wounds of commission.

Finally, simply "trying on" another perspective can be a real eye-opener (excuse the pathetic pun). Have you ever put on someone else's glasses because you thought you'd look good in them, only to discover their vision is *very* different from yours? Try to actually BE like someone you admire for half of a day. ("What would John do in this situation?" "What would Heather say right now?") Think of the thing about yourself that drives you most crazy, and fix all your attention and energy on being the opposite for a week. If you simply cannot imagine being able to be like the healthy person you know, it could mean some lie has rooted deeply. If it feels radically different, impossible, or perhaps even freeing, these might be signs that you have an unhealthy lens in place.

One other indication of an implanted lie is that sometimes we have equations where our "wires have gotten crossed." For example, consider how you would fill in the blank to this question (without thinking about it much): Love equals _____. For the sexual abuse survivor, love can unconsciously equal sex, being controlled, or doing things for other people. While anyone reading this can see how clearly distorted that is, just the other day in my office a beautiful woman wondered about her husband's love for her because he wasn't as sexual as her boyfriends had been. It can be telling for us to examine how we might have gotten some wrong equations due to hurt. Sometimes I have found myself believing that if I am noticed, that means I am irritating to others. Distorted equation. For some, being financially provided for equals love, over and above commitment and trust. Another woman and I talked recently, only to discover that she has the equation "weakness in a man equals showing emotion" and finds herself detesting when her husband shows a modicum of moodiness. Closer examination of some of our equations can also be a route to uncovering what lies have taken root. All such exploration is for the purpose of rooting them out and replacing them with God's beautiful truth. Such work is explicitly described in chapter eight.

Romans 6 addresses how we can perceive life. It essentially offers the truth that we can see ourselves from one of two vantage points. We can be slaves to sin or slaves to righteousness. The principle here is that we "are slaves to the one whom (we) obey" (2 Peter 2:19). It is our choice to receive the gift of freedom, or to continue living under sin-laden viewpoints. After the Emancipation Proclamation, many slaves stayed on the plantation. Oh, let us read on of God's truthful perspective, that we not remain enslaved to previous owners! We have a powerful choice in that having been set free from the old, we can live to God and from his perspective in the new. Vile lies from our wounds of commission need not rule us one more day. Neither do the effects of our wounds of omission.

Clues to Assessing Wounds of Omission

It is actually frightening to me how many people walk around life unaware that they are trying to get empty buckets filled up, never realizing those buckets have huge holes. While the desire to be filled comes from many sources (we are longing for our true heavenly home, we were created to want deep relationship, we have been hurt and want it fixed), when the reason for our efforts is from past wounds of omission, we are in trouble. Not only will those wrongs never be righted, our lives can become exercises in futility without us even knowing why. Do you know someone who is clearly "stuck?" Is it you? That feeling of being caught is the result of being in a dead-end pattern from living out of one's deficits. As with wounds of commission, there will be evidence that shows a person if they are living from wounds of omission. I explain seven such indices here.

<u>Can't Get No Satisfaction</u>

A quick glance at what happened in the Garden of Eden reveals how evil tempts us regularly. Discontentment. Both Adam and Eve were baited to be discontent with all the wonderful beauty and freedom all around them and instead focus on the one little item withheld from them. Soon thereafter, both expressed discontent in their relationship with each other ("Well, she…" "But he…"). Is this not a picture of what we so often do? We focus on the small area we don't have rather than focus on all the good that we *do* have – whether in a person or in our circumstances. As such, it is safe to assume the attack continues on to make us dissatisfied.

Therefore, we might be wise to examine our level of displeasure with the significant relationships we have. Widespread disappointment (dissatisfaction with every person) is an indicator that a problem exists.

However, as mentioned above, we often fail to see that *we* are the most common denominator. How many times I have heard someone decry that every roommate or boyfriend or boss they have had has been unfair, unkind, or unjust? At what point do we then turn the tables and realize the most common denominator – the one constant – in all those situations is us? Looking to your own bouquet of relationships, if each seems deficient in some way, you could be unwittingly living out of the scars of your previous wounds of omission.

As Erin shared about the struggles in her marriage yet another time, certain phrases emerged. Her statements pointed to a pattern of constant dissatisfaction. Her quiet husband, John, shared that he felt like she had too high of expectations, saying "I feel like I can never make you happy; I can never be what you want." The fact that he was involved in counseling with her proved he was committed to working towards change. Some husbands feel the way John expressed and yet don't try to change. However, if one party in a relationship is trying to improve in ways the other person is asking and feels as though it's not enough – that the high bar just keeps being raised – then it's likely deficits from past hurts are coming into play.

Erin humbly explored whether this was the case for her. Surveying her history, she realized her serious high school boyfriend, various girlfriends, and now her husband all echoed the same refrain. While saddened by the awareness, Erin pinpointed her most significant deprivation of unconditional love as coming from the eight to 13 years of age corridor. It was at this critical formative time in her life that her dad's explosive temper was at its worst. She never knew who would walk through the door – the alcohol-influenced-drunken-abuser or her normally emotionally distant but not violent father. When asked what she felt like she missed from this deficit, she said, "…for my dad to help me know who I was and really like who I was."

Reflecting further, Erin was able to see how her internal dissatisfaction and insecurity became displaced onto the people in her life. In other words, when her own father did not mirror back to her the various strengths and weaknesses she possessed or give her feedback about her different or special gifts, this created internal unsureness about who she was. Without her own secure view of self, she did what virtually everyone in that situation does – look to the people around us. Immediately, very Eden-esque, we blame them.

Subtly, codependency develops wherein "if you feel good about me, I feel good about me" or "if you are unhappy with me, I am unhappy with me." If this occurs, we scrutinize every move, word, facial expression and utterance of the other person to try to fill up that internal deficit of wanting peaceful self-understanding. Our inward fault-finding becomes projected on our intimates, and they then become the screen for our self-esteem. As is obvious, the problem is that no matter how excellent that person, friend, or spouse is, he or she cannot undo our inner longing for those close connections we were meant to enjoy as we grew and developed. No one in the present can fulfill our past. The perfect husband can never (and should never) be the perfect daddy, dad, or father. Therefore, if we are not aware of what we are doing, we can unintentionally place unmeetable expectations on the people we love and appreciate the most. Pervasive discontentment is often evidence that we have residue from wounds of omission.

Looking for the Perfect "15"

We were meant to enjoy everyone who has a "vat" in our life in a mutual interchange of blessing. Let's say we can enjoy them on a scale from one to 10. As his wife, I'm going to try to appreciate and take pleasure in Mike to a 10! You are permitted to relish your wonderful boss for the full dose of 10. We're not talking about the level of unconditional love you feel *from* them (how full you think their vat is), but instead how much you love, are intrigued by, and take delight in them as well as appreciating the blessing they are to you personally. So, we can indeed attempt to have a great relationship – to shoot for a "10."

Problems only come when we either try to put them into other people's emptier vats, or when we begin to desire too much from that person. In other words, when we start to attempt to get a "15" from a friendship, we are setting everyone involved up for a disappointment. If we want a "20" out of an already great relationship, this could be a strong indicator that we have past deficits seeking to be completed. Because my relationship with Mike is great, and I enjoy him immensely, when I start wanting to wrestle a "17" of enjoyment out of our relationship, I'm trying to get him to fill another spot, which is not his to satisfy. This is wrong; it is an injustice against another. He's a spouse; he's not a daddy. She's a friend; she's not your mother. If we project our "stuff" on other people, we unwittingly sabotage the glory of God in that relationship, because we are falling prey to the same thing to which we fell prey in the garden – discontent.

Knowing our past wounds and ourselves helps us recognize when we are acting out of them. If we can step back and realize what we are doing, we can then ask ourselves the question, "How would a ____ year-old interact with a good ____ year-old friend?" or "How much time would be appropriate for a ____ year-old to spend with a great coworker, or boss, etc.?" Such evaluation helps us to know when we are dysfunctionally looking to others for too much. Noticing when our thoughts about someone cross over into what you would consider "obsessive" for yourself is another index. One of my clients depicted a couple she knew who obviously didn't know they were trying to push each other into their unfilled vats by saying, "They eat each other alive." If you've ever had a friendship or relationship that befits such a description, the concept of fillings past voids is probably apropos.

<u>Is it Stamped on my Forehead?</u>

I'll never know precisely why it is that some people who have been hurt seem to endure further hurt in the same form time and again. Too numerous to count are the times when my clients have said, "Do I have 'abuse me' written on my forehead?" or "Why does it seem like I just get criticized/lied to/used/ignored/rejected over and over again?" While the answer to that question may not ever be completely understood, it does seem that others can sense, or what I call "smell," damage from another's wounds. Clinton and Sibcy describe it thus:

> Have you even wondered why people with horrific pasts, instead of…living later lives of calm and order, tend to experience more catastrophes later on? When asked why, they might tell you they're convinced that tragedies stalk them, seeking to corrupt their lives like unholy phantoms. Of course, those unholy phantoms are usually themselves, and their misfortunes are a result of their own poor choices... They don't see it, although everyone else does. They generally think they've just had bad luck, or others have had them in their cross hairs.[1]

With compassion paramount, we must wonder about this. I have known individuals who struggle financially whether they are unemployed or have an excellent job. I have seen people be in abusive relationships, only to get out and then later are "just not attracted" to someone who treats them well. You know how it continues – they soon find themselves being mistreated by yet another person. What is this about? We must ask ourselves about our own patterns. Do I do this in some way, also? We are wise to think long and hard on the assertion that people unintentionally recreate their trauma in some form for themselves.[2]

At some level, this occurs because the undone cries to be righted. That which has been unjust in our souls will not simply "go away." Especially if something was supposed to happen for us and did not, this sets in motion deep within us an urging. We will continue to search. It's as if the soul says, "No, no, no. Keep trying. It'll happen." It continues to sort of circle around and, in doing so, explains why the man who felt rejected by his mother marries a critical wife. You'd think he'd find a nurturing gal to latch onto, but instead a subterranean part of him realizes "Here is a woman who is like my mother who appears to love me. *She* will not reject me." Is the wrong righted, however? It can be why you constantly choose friends who are opinionated. It might explain why it seems all your bosses seem boundary-less, requiring more and more of you. Could it be that somewhere deep within, this present person has characteristics of a past figure in your life, so you gravitate toward them in the hope that *they* will respect you, love you, or appreciate you? This is a difficult concept, but it is an important exercise for us all to consider what "signs" we might unwittingly wear.

Past omissions definitely can create this consuming cycle, pulling on us to be completed, and therefore can drive our present-day interactions. In her middle thirties, Valerie is attractive, talented, and successful, yet her heart breaks as she remains single (because she wants so badly to be married). As I survey her life, only one reason makes any sense at all about her pervasive loneliness. She fits in the category of a person who is looking to get. She will give to people, but ultimately only to get something in return for herself. Her past has significant deficits in it, and she keeps trying to fit present friends into her Mom vat, and wants a husband so badly because it might shut that Daddy vat up. When she gets a friend, she stops by their house and asks them to do things multiple times a week. She can't get enough. When she's had a good time with someone, she's already initiating for the next outing. At some level, I believe Valerie's friends know she is looking to them for something they cannot give, so they gently back away. Proverbs 25:16 and 17 is striking: "If you find honey, eat just enough – too much of it, and you will vomit. Seldom set foot in your neighbor's house – too much of you, and he will hate you." She has discovered the honey of other relationships, but is suffering the consequence of wanting a "15."

Jacqueline knew she had deficits and that she looked for them to be filled. She described herself as feeling "like Oliver lifting my bowl for more gruel" when with others who treated her well. She was in touch with the inner throbbing from past hurts, and has learned well how to manage the effects of being a sexual abuse survivor. However, she admits that if she did not, she might have become an overly sexual person, and likely would have channeled that toward females. She knows that for her, lesbian feelings are a result of starving to death for nurturing love. It is devastating, but true. When someone is physically starving to death, they will eat things they never would have even considered were they not excruciatingly hungry. The same is true for us emotionally. There are men who have faced such tremendous rejection from their fathers that anything will look like food to their souls, especially other men. I'll never forget Thomas who sat crying with me, saying, "I just let him use me over and over. He ravages my body and I let him. I hate this, but I can't stop." He was afraid of women and still longing for the male protection and attention he always dreamed of from his distant dad. Another Proverb bespeaks to this treacherous truth: "…to the hungry even what is bitter tastes sweet" (Proverbs 27:7).

If you seem to experience the same type of hurt over and over, you might be operating out of your deficits. Wounds of omission could be pulsating to be righted, and you might unintentionally be looking to people similar to the ones who hurt you to treat you well, and take away the hurt. We are foolish to remain out of touch with past hurts and unaware of the greater spiritual battle from which their personal struggles stem. Let us no longer allow undone elements of our lives to drive us. Let us be spurred on by the depth of God's love, the sweet tastes of freedom, and the hope for true victory.

A Little "Jumpy"

When you get a bruise or a deep cut and someone accidentally comes near it, what do you do? You pull away. We all get a bit "jumpy" when we have a significant pain, and tend to be over-reactive to anything similar happening again. Likewise, if we find we have some knee-jerk reactions to others and oversensitivities to certain people, we could very well possess wounds of omission. Do you have some "jumpy" areas that when others approach, you overreact? When someone new initiates getting together with you, do you immediately think "What do they want from me?"? How about when a friend leaves a message that says, "I need to talk to you"? Are you frozen in fear at what you anticipate to be their rejection or disappointment? I know people who interpret an unreturned phone call as "They don't like me." Others translate people's questions as interrogation, rather than interest and enjoyment. Still others doubt one who gives them a compliment, certain that they are insincere. Do such overreactions come from years of yearning for parental love and affirmation unmet, sort of like "I remember hoping for that before, so

I'm not going to put myself in the position of getting hurt like that again"?

The way that being oversensitive relates to having wounds of omission is that we don't want anyone near this area of hurt, so once they start to get near it, we get quite uncomfortable. So, if I spent years longing for affirmation, when someone gives it, I become over-analytical and second-guessing. If I wasn't nurtured, I am strangely drawn to, and repelled by, nurturing people and acts. A clear sign that we are oversensitive because of past omissions is when we have a reaction out of proportion to an incident.

For instance, if your spouse forgets to pick up the item at the store you requested and you go ballistic, it is likely you are overreacting based on a past hurt. In other words, if an offense or slight or hurt is given you that would rate a "5" on a scale, but your reaction is a "25," then your emotion is siphoning off from some other unhealed wound. Mike not recalling what I said yesterday is not worthy of asking him to sleep in another room for the next month (which has never happened, mind you.). However, it could indicate that I am oversensitive to people not really listening to me. The next time you find yourself obsessing about a comment, you might want to examine why your reaction is so big in comparison to the small statement it was.

Basically, our oversensitivities are like the lens concept examined above. Wounds of omission also cause us to wear untrue perspectives through which we filter information. For example, Candy bemoaned one day that her husband "doesn't make me feel special" and instead made her "feel invisible." When we focused on these feelings, it became clear this was an oversensitivity of hers. She relayed how she would become angry when her bosses at work would disregard her input, and how furious she would feel when her co-workers did not read her written reports. In her healing process, Candy rightly identified that her greatest deficits were in adolescence, at which time both parents were completely detached from her. Just when she was needing affirmation that she was developing into a person who could think and act well for herself, instead her parents were nowhere to be found – her dad having moved out and her mom focusing solely on living her own life. In this way, Candy's deficit created a template through which she viewed her life. She was oversensitive to being ignored and feeling invisible. In fact, people with certain wounds of omission almost expect to be betrayed and abandoned, because in the past, their support figures have repeatedly let them down. Our past can set the stage for how our current relationships will unfold, especially if we wear some diabolical lens that other people are not reliable, dependable, or trustworthy when it comes to my needs.

When I think of my own oversensitivities from wounds of omission, I envision it to be much like a fishhook that catches the corner of my mouth. It's akin to a fish that sees a worm that looks good to eat, and so without examining it, takes a bite and is then "hooked." I refer to this as "being plucked." The sense of being plucked is the idea that my hunger drives me to be open to what will not be best for me. Some days I will interact with a male who is in charge, and I'll be fine, acting and reacting within our adult-to-adult relationship. Sometimes, however, especially when I am caught off guard, I can look to that person for too much. The "worm" is the potential for a person in authority to give me affirmation. I can quickly be moved to try to take a bite of that, only to realize it is not the true love I seek, and that it actually hurts me in the process because of how that person cannot provide what I am looking for. Conversely, I can also be deeply bothered if that same authority figure seems to withhold affirmation from me. I am plucked by being overly concerned with whether this person thinks I am valuable, worthy, and acceptable. Wrong person, wrong desire. My past is breaking through, and I am "hooked" to do whatever it takes to gain that desperately desired approval. Thankfully, I can then backtrack and re-situate myself. The idea of "being plucked," though, is helpful for us to realize when we are oversensitive or overreacting to something. What plucks you?

Despise the Desire

Some people who are "plucked" to want too much from people conversely go the other direction. Instead of oversensitivity, they attempt to deaden themselves from the longings which remain from their wounds of omission. Theirs is a life of "numbing," or denying their yearning for love and approval. Any attempt to kill desire is likely a result of significant wounds of omission. "Hope deferred makes the heart sick," Scripture says (Proverbs 13:12). They hoped for love so very deeply, that when that hope was dashed time and again, in essence they developed "sick hearts." An example of a sick heart is one where the most basic desire of all human beings – to be loved – is essentially hated and repudiated. There are many people in this day and age who cut – who mark their bodies by using razors, knives, and fingernails to draw blood. While there are a variety of reasons why people do this, often cutting is a person's way to punish him or herself for neediness and desire. If you harm yourself in any way, the root might be a wound of omission.

Emotional Time Warp

How old do you feel inside? Do you feel ten? Eighteen? Twelve? When surveyed, it's amazing how young most people feel on the inside. I've talked with millionaires who feel nine and college professors frozen at fourteen. Do you know what that is a clue to? It's a hint to our woundings. It's a shadow of a place we got stuck, emotionally. You see, when deprivation takes place, a child suffers an injury to a part of the budding self. The growth process in this portion of the self stops, and a part of the soul begins to atrophy. It stays behind, out of time, while the rest of the person continues developing. That's why brilliant scholars can be socially inept and incredible mothers can't navigate a peer friendship. Assessing what age you feel inside can help you understand what was going on with you around that time of life that caused a "hold" to occur. Many times, we feel inside like whatever age we were when our needs for love, understanding, and nourishment were not met.

Wounds of omission can cause us to feel quite young on the inside, something we hide from others. We long for people in ways that feel childish at times. Another contributor to feeling young inside is if you started abusing drugs when you were twelve, or started drinking alcohol when you were ten, you could very well be stuck there. A part of you can remain at that emotional age because instead of learning how to deal with the many emotional and sexual feelings of that period of life, you got used to numbing yourself from the situation. For a time, the substance allowed you to "escape" from difficulty and intense emotion. In doing so, you became exempt from having to develop capacities for facing pain and hurt. This exemption now causes you to sense you are younger internally than your actual age, and can be an indicator of wounds of omission.

<u>Hating the Addiction I Love</u>

Finally, when we become addicted to something – and this can be *anything* – it could signal unhealed wounds of omission. When we develop a pattern of attempting to fill our deficient love vats with something, that something can insidiously become our everything. The depth of longing for love and nurturance became so intense that we unintentionally become enslaved to the thing that "took the edge off" for even a short time. That's why addictions of any sort are so hard to break. They mean so much. They've been used to replace, literally, what can't be replaced – relationships. Two authors aptly describe:

> The man addicted to pornography (i.e. the woman who is always available to him through books, magazines, or the Internet) creates a false intimacy. Even positive addictions and rituals – like studies, sports, and religious activities – can create a false sense of closeness in which habits and things replace our need for relationship.[3]

This last point is instructive for many of us. God's word informs us that "death and destruction are never satisfied, and neither are the eyes of man" (Proverbs 27:20). When we look to something to alleviate the destruction or loss (death) from our past, it will never be completely fulfilling. That latte that you've come to so enjoy could actually be more than just your morning drink. The way you love to shop immediately after a fight with your spouse is not a coincidence. Messing with your computer games, having a nightcap, and that pornographic secret can all come from those screeching empty buckets. Especially if you are desperate to break this addiction, and have tried over and over, this could definitely be a sign that you are battling wounds of omission.

The Hallmark of Shame

A major billboard advertising the presence of one or both types of wounds is shame. When we receive wounds growing up, we often come to believe that some part of us, maybe every part of us, is marred. It happens when we think the things that have happened to us were somehow *our fault* – that I deserved it. If only I had been prettier or smarter or done more or pleased them, somehow it wouldn't have happened. I would have been loved. They wouldn't have hurt me. This is how shame comes to exist deep within.

> Shame enters in and makes its crippling home deep within our hearts…Shame is that feeling that haunts us, the sense that if someone really knew us, they would shake their heads in disgust and run away. Shame makes us feel, no, believe, that we do not measure up – not to the world's standards, the church's standards, or our own.[4]

One of evil's goals of wounding us with lies is to invoke shame because it says we are unworthy, broken, and beyond repair. Remember the truths of God in chapter one – that we are entirely worthy because of Christ, and a beautiful piece of His craftsmanship intended for purposeful power as we move about planet earth? Shame wins when it trumps "I did something bad" with "I *am* bad." Moving about our daily affairs with a sense of godly propulsion to pour ourselves out, looking to freely give is sabotaged when we believe we are utterly defective. Shame (not godly conviction) is a strong gauge for us to know if we have deep wounds of omission or commission. Let not another moment pass before you stop living under this heinous oppression.

"Oh, Lord, Search me and Know Me…"

As has been evident thus far, recognition is key. As you pray, "Oh, Lord, search me and know me," ask the Spirit of God to show you specifics. He will. Falling prey to an addiction you can't break, feeling young inside, trying to squelch your desire for being loved or punishing yourself for having such wants, having oversensitivities to certain types of people, sensing you have a "sign" on your head, wanting a "16" out of a relationship, overreacting to certain situations, or struggling with being discontent in, or dissatisfied with, all your relationships are some of the indications that wounds of omission might be at the root of your present struggles. If residue from wounds of commission is the culprit for you, you could be burnt out, depressed, unable to imagine yourself being like confident or healthy people you know, deeply convicted by God's truth about you, or rejecting of any positive feedback given you. The reason to engage in such an internal survey is so we can appropriately identify the type of wound to assure the right process of reversing these evil effects. God has a plan to glorify Himself through your life and person, a plan that is an amazing, fulfilling path of maturity, freedom, and victory in Jesus. *Let us press in to truth, recognition, and awareness and run this healing race with endurance!*

5

REAL FILLING

*You have made us to be toward yourself, O Lord,
and our hearts are restless until they find their rest in Thee.*
ST. AUGUSTINE

*O God, you are my God, earnestly I seek you; my soul thirsts for you, my body longs
for you, in a dry and weary land where there is no water.*
PSALM 63:1

For some of you, this previous section has been intense, as you
have seen yourself in multiple examples. For others, you have rushed
forward, with a sense of urgency, agreeing that the battle for your soul
has included effects of wounds, and wanting solutions. Because the point
cannot be overemphasized, such exploration is important in order that
we "not be unwise about the devil's schemes" (2 Corinthians 2:11).
Dallas Willard says we are in danger of missing the fullness of life offered
to us and challenges, "Would he (God) leave us even temporarily
marooned with no help in our kind of world, with our kinds of problems:
psychological, emotional, social and global?"[1] His contention is that God
is involved in the "awesome needs of present human life," that He is
quite concerned about human character, and that some have minimized
the goal of the Christian faith to nothing but death and after. It is a true
and glorious fact, as Willard intimates, that God is truly Emmanuel – a
God who is *with us* in every sense possible.[2] With Emmanuel as our

foundation, there is nothing that can ultimately prevail over the freedom and victory of our souls in Jesus Christ.

If you haven't already been thinking it, at some point you'd likely ask where the work and person of Jesus comes into this internal picture we've been exploring. Where does God fit into this "vat" configuration? When we accept Jesus Christ as our Lord and Savior, we'll often expect Him to *fill every need we've ever had from every human who's ever hurt us.* If someone has deficits like "I so long for a comforting mom" or "I would give anything to have that gentle, approving, involved dad," then it's easy to see how when that person accepts Christ and looks to Him for fulfillment, he or she would assume Christ fills the void, thereby "fixing" the problem. Our mostly unspoken and unconscious assumption is that Jesus completes us where we are incomplete. And while there is a truth in that equation, we are mistaken when we naively think, "If I accept Jesus, I'll just feel better about all of the major damage that was done to me when I was young. It's not going to hurt so much. Diagram five shows us the mistaken belief many Christians possess.

While it is true that we are reborn (1 John 5:1), regenerate (1 Peter 1:23), new creatures, and that the old has gone and the new has come (2 Corinthians 5:17), *there is no Biblical basis that He* **undoes** *what was done to us in the past.* He doesn't usually erase people's memories. He doesn't usually grow someone's arm back after they've had it lopped off. In the same way that we have emotional wounds, He does not come and compensate and take away the damage that was done to you by some gaping deficit. So where is He in this whole thing? Paul didn't forget that he had persecuted so many Christians. Joseph didn't have the memory of his brother's betrayal erased. The father of the prodigal wasn't naïve about how much pain his son had caused him. Such inner

<u>Diagram 5</u>

awareness is crucial because so many of us are walking around
disappointed with God for not doing what we thought He would,
especially when it comes to healing our past wounds.

However, what God *does* do with our past troubles is consistent,
transformative, and wonderful. He time and again demonstrates that He
is in the business of taking what was intended to damage or harm us –

what Satan intended to put us "down for the count" – and He turns it around. He is all about redemption. His promise is to "restore the years the locusts have eaten" (Joel 2:25). And in the middle of our personal redemption story, He is the one who bears our sorrows, the one who collects our tears in a bottle, our primary comforter who says, "Come to me, and I will give you rest" (Psalm 68:1, Psalm 56:8, Matthew 11:28). So where *IS* He in this whole thing?

Theologically, there are no bounds to God. He doesn't have a "vat," per se, but if we stay with our conceptualization of internal vats for purposes of discussion, God's "vat" would be humongous. While in actuality, His unconditional love for us is boundless, if we tried to depict it in vat diagram, every square inch of God's enormous vat would be full. The one-way, delighting in, valuing love that meets the deepest human needs is complete in the Lord. Saying that His vat is completely full means that every time we go to Him, He will never disappoint. Any need we take to Him, He promises to meet (Philippians 4:19). Anytime we come to Him with a prayer request, He promises an answer (John 16:23-24). He is the unconditional One. He always responds to our needs. His rebuke is gentle and loving. He is the One who gives more than we could ask or imagine, but unless we take our eyes off our deficits and turn to see all that He is, we will not experience Him for who He is (see Diagram six).

What we do instead, often, is to just keep focusing on, "Why isn't He fixing this? Why is this not going away? Why isn't He reversing the effects of this?" When we focus on our pain and woundedness, we miss what He has for us and who He is for us. You see, when we look for Him to be there for us in definite, specific ways, we are just like those

<u>Diagram 6</u>

who missed the Messiah. When we cry out for deliverance *on our terms,*
we miss Him. Why did many who longed for the Messiah miss Him?
They had been anxious for His arrival. They were looking for a political
ruler who would come in with military strength and rule in might.
Instead, He came in on a donkey and ruled in humility. Although they
were searching for their Savior, they missed Him because *they had their
focus in the wrong place.*

If we're looking for God to cause our abuser to repent, our parent to change, our friend to apologize, or our innocence to return, we are unwittingly dictating how our deliverance should look. When we expect God to be the mother we never had, the boss who didn't sabotage our career, or the pastor who didn't disappoint us, we are focused on a specific type of healing. Whether consciously or unconsciously, when we presume God will completely alleviate the hurts of life, we are telling Him we want His provision on our terms. Focusing on the wrongs done to us, the pain from our wounds, and all the resultant present-day issues sets us up for further disappointment. When we come to God with a certain picture of just how He will heal us, we can end up in a faith crisis.

It is impossible to gaze in two directions at one time. (Try it!) This reality is also true for what Scripture calls the eyes of our heart. We cannot be firmly locked onto the Lord and simultaneously engrossed in areas of pain. To affix your gaze to Jesus means you cannot be intently staring at your hurt. The Bible is abundantly clear about how we are to focus: "let us fix our eyes on Jesus, the author and perfecter of our faith" (Hebrews 12:2), "forgetting what lies behind, and straining towards what is ahead" (Philippians 3:13), "so we fix our eyes not on what is seen but on what is unseen" (2 Corinthians 4:18). Please hear this, though. To focus on Christ does not mean to deny or ignore our wounds. That would fly in the face of the awareness plea I've been making all along! What I want to make patently clear, though, is that if our deficits, injustices committed against us, and personal pain are what we *indulge* on a regular basis, then healing will be far from us.

When we steady our gaze on the Father, what do we behold? Remember, the vat within us with His name on it is entirely full to the

brim. Authors Clinton and Sibcy remind us God is the ultimate
attachment figure.

> He will always be there. He applauds our uniqueness, He cheers
> our joy, and He weeps with us in our sorrows. He will never die.
> His presence is eternal and His love is everlasting. He fills a
> place in our hearts that only He can fill. He'll work in every
> aspect of our lives – our brokenness, our rebellion, our beauty,
> and even in our plainness.[3]

Such love is overwhelming! He sticks closer than a brother (Proverbs
18:24). He promises to never leave us or forsake us (Hebrews 13:5).
There is no condemnation for Christians (Romans 8:1). He has adopted
us and is our most tender Daddy (Romans 8:15). He delivers us from all
fear (Psalm 34:4). He has made us His heirs (Romans 8:17). He has
given us all the counseling we need for life in the indwelling person of the
Holy Spirit (Romans 8:23). There's not one thing happening in our lives
He isn't working for our good (Romans 8:28). We have total freedom in
Him (Romans 8:21, 2 Corinthians 3:17, Galatians 5:1). His love for us
will never wane or end (Jeremiah 31:3, Romans 8:39). I could quite
literally go on and on with truths about all that He is and does (realize
most of these verses were taken primarily from just one of the 1,189
chapters in the Bible!).

Such unbelievable truths are there for us, just a glance away. If
we stop staring at the gaping wounds we have, the scene of the accident,
and the ones who hurt us and instead look upward at the doctor kneeling
over us, only then can we realize how very close our healing is. Such
"turning" – turning the eyes of our hearts to God – is why the old hymn
has had such transgenerational appeal: "Turn your eyes upon Jesus, look
full in His wonderful face, and the things of earth will go strangely dim in

the light of His glory and grace." The truth therein has resonated with humankind. We've experienced it, even if just in snippets.

Scripture is full of allusions to opening our mouths so that He can satisfy us with good things. Are our mouths open to Him for filling, or are we looking to that person or people who hurt us to undo that hurt and fill us instead? Turning to Him instead of our throbbing wounds, opening ourselves to His filling involves a stance much like the Roman Centurion in Mark 9. At his daughter's graveside he said to Jesus, "I believe. Help my unbelief" (Mark 9:24). My sense is that you are reading on in this book because you believe. You trust that the sum total of your life thus far is not the end-all of what God has promised for those who hope in Him. However, you struggle and doubt, especially when you don't seem to be changing or growing like you'd like. In your bed at night, the questions sometimes come loud and pictures from the past seem clearer than ever. You think that this can't be *it* – all there is. Thanks be to God, it isn't.

However, there is an undeniable sense that we must reach out and grab the abundance. We must *apprehend* the truth. We must *embrace* Christ. It is necessary to *turn* our eyes upon Jesus. It doesn't have to be pretty, or even super spiritual, but when we're willing to say, "I believe. Help my unbelief. I don't know how you're going to do this, Lord," He honors it. When we come to Him not with "fix this, God," but because we believe Him, in this moment, real change begins. When we come to Him just for who He is, when we trust in Him, when we look at what He says He is and who He says He is, and believe Him on those terms, be assured He will honor this. When we can by faith say, "I'm going to trust that You're good all the time even though I can't see it. I'm going to trust that You're completely consistent in your character. I'm going to trust that You are faithful, faithful, faithful, even unto the ends of the earth," then He's going to start showing Himself to you. More accurately, you will finally begin to have eyes that see.

Anytime we lay down our own agenda for how we want Him to meet our needs and how we want Him to come into our lives and make everything all better, we give ourselves a chance at true healing. Instead of coming to God with our list of things that need fixed, true liberation begins when we say, "I believe you are all I need, despite my pain. Help my unbelief." When we get to that space, we can then and only then let Him do the deeper work of being the One who says, "I can do more than you can ask or imagine" (Ephesians 3:20). Philippians 4:19 is stunning: "And my God will meet all your needs according to His riches in Christ Jesus." *All my needs?!* God will handle my emotional swings, sexual fits, and financial burdens? The answer is "yes." More so, it's not just a stingy, parsed out meeting of our needs, but "according to His *riches* in Christ Jesus." There is such a level of extreme generosity here that it takes my breath away. He died to give us the best of the best. Do you believe this? It is what God promises: "I'll meet all needs, but you must stop coming to me with your limiting bill of goods that you mandate me to fulfill" like: "Can you please give me a boyfriend?" "I need a better job." "Can you please make me the leader of a small group?" He has much more to give than such simple things. He wants to give deeper realities, like abiding peace and joy, which are beyond imagination and outside our comprehension.

Megan had an earthly father who beat her, abandoned her, and abused her. She has memories of him striking her in front of her friends, of him screaming at her to the point where the neighbors could hear, and of blaming her for his anger. Understandably, the wounds she now struggles with are many: trusting others, self-protection, self-hatred, perfectionism, isolating, depression, and panic attacks. Certainly the idea of turning to a God who calls Himself Father for unconditional love was a huge hurdle for her. While she had confessed Christ, the concept of God as a loving Father never connected with her. One Sunday at church, the message was on Romans 8 wherein God refers to Himself as "Abba." The literal interpretation of the word is "Daddy" and is meant to convey the idea of a tender, involved, gentle, attentive Father. She internally bristled as the pastor explained that God's desire is that we call out to Him as daddy, with arms open, and fully trusting Him to meet our needs.

That afternoon she was at a party. The face of one of the men in the crowd gripped her. Ever vigilant around any man, she followed his intense gaze, and then watched him push his way through a crowd of people to run to his little daughter and pick her up just before she stepped unknowingly into peril. Watching for a chastisement or stern warning to be careful, Megan's heart melted as she saw this daddy kiss the little girl he had scooped up. Apparently, he felt no need to scold, but instead smiled and laughed as his precious one scurried down his side and on her merry little way. In that instant, Megan saw an "Abba." His focus was on his child, even amidst the crowd. His watchful eye was always on her. He rescued her without her knowledge. He delighted in her uniqueness. He scooped her up and held her tight. He gently kissed her cheek. He let her freely run and play. Megan knew this day God had given her a picture of Himself. It was no coincidence that she was exposed to this interaction the same day as the message on "Abba." It matters not whether you are a male or a female. Do you need to shed yourself of some tainted view of God as Father because of your own experience of "dad" thus far in life?

The foregoing discussion boils down to this: *We must come to God for God, not for what He can do for us.* Healing actually accelerates when we turn to Him for who He is and not for how He can heal us. One client of mine said she felt like she had been stuck in a pattern of treating God like a vending machine. "If I put in my coin, I feel I should get what I want in return," she said, "and when it doesn't work, I find that I want to shake the machine, because I'm not getting what I ordered." God is not a vending machine, Santa, or the Starbucks clerk who gives me just exactly what I order in timely fashion. Larry Crabb suggests Christians today suffer from this "If-I-do-what-I-should-then-I-should-get-what-I-want" mentality. He says our hope has become "a responsive Christ who satisfie(s) His hurting people by quickly granting them the relief they demand."[4] If this has been our hope – "Undo the hurt caused me in life and take away my pain, God!" – then I am certain we remain stuck in patterns, and frustrated with ourselves and others.

What are we to do, then? Everyone knows our troubles drive us to God more than times of ease. Our hurts cause us to cry out for healing more than times of calm. Perhaps this is not a problem at all. Perhaps it could be even part of a blessed plan to keep us close and dependent upon Jesus. (Remember Paul's thorn in the flesh?) The problem, then, is not when we come to Him out of our difficulty, wounds, and hurts. It never works, though, when we come to Him demanding for Him to fix us, others, or something about our lives. His constant plea to us throughout Scripture is "come to Me" (Matthew 19:14, John 7:37). He even promises to carry our burdens and give us rest (Matthew 11:28). The coming to Jesus, though, must be because we believe in Him and who He said He was, not because He will fix my problems like some cosmic repairman.

While the difference is subtle, it is critical. The result is significant. It's huge. When I interact with, choose to worship, and proclaim my trust in Christ because I believe He is who He says He is, *then* healing and deliverance commence. My relationships are transformed as I commune with God because He is God, not because I keep waiting on Him to change them all. Anglican Bishop Stephen Neill explains that all of a Christian's life "…depends on a certain inner relatedness to the living Christ. Through this relatedness all other relationships of a man – to God, to himself, to other people – are transformed."[5] If we want a different external life, our internal life must be different, too.

While we are going to discuss more specific aspects, patterns, and tools of the healing process in chapters eight through eleven, what we are discussing here is the foundation for all else. If we want to be *transformed* (completely altered, not just a tad better), Romans 12:2 tells us how: "Do not conform any longer to the pattern of this world, but be transformed by the renewing of your mind in Christ Jesus." Do you hear it? *Turn your eyes upon Jesus.* Lenses that we have in place from wounds of commission are changed through recognition and replacement with the truth. Deficits from wounds of omission are addressed fully through identification and interaction with Jesus. Addictions, shame, patterns of discontentment, struggles with identity, purposelessness, depression, anger, and the whole host of other hellish schemes against us are defeated only as we run back to our Abba, with arms open, crying out for help. Every time we do, we'll bump into the fullness of His vat. His love is unconditional, endless, and lavished upon us (1 John 3:1). We will not "see" Him in this light unless we first turn our eyes away from our hurts.

The critical, can't-move-forward-without-it, won't be healed-unless-we-have-it foundation is a fundamental, deep, abiding and trusted security in God. This includes the belief that you are His, made for His purposes, and that your truest life will only be discovered in Him. This is the all-important first action of real change – assuring that you have this foundation. And please, *stop here* if you don't have it. Wrestle it out. Get in the word. Have friends pray for you, but don't move on, because nothing else will work. Even if you have great tools, you can't use them well unless they are placed firmly in a secure toolbox. If not, they'll be scattered about and used willy-nilly, with no rhyme or reason. Maybe that's why all the seminars, counseling, and reading you've already done hasn't really worked. You don't have deep, abiding trust in Christ. Real trust that says He is good and His ways are right no matter what I think or feel.

With great sadness I am reminded of a woman who spoke with me after a presentation on communication skills I gave for a business group last week. She apologetically approached me and said, "I want to tell you that I've done everything and I just can't seem to get better. I've been to 10 different counselors in the last 15 years. I've done hypnosis, biofeedback, Freudian analysis, positive thinking, group therapy, meditation, behavior modification, and inner child work." I knew what was coming next. She said, "But none of it has worked. Nothing I've tried has made me any better. As a matter of fact, I think some of it has actually made me worse." I was sickened, as I have observed this reality with my own eyes in all the training hoops I've been required to jump through. Counselors get richer while people are none the better. Why? Because true healing only occurs in Jesus Christ. Some symptoms are alleviated for awhile, but deep, lasting change only happens as people choose to believe God and plant themselves on Jesus. It's a fact that with a solid foundation, complete restructuring can occur! Incidentally, I thanked her for sharing so vulnerably with me, and admitted I had only one thing to offer her. When I communicated that all my personal and professional experience has shown me there is just one answer, Christ, she burst into tears. She said, "I don't know why I'm crying, but no, I haven't tried God. I'm an atheist." I wondered if she would ever understand the tears that ran down her cheeks, seemingly by themselves, were the very validation she needed that her soul longs for Him.

It is being included in the eternal life of God that heals all wounds. Seriously, what really matters once you are included? You have been *chosen*. By GOD. "God's demonstration of love at the Cross should end all doubt as to whether God is for us."[6] This message of the kingdom is the only one that allows us to stop demanding relief from our pain or escape from our troubles. God says, "I will give them a place forever in my house, and a name better than sons and daughters, a name that will stand forever" (Isaiah 56:5). This was spoken to the non-Israelites who felt on the outside looking in and the eunuchs, who could never have a family of their own. Haven't you felt on the outside looking in at other people who seem healthy, who seem to be able to rest in God, and who aren't controlled by their pasts? In your life, you must choose to believe the goodness of God or you will not truly be at peace with him. From this place come rivers of healing.

We believe, Lord. Help our unbelief.

6

SPACE IN YOUR SOUL

Until we acknowledge painful disappointment in our circumstances and relationships (particularly the latter), we will not pursue Christ with the passion of deep thirst.
LARRY CRABB

Though he brings grief, he will show compassion, so great is his unfailing love.
LAMENTATIONS 3:32

When my mom fell down some unfamiliar stairs last Christmas Eve, she broke her foot. One eye socket became a stunning shade of chartreuse, while her four stitches served to complete a trendy look for the new year. The unique melding of yellow and brown perfectly complemented her new fashion statement so that all eyes were on her! Wherever my mom went, she caught second glances and had to answer the question, "What happened to you?" Now, consider, did my mother choose to have this happen to her? Did she do it on purpose? The stares, the doctors' appointments, limited mobility, a less-than-perfect holiday…she was faced with dealing with the effects. In other words, although it wasn't her fault and she certainly didn't choose to receive those wounds, she had to deal with the consequences of them.

We have to accept – and this is hard – that our pain, our hurt, our suffering, while not our own fault, is still our problem. Our wounds and everything that has resulted from them are now our responsibility. In other words, no person will ever experience healing and freedom unless he or she grasps the personal accountability in it. We have all seen ones living out of a victim mentality, never moving on in maturity, because of a refusal to accept this hard truth. Whatever was handed us in the past now sits fully on our lap in the present. If someone, either accidentally or on purpose, gashes me with a knife, it is now my responsibility to handle. I must take action for healing to occur. If not, significantly worse damage could result from neglecting a wound. In the same manner, unless we actively pursue healing of our emotional wounds, more damage can occur as a result. If I need help in dealing with my physical wound, I must get it. I must actively apply the healing elements and follow any prescription given. If someone places a burning coal in your lap, most likely you will not wait for that person to then remove it. It is indeed a difficult and unjust truism: although we would have never wanted to be wounded, we alone must now take responsibility for that very wound. If we have been handed a heritage of alcoholism, violated through sexual abuse, neglected by self-centered parents or betrayed by trusted friends, we haven't chosen to be hurt, but we must take ownership for ourselves and our healing.

Acceptance is a Decision

All of this hinges upon acceptance. We have to behold our injury and accept that we have been injured before healing can commence. Acceptance is a hard pill to swallow. Do you understand that the harsh words spoken to you when you were younger leave you to deal with the consequences? If you're waiting for the other person to make it right, it's a long life. If we're waiting for the one who wronged us to undo the damage, we are waiting for the wrong thing. It's now ours to handle. This critical turning point for anyone who is impeded by past hurts is to realize "It's now on me." If I was formed in a household of anger, I have to assume responsibility for my own temper as an adult.

Having been reared in a context of financial mismanagement does not excuse my personal financial distress today. We can spend life saying, "I didn't want to be handed this! I didn't want this!" or we can realize the first step in the healing journey is saying, "It's mine, and I must accept it." Healing begins when we turn this corner.

That the effects of our wounds are now our responsibility can cause us to quickly look around at others. "Why do I have to have *this*?" "What about her?" "It's not fair!" However, the quicker we can realize everybody has his or her burdens to bear, wounds to tend, and obstacles to overcome, the better off we'll be. Would you ever wish to have her cancer? His sexual abuse? The point is, can you just say yes to the thing that has happened to you? Can you say yes to "I have been wounded?" Can you say yes to "I accept that, and it means I must deal with the consequences, even though I didn't choose it?" That's a big step of maturity. To be clear, saying yes doesn't mean jumping up and down for joy, but rather acknowledging and adjusting to all that life has for you. Only those hard after Jesus can really say, "I accept that, although I did not want this abuse to occur to me, I now have a trust issue to deal with. It's my issue now." "I accept that even though when I was young these words were said to me that caused me to question what I looked like, I accept now my eating disorder is my issue." Can you see the transfer? Such a step is not easy, and involves many emotions, yet if we become people who say, "Yes, Lord, I'll accept it," we take the first step toward a very significant amount of healing.

What has your past handed you, for better and for worse? Have you taken those strengths and talents and positive experiences and run with them, capitalizing on having such a skill in your gift set? Likewise, have you agreed to shoulder all that the hurts in your life have wrought?

Do you accept that your propensity towards lust, overspending, judgmentalism, depression, or self-loathing, is *yours* now to deal with, even though you would have never chosen to possess such a thing?

However, if we continue to ask, "Why me? Why couldn't I have had her dad? Why couldn't I have had that brother over there, who wouldn't have done that to me?" we will be fighting the wrong battle, and putting our energies in the wrong place. We have to be willing to take ownership and admit our patterns, our addictions, our relational issues, and our lies. So, as the damage has surfaced during your reading of this book, it's important for you to now realize you cannot be a blamer, a denier, or an avoider. Those things destroy ownership. My problem is still my problem, even though the source is not mine. Are you willing to go there and take huge steps toward maturity this very minute? Have you told the Lord that you accept the painful and challenging things in your life? Will you now? Doing so is a crucial first pillar on the foundation of trusting His character, as we talked about in the last chapter.

Grieving What Could Have Been

When we cross the threshold to acceptance, it is virtually always accompanied by grief. The picture I've observed not only in my office for the last 13 years, but also as a pastor's wife is that healing occurs in this fashion: (1) increasing awareness of the larger spiritual battle wherein evil is bent on our destruction, (2) becoming acquainted with the type and degree of our woundedness, (3) choosing to trust that God is *enough* based upon His revealed Truth (this is the foundation upon which healing is built), (4) accepting what soul injuries we have had, including accepting their effects in present-day life, and (5) grieving the losses associated with all the previous elements. While grief is not where the process ends, it is a critical point for forward movement through our issues.

Grief is a part of our everyday life, if we have eyes to see. Not only are we all grieving for losing the innocence of Eden, but some of us also have much else to grieve. When I made this point during a seminar, a young lady whose mother had died in her teen years approached me. She wondered why much of her life she would talk with lots of people, sharing too much about what was going on with her life with practically anyone who would listen. Then she told me, "I shared everything with my mom." Notice, there are two significant losses here. What's the first one? Her mother, of course. What's the second one? The person who listened to every word she had to say. There is grief for every legitimate loss, not just for the ones that involve caskets.

This is the challenge – many people associate grief so closely with death and tears, that unless those are present, they are not aware of their own grief, or need to grieve. Grief is actually a healthy part of life. Grief is good. It helps to heal our hearts. Consider, Jesus himself was a "man of sorrows and acquainted with grief" (Isaiah 53:3). Grief is a much larger concept than simply crying. It has been defined as "heartache, heartbreak, brokenheartedness, pain of mind on account of something in the past, mental suffering arising from any cause, and sorrow or sadness".[1] Grief is simply the reaction to any loss. Losses can range from loss of employment, pets, status, friends, or possessions, to the loss of the people nearest to us. While different losses may have different circumstances and intensities, nearly all involve similar grief processes.[2]

"Grief" is often a misunderstood or minimized word. Yet it is a crucial, can't-get-around-it aspect of any true healing. Said as succinctly as I can put it, grief is what happens when we ponder "what might have been." Sitting in front of the casket of a young person, we mourn what their life could have been. At the more predictable funeral of an older person, grief brings into focus what we have lost. Grief over emotional wounds encompasses both facets. It comes when we consider, "What would I have been like if _____ hadn't happened?" "Who would I have been if this hadn't happened?" "If my parents had never gotten divorced…." "If he had never laid a hand on me…." "If she hadn't said that to me…." That's when grief comes, as we interact with those types of thoughts. "What would I be like if I didn't have to fight this inner insecurity/self-hatred/eating disorder every day?" "What kind of woman would I be if not for the sexual abuse?" "What would my life have been like had not my dad died?" "Who would I have been with the love and support of two committed parents?" "How would I be different if Sarah hadn't betrayed my trust so violently in seventh grade?" The answers to these questions and their accompanying emotions open the door for grief. Have you really ever entertained how you and your life would be different were it not for your wounds and their effects?

Brenda was fantastic by pretty much everybody's standards. She had been a successful lawyer prior to having children and choosing stay-at-home parenting. She was beautiful, outgoing, friendly, dedicated to her family, and seemed to have it all together. She was even a strong Christian. When she came to my office in her early forties, it struck me that she had carried around a horrific secret of ongoing sexual abuse from her brother for many years. Although she had disclosed it to family members, she had never explored all the consequences of it. As we spent time identifying her pervasive lack of trust, self-protective stance, performance-based evaluations of herself, poor choices in relationship, and constant plaguing dissatisfaction with every relationship, it began to sink into her that many of these patterns were the result of being sexually abused by a family member right under her parents' nose. Without any prompting from me, she looked at me and said, "What would I have been like if all this hadn't happened?" "What would I have been able to be and do?" "How different would my life have been if this hadn't happened?" As she did, the first tears of all our sessions began to come. Brenda had never grieved all the legitimate losses in her life.

Have you? There is the loss that says, "This is the way I thought my childhood was supposed to be, and until age nine it was, but at age nine, then _____ happened." There is the loss of trust the first time someone lets us down or betrays us. That one always hits us hard. There is the loss of innocence. The other day when my son came home from football practice, he asked me about a certain word he had heard there. I told him it was a swear word. He exclaimed, "Another cuss word?!?" and he looked upset. Because we don't use profanity in our household and he attends a Christian school with high standards, it's not been until age nine that he is becoming acquainted with the concept of swearing, and actually hearing people do it. When he threw his hands in the air, I can honestly say there was disappointment on his face that seemed like grief. When he then said, "I wish I didn't have to hear that," I knew his young soul was feeling the loss of his own innocence, though he couldn't articulate it. Grief is literally interacting with the thoughts and the feelings that come with contemplation of our losses in life, and the consequences thereof. When it comes to what we've lost through our hurts, grief is a form of validation. Grief says the wound mattered, and you mattered. Grief underscores that's not the way life was supposed to go. It is the sober confirmation that I have lost some of who I would have been had I not been wounded.

Grief is natural over every loss. The man who lost his arm as a child must certainly reckon with "What would I have been able to do if I had two arms? How would my life have been different?" We can appreciate how grief is necessary for him. Yet every loss is a loss, and all losses, to be fully accepted, must be grieved. We don't malign the person who grieves over a lost pet, and yet we are willing to disparage ourselves for not being able to "just get over" our past hurt. "Sucking it up" is counter to grief. Allowing oneself – and actually putting oneself in that place on purpose – to grieve over emotional wounds is necessary for healing. Because grief over emotional wounds is more "optional" than grief over a physical loss (such as death), we often keep ourselves from it for a very long time.

I hope you are sensing how grief is a much larger concept than merely tears. That is a limited and narrow conception. Grief is the contemplation of all that loss costs us, and any emotions companion to such thoughts. While overwhelmed with joy and gratitude for my amazing boys, I grieve that I don't have a girl. I grieve that I lost my twenties on searching for the approval of others. I grieve that my family of origin didn't stay intact. I can honestly say that I grieve not being in Eden. What would my life, me, this world, be like were it not for sin? Little griefs and large griefs combined are natural to every person who's breathing.

True-life Example

To make practical and further elucidate these concepts, we'll follow a young woman's real-life journey through the waters of acceptance and grief. Maureen, we'll call her, sat in my office, coming to the realization she had done it again. She had unconsciously jumped out of reality into a fantasy world. Knowing her reality, it is an understandable movement. In her early twenties, Maureen was facing the devastating effects her father's alcoholism had wrought upon her soul. For some time she had blamed God for her miserable lot; pointing to the fact that not only is He all-powerful and almighty, she had seen miraculous turnarounds in the lives of others' parents. This is a critical point of note - God is often mistaken as uninvolved, or worse, unconcerned when it comes to how human beings hurt one another.

However, we cannot pick and choose the attributes of God. If it is believed that He is all-loving and all-powerful, it cannot be denied that He is also just and all-knowing. His attributes are, frankly, beyond human comprehension. In His stated position of delaying the return of Christ "that none should perish," His love is evident. His position is that He waits with longing for all to enter into a salvific, love relationship with Himself through embracing the sacrifice of Christ. His great love causes Him to essentially withhold His own power.

Yes, He *could* "zap" that situation and fix it for you or me. However, because He is perfect in every way, He cannot be inconsistent. Inconsistency is imperfect. God is anything but wishy-washy or willy-nilly, as struggling people often accuse Him of being. He has chosen to be more than a puppet master. Instead of controlling a human's will, He allows the freedom to make choices. Therefore, if on the one hand He is taking himself captive, so to speak, by withholding His power, then, on the other hand, He cannot simply release Himself to violate human choice. To do so would be *inconsistent*. Because of His great love, He restrains His own power to violate and even control a human's will, so that all will be drawn to Him for eternity. That is why He will not automatically violate a person's will to stop hurting me when I ask Him to do so. It would go against His own character.

After Maureen began to see her father's own choicefulness and volition more clearly, her anger began to shift away from God and toward her father. It was an important step for her to clearly demarcate her father's active choices and to stop blaming God for not just making it all better. She realized that to demand God "zap" her father to do exactly what He (and she) wanted would be, in a sense, to ask Him to completely alter the great love and sacrificial plan that gave her the ability to so freely ask of Him in the first place!

It was hard for her, though, because she had lived for so many years under "it'll get better" hope. That's where fantasy came in. It became the salve to ease the pain of the present. When reality was that her father had yet another beer in his hand, she would train her mind to think of when he would soon hold her instead and laugh with her. Whatever devices we develop in childhood grow and morph into bigger ones in adulthood. Therefore, now in her early twenties, Maureen would often watch movies, read fiction, and play computer games. She hadn't realized these were unconscious escape mechanisms to keep her from having to face the full amount of pain at her dad's hurtful choices over and over again.

As I have disclosed at other points in this book, I am sensitive to being perceived as talking about psychology-like things for psychology's sake. This concern has driven me to stop, pray, seek, and wait for my Lord's confirmation at many points in the work of writing this book. When I was at such a point in this section, that very afternoon I was seeing clients. One came in who said, "I have talked about, taught about, written about, and thought about my hurts in life, and the things I do now as a result of them. However, I've never grieved them until these past three weeks. I've kept it all locked away for 45 years." Sam, self-described as emotionless, also came in that day and we discussed from where the patterns wrecking his marriage originated. When I asked him if he could imagine who he would be if he had been formed in a different environment, his eyes became emblazoned as he said, "Yes. Yes, I can." He began to describe a friend he has, whom he enjoys very much. Tears came as Sam choked out, "I would be like him." Sadness over the loss of innocence, joy, and childishness washed over him like a wave.

When I think about ones like these, the myriad Maureens, Brendas, and Sams who have boldly opened their hearts to the Lord in my presence, I am compelled to write on. Each special person who has allowed me to participate in their heart's healing journey has taught me something, and I have been incredibly blessed to have witnessed true miracles of emotional healing. In this way, I often feel as though there is an unseen cloud of witnesses who write with me, and to whom I am deeply indebted for their amazing bravery. They have instructed me in particular about these matters of acceptance and grieving.

Filed Under "Later"

The thrust at this point is towards acceptance, which is accompanied by grief, both upon the foundation of deep belief that God is who He says He is. Some of you have grasped this, and begun to identify losses you have or have not grieved. Many people, however, in reality live like this: just push the stuff down. It has become a way of life. Numb out. Shut it off. Keep busy. Pull it together. Whether consciously or unconsciously, countless people ignore their emotional states and simply shove it away, out of sight.

Many, many of us have developed a habit of shoving hurts down, mostly because we didn't know what else to do. It's as if we have a huge armoire (you know, big chest) that houses the hurts we don't feel, the losses we don't grieve, and the pain we don't acknowledge. When some difficult feeling appears on our laps, so to speak, we either pick it up, look at it, and handle it or we quickly shove it inside a drawer of that armoire and shut the doors. Any time more pain comes our way, we are quick to move it as fast as we can into that armoire. It works for a while. But then, depending on what we've been through, the first couple of drawers get full, and then others. The job loss, the health problem, mean words spoken between spouses, the friend who "drops" you without explanation, all the hurt is not really felt, just knee-jerk-like filed away. We keep doing this until the entire cabinet is full. The point of the picture is that at some point, there is no more space. There is no more room inside for any more hurt. As stated previously, it is again obvious that what once might have been helpful now becomes our enemy.

Sadly, I've found that people who live this way not only *seem* successful, but are also often lauded as "spiritual." We admire Christians who look like they've got it all together by their constant smiles and well-ordered lives. We "stuff" our feelings, especially the challenging ones, because we aren't seeing many examples of how to deal with them. However, the armoire only has so much room. For the most part, this will work for you through your twenties and mid-thirties, and then guess what? It does not work anymore. *It will not work forever.* There's no more space inside your soul to keep it all down. That's not how we were meant to live, by the way. If this is truly the pattern, though, even the ones who are really good at shoving away their pain reach a breaking point. It's often in one's early forties that depression sets in, a temper becomes unmanageable, or burnout occurs. The armoire is full. The soul can only contain so much pain until it shuts down.

Seen through this formulation, depression seems to me to be a message from one's emotional system: "That's it. We're done. There's no more room here. There is not one more square inch of space to house unfelt emotion." Almost everyone I've ever talked to with acute depression completely resonates with the armoire idea. Jill, a pastor's wife, mother of a severely handicapped child, a homeschooler, and daughter to ailing parents approached me after a seminar with eyes full of emotion and tears dripping out of them like an overflowing cup. She said, "When you talked about how a person can keep painful emotion shoved away in their 20's and 30's, but it starts to fall apart in their 40's, I knew it was me. I've been living this way without knowing it for so long, I don't know what to do."

We are equally emotional beings as we are physical ones. It's true, yet we attend so much to the physical that it's hard to grasp that our emotional self is just as important. It almost seems funny to think about nourishing, attending, exercising, and resting our emotional being. How much healthier we would be, though! When we do not use a muscle, it atrophies. The same is true of the equivalent of emotional muscles. When an armoire philosophy is used, emotional muscles for handling sadness, hurt, pain, grief, betrayal, disappointment, abandonment, and the like are weak and useless. Perhaps this is why study after study shows the relationship between one's emotional health and physical health to be quite significant. Researcher James Pennebaker has provided numerous fascinating studies on the topic, and with great breadth has found that unexpressed emotion, pain, and secrets have a significant effect on one's physical condition.[3]

A person who has dealt with pain by slamming the armoire doors time and again does have one emotional muscle that often gets used. It's the anger one. Why? Well, think of it…when the armoire is full, the emotional system is in the process of shutting down. If it encounters another difficulty, what it is to do? The doors are opened, the space surveyed and there is *no room* for the pain. An anger outburst essentially is the taking out of a drawer, dumping out a bit of what is there and then the shoving of that pain into the space just cleared by the anger. Think of the people you know (perhaps it's yourself) who can "spew" an emotion with great force for a minute or two, and then be completely fine one half-hour later. It's a little disconcerting (freaky), isn't it? An anger outburst is the equivalent of tipping a very full cup just enough to create a little space at the top. Then that teaspoonful looking to get in now fits. People who have patterns of angry outbursts without too many other emotional expressions might quite literally be "pent up."

Anger is what is called a secondary emotion. It means that something else always comes first. The overwhelming majority of the time, we are never angry first in a situation. Instead, we're probably hurt, embarrassed, frustrated, or sad. Anger acts as a type of cover for the more painful raw emotions. Have you ever seen someone fall down the steps and yell at the steps or the person coming the other way or themselves? What came first in the situation? Probably shame or embarrassment. How about the wife who is furious when her husband arrives home late for dinner after promising he wouldn't? Certainly, hurt came first, and because that is just too raw a feeling to stay in for very long, anger allows us to feel an emotion and continue functioning. Hurt is just too excruciating to feel. Anger is less vulnerable, and in this way a more "acceptable" emotion for us to have. Think about yourself, and whether you'd rather be angry or hurt. Anger is actually like a blanket, and almost always, hurt is what is being covered. Therefore, whenever I encounter someone with a great deal of anger, I imagine they must have a large degree of hurt underneath. If you struggle with anger, perhaps you might consider whether or not you have significant hurt in your heart. In this way, struggling with anger can validate that you indeed have been functioning armoire-style.

Many of us have indeed tried this "push the thing down" approach. "I've got space. Keep shoving!" Satan just keeps trying to "trump" that thing and "trump" that thing to get IT to come out. Then something happens. What feels like a monster comes up and we try and push it down and that's when we think, "Who am I?!" In those moments the suicidal thoughts come at you like a tsunami. When the anger comes on you, you think, "I don't have a temper!" and yet experience a black rage wherein you scare yourself. You would be mortified if ever anyone knew where your thoughts went in those moments. The reason it all feels so monster-like is because it has become so huge over time. You let the armoire get full. Nothing in there is huge by itself, but left unattended to, the sheer volume of that which we know we haven't been allowing ourselves to feel seems overwhelming. I've had person after person look at me and say, "I'm afraid that if I open it up, I'll never stop crying," or "I really think if I 'go there,' I won't be able to continue functioning in my life." While your armoire may seem to have been helping you, it will eventually let you down. Whether depression is setting in, anger outbursts are becoming more regular, or your thoughts have taken you places you never thought they would go, please see how the armoire prevents us from living free, authentic, hopeful, peaceful lives in Jesus.

And this IS the goal. For my own conscience and the loathing I feel for a self-focused, self-involved, self-analyzing society, I must interject the big picture here. The sole reason I write about the armoire? People have found it a helpful way to move towards greater freedom in Jesus. Why do I speak at such length about grieving? Without it, much of our internal condition becomes stunted, hidden, and requires great effort to keep it that way. Not only are these antithetical to "it is for freedom that Christ set you free" (Galatians 5:1), it is also robbing us from "running the race with endurance" (Hebrews 12:1).

Casting Aside Crutches

An important word about childhood coping mechanisms is this: what was once our friend in childhood often becomes our enemy in adulthood. In other words, that which helped or even saved us as a child now hurts us as adults. The crutch that helped us walk now becomes our impediment to being able to run. So often, what preserved our young souls in childhood now becomes our downfall in adulthood. Of course, we are talking about that which becomes unhealthy as we age.

For instance, dissociation, or splitting off, is something that quite literally delivered a sexually abused child from death. When Mary Beth was abused, she would "go into" the picture on her wall. Plenty of people describe having memories of being in the corner of the room looking down at themselves in a particular situation rather than being *in* the situation. To stay present at the time of violation would devastate a soul. It was a helpful escape. However, now when that same woman encounters a challenge in her job, it is now hurtful to her that she is "not there." When she disengages in adulthood, it becomes anathema to her own goals. Similarly, the boy who learned to deal with his mother's life-threatening illness through humor now sabotages intimacy with people in his life through it. Maureen coped with the painful reality that her father chose himself over her by escaping to a reality concocted in her mind.

Today, she shoots her progress in the foot by her propensity to fantasize about when "it'll get better."

Staying in the reality of her situation was an important next step for Maureen after placing responsibility for her losses squarely on her dad's choices. With resignation, Maureen began to assume full responsibility for the damage done her and the resultant lens, lies, and patterns. It is with such regularity as to be predictable what happens next in such a process. As intimated earlier, on the heels of acceptance of both reality and responsibility comes grief.

Maureen had a dream shortly after she had begun to lean into the reality of her past wounds and their effect on her present. She saw her father in the dream, but couldn't reach him. In it, she had the knowledge he was going to die young. Staying with this likely reality (her father's earlier-than-normal death) instead of dismissing it as just a dream, Maureen's grief came forward. Here's what she said: "It almost feels as if it would be easier if he weren't alive and then I'd stop trying to get him to choose me. I just think of all his great qualities and then what kind of a dad he'd be – could be- what never will be now. It's like that daddy need will never be met. It'll never be satisfied...I just wish somehow I'd be worth it to make a different choice...I just want someone to look to for answers; to be guided; to be given guidance." This picture of grief is intermingled with her acceptance of her wound of omission. Her expression of sadness came in conjunction with awareness of who wounded her and what was lost.

Maureen also certainly resonated with the armoire concept. As she described how she never had friends over, never showed people her family's picture, and couldn't bring herself to read a book about alcoholic families, she began to see all the more how acceptance and grief walk hand-in-hand. Until she accepted the reality of her situation, she kept filling her armoire. The first steps for her involved letting other people into her world. She showed a friend a picture of her relatively young father, who looked very old from the ravages of alcohol. On the staff of a Christian ministry, she added, 'I'm dealing with family stuff' to the prayer list she weekly gave the other staffers, normally filled with only names of others to whom she was ministering. One of the biggest hurdles for her was to actually say, even just to me, "I am a child of an alcoholic." Wanting to go to Al-Anon for years, she could never bring herself to, for fear of those words.

We all know how very much energy it takes to keep a large beach ball under water. So it is when we have a large amount of anything we are keeping from the light. There is a Biblical truth that, loosely said, offers the principle: *what's in the dark grows, what's in the light shrinks.* In other words, whatever is hidden tends to increase in pressure, strength, or power to consume. Whatever is pent up inside of us, whether it be a secret, an area of shame, a sad memory, or pockets of emotions, will eventually control much of our external life. Pain withheld, locked inside, grows and unless we deal with it, it will consume us. Sadly, we have all beheld bitter angry people, who, as their physical bodies fade, their inner selves emerge. Such ones have never accepted or grieved whatever might be in their armoire that still holds them captive. This is not the intended destiny of a child of God. I write about such things because I am a champion of the freedom for which Jesus paid so dearly. I pray He would use these very words for His purposes.

Opening the Doors

Obviously, if acceptance and grief are necessary components to any healing process, that requires opening up the armoire. Returning to the body analogy, it's true that many times for a wound to heal, it needs to be exposed to the air. Jaundice requires more exposure to the sun. Similarly, if you and I want to move through our struggles and grow past living lives walking around the shards of pain in our past, we must be willing to open up and let our inner reality come out. In a variety of ways, spiritual maturity is moving from darkness to light, from concealment in fear and shame to confession and repentance in love. "Satan wants darkness for us, because there the truth of our loved state in Christ can be denied. The opposites of the lies of darkness are the love and truth of God's light."[4]

For the Christian, hiding always has some fruit, or symptom. In other words, you and I can detect what is hidden in our lives by the problems it causes. Your self-protection and aloofness suggests hidden hurt of betrayal and resulting distrust. Another's constant self-deprecation and inability to receive compliments belies a deep sense of unworthiness, from a wound or perhaps a secret. When we hide, a part of our character is pushed away from relationship into a spiritual darkness. The isolation of some part of our soul will always produce a problem. This reality often prompts me to declare: *deal with your stuff or it will deal with you.*

Not grieving can lead to a low-grade depression that can last for many years.[5] People who have finally looked fully in the face of their sadness, pain, shame, or longing and felt the feelings that come, often say later that they can't believe how much lighter they feel. Instead, however, we'll go to great lengths to avoid the inevitable. We'll stick activities and people into leaky areas, plugging the dike damming back life's unavoidable grief. One author describes her failed attempt to hold back the grief of losing her father and admitting to plugging others into his vat:

It was terrible. Just terrible...I almost began to keen with grief. How could you even *begin* to live with this desolation, with no longer having the love of your father?...I started to cry then, and I cried for a long time without making much noise. I cried and cried like a little kid...I'd always known that one day it would happen, and I had even wanted it to, in an abstract way – you should see some of the men my girlfriends have stayed with for years to avoid this reckoning. Bad men, sadistic, men, any port in a storm...I handed over my hope and belief that I did not have to have a dead father. Or that any of these men I'd taken hostage would fit into the space my dad had left behind.[6]

While I can't quite pinpoint why, when it comes to grief and opening up, there really is something huge about speaking and hearing yourself say the things that are true deep within. Clients who have written letter upon letter to a deceased parent have often collapsed in grief when I've asked them to read it aloud. The hurt and the healing seem to fuse in some exponentially increased fashion when we speak out loud that which has been buried, or is most real. Indeed, some of the hardest words I've ever seen people try to muster are, "I've been sexually abused," or "I am from an alcoholic family," or "I'm so very lonely." Edward Hallowell relates his experience of wanting to keep the doors closed:

I have always felt, *If people knew my story, they would think less of me.* I have always felt, at some deep unspoken level, that I was a tainted person because of what happened in (my past), and no matter what I did, I would always be impure at the core, flawed in the eyes of others, if they knew.[7]

It's true that opening the armoire will probably not be pretty, nor will it be easy. It might reveal pain, shame, sadness, fear, or a whole host of other intimidating emotions. For instance, if you've been hurt by a parent, there's undoubtedly anger at the parent who didn't protect you. Mary Anne couldn't stop wondering why her mother ever let her get in the car with her father when he was drunk time and time again. Leslie welled up with intense sadness and anger whenever she would think of how her sibling abused her for years "right under mom's nose." Candy would become furious when her father would now try to buy her gifts or take care of her family. She wanted to scream, "Don't just love me now. Why didn't you take care of me then?" Her revulsion at his present-day loving acts came as a result of not having grieved her past hurts. In Fran's reckoning with her past, her grief came forward as she expressed, "All that I longed for was just not there." Crabb describes how grief comes as we contemplate our losses in opening up:

> When what I do seems unimportant, when evidence mounts that I'm not able to do what matters deeply to me, when people I care about don't care about me, when I suffer the loss of a relationship that deeply mattered, I feel a horrible emptiness within that hurts. Physical pain can sometimes be easier to bear than the anguish of loneliness, rejection, or failure. When critical longings for relationship with others and activity that makes a difference are frustrated...I feel a deep sorrow, an immobilizing lostness that, at least for a time, empties my soul of energy to continue.[8]

When you are willing to open up the armoire and face what's inside, including the myriad emotions, grief at what might have been is virtually inevitable. On this topic, John and Stasi Eldredge encourage:

> Let the tears come. It is the only kind thing to do for your woundedness. Allow yourself to feel again. And feel you will – many things. Anger. That's okay. Anger's not a sin (Eph. 4:26). Remorse. Of course you feel remorse and regret for so many lost years. Fear. Yes, that makes sense. Jesus can handle the fear as well. In fact, there is no emotion you can bring up that Jesus can't handle. (Look at the psalms – they are a raging sea of emotions.) Let it all out.[9]

142

There are indeed many unwept tears in that armoire. The Eldredges say they are the tears of a child "who is lost and frightened. The tears of a teenage girl who's been rejected and has no place to turn. The tears of a woman whose life has been hard and lonely and nothing close to her dreams."[10] It is precisely because we know we will feel many emotions when we think about our lost dreams or when we consider that we never got to have the caring, tender love of a mother or the wonderful time and attention of a father that we often keep ourselves from grieving our losses. However, holding back grief is counterproductive to not only all that God has for us, but also to all that we long for ourselves.

When we are willing to open up, air out the armoire, and accept that grief is a part of life, it is important to realize how this will look. Indeed, many of you are intellectually agreeing with your need to live a different way, but wondering if this means you will suddenly begin to wear your heart on your sleeves. In actuality, grief seems to come in waves. While unpredictable and unbidden, if we can imagine that we need to "ride the wave" of grief as it comes, we will see that it indeed does come, and go. However, if we fight the feelings and shove them down, they will only come back knocking with greater force. Ann Lamott paints a poignantly apropos picture of permitting oneself to grieve, and although it is rather lengthy, I encourage you to read it in its entirety to get a first-hand idea of grief in everyday life.

> All those years I fell for the great palace lie that grief should be gotten over as quickly as possible and as privately. But what I've discovered since is that the lifelong fear of grief keeps us in a barren, isolated place and that only grieving can heal grief; the passage of time will lessen the acuteness, but time alone, without the direct experience of grief, will not heal it…I'm pretty sure that it is only by experiencing the ocean of sadness in a naked and immediate way that we come to be healed – which is to say,

that we come to experience life with a real sense of presence and spaciousness and peace…

Grief, as I read somewhere once, is a lazy Susan. One day it is heavy and underwater, and the next day it spins and stops at loud and rageful, and the next day at wounded keening, and the next day numbness, silence…

And this is God's own truth: the more often I cried in my room…and felt just generally wretched, the more often I started to have occasional moments of utter joy, of feeling aware of each moment shining for its own momentous sake.

I was terribly erratic: feeling so holy and serene some moments that I was sure I was going to end up dating the Dalai Lama. Then the grief and craziness would hit again…

The depth of the feeling continued to surprise and threaten me, but each time it hit again and I bore it, like a nicotine craving, I would discover that it hadn't washed me away. After a while it was like an inside shower, washing off some of the rust and calcification in my pipes. It was like giving a dry garden a good watering. Don't get me wrong: grief sucks; it really does. Unfortunately, though, avoiding it robs us of life, of the now, of a sense of living spirit. Mostly I have tried to avoid it by staying very busy, working too hard, trying to achieve as much as possible. You can often avoid the pain by trying to fix other people; shopping helps in a pinch, as does romantic obsession. Martyrdom can't be beat. While too much exercise works for many people, it doesn't for me, but I have found that a stack of magazines can be numbing and even mood altering. But the bad news is that whatever you use to keep the pain at bay robs you of the flecks and nuggets of gold that feeling grief will give you. A fixation can keep you nicely defined and give you the illusion that your life has not fallen apart. But since your life may indeed have fallen apart, the illusion won't hold up forever, and if you are lucky and brave, you will be willing to bear disillusion. You begin to cry and writhe and yell and then to keep on crying; and then, finally, grief ends up giving you the two best things: softness and illumination.[11]

The previous passage illuminates a point worth underscoring. Opening up is not for purpose of indulgence. Encouraging grieving is not advocating emotional gluttony. We live in a society bent on shallowness, with the ultimate goal of feeling good. Even moreso, we live in a culture where self is supreme. Certainly, the lifestyle Jesus calls us to is antithetical to self-indulgence. However, living life with an internal armoire full of hurt, pain, and sadness *is* self-indulgent. It's essentially disallowing God access to and full handling of our emotions. Carried to its extreme, attempting to live life on our own terms in any way is like saying, "I think I'll do a little better on this one than you, God." Self-protection in any form is signaling to God that "I have this one under control," because His ways might leave you just a little too vulnerable. We cannot live authentic, free, victorious, and fruitful lives if much of our energy is going into maintaining our own hiddenness (in any form).

One explication of how grief works is summarized in the acronym "TEAR." The first aspect is "T" - to accept the reality of the loss. The previous discussion lends support to the necessity and importance of acceptance. "E" is to experience the pain of the loss, which is exactly the point we're on. The next two components are "A," adjust to the new environment without whatever was lost and "R," reinvest in the new reality.[12] This picture is precisely why I am suggesting that grieving is so very important – *we have a new reality in Christ in which we must invest.* When we even unintentionally carry about an armoire full of anything, our investment and energy is in shouldering that load. To actually be able to fully embrace – wrap my arms around, grasp with my hands – some new thing, I must let go of that which I am presently carrying.

Thirst

As we walk ourselves into areas of acceptance and the inevitable grief, we will soon see a few other items of note along this path. I will say clearly here what has been alluded to prior: Some of the grief and disappointment in others and life that we feel is in actuality an innate longing for heaven. We will have this desire with us until we see Him face to face. Larry Crabb points out a false message in this regard. He purports that unlike the Biblical picture, present-day Christianity has tended to promise to take away the pain of living in a fallen world. He says the message, whether from fundamentalists who advocate living by a set of rules or from charismatics who promote a deeper experience of the Spirit's power, is "too often the same: The promise of bliss is for NOW! Complete satisfaction can be ours this side of heaven."[13] The reality is that we will never feel totally satisfied, fully restful or completely satiated on this earth. While it is important to dive into these unmanageable feelings and determine whether they are from deficits in our childhood, pain pushed underground, or some other unresolved issue, it is critical to realize we will always have a part of us longing to be with Him.

Becoming familiar with our inner thirst is excellent, because this very desire can drive us to deeper intimacy with the Lord. Let's face it; everyone we know is quite thirsty. We were designed for the very purpose of living in relationship with someone unfailingly faithful, loving, and full of strength, who has created us to fulfill an important purpose for which He designed us. "Without relationship or impact, life is profoundly empty. Nothing can fill that hollow core except what we were built to experience. Not imperfect friends, not impressive work, not excitement, not pleasure."[14] In short, nothing can satisfy our deepest hunger except the sort of relationship that only God offers. Evil wants to fool us into thinking that our thirst: (1) shows us we're messed up, as if thirsting is something to be ashamed of, (2) is what must be focused on and fixed, or (3) will go away if we are healed. While overfocusing on our thirst is just as treacherous as ignoring or denying it, the clear reality is that our inner longing for more is meant to drive us to deeper relationship with God.

Pain is an integral part of that path. We certainly know that human propensity keeps us from running for help when we're doing fine. We aren't quite as faithful with reading the Word or prayer when everything is going well. However, whenever we are in trouble, we are much quicker to call out to our Creator. Therefore, facing our inner reality allows us opportunity to experience a greater depth in our relationship with the Lord. Grief hurts, and hurt is painful, and pain drives us to God. Crabb spells out, "Until we acknowledge painful disappointment in our circumstances and relationships (particularly the latter), we will not pursue Christ with the passion of deep thirst…we rarely learn to meaningfully depend on God when our lives are comfortable."[15]

Our Lord does indeed promise us daily bread. He does promise abundant provision. However, these promises in no way guarantee us pain-free living. Instead, because He wants to draw us deeply to Himself, and because we have an innate longing for life with Him, we have to admit deep sadness and disappointment – sometimes unbearable – as we think about our human relationships. As we do, acceptance rises, our armoire is opened, grief comes forward, our longings become more intense, and healing in Jesus commences. While grief and acceptance are amorphous, fuzzy concepts, they are a must for your forward progress.

7

HIDING OUT

The tragedy of life is not in the fact of death,
but in what dies inside us while we live.
NORMAN COUSINS

Surely you desire truth in the inner parts;
you teach me wisdom in the inmost place.
PSALM 51:6

In the last chapter, we discovered the primary components to
living a life beyond our hurt and pain, experiencing freedom and joy, and
knowing the perfect peace Christ bought for us. Committing to believe
God is good, trustworthy, loving, and faithful is a necessary foundation
for any successful negotiation of life. Accepting that which our lives have
contained, and grieving the natural sense of loss that accompanies it, are
pillars raised upon the foundation of God's character. Such is the
mandatory beginning to the process of soul healing. Recognizing our
wounds, while helpful, is not enough. Knowing truth, while critical, is
alone not enough. We must also begin to move through the rocky terrain
of our emotional selves. If we do not, dangerous results occur. In this
chapter, we will briefly discuss the all-too-common fallout from an
unwillingness to move forward into deep truth — about God, others, and
our own internal condition.

"I Swear"

If we are either unaware of how our wounds have affected us, in agreement with lies that have been implanted, or unwilling to turn the corner to acceptance and grief, this will often cause us to make inner commitments to protect ourselves from further hurt. What comes to your mind as you ponder that statement? Shielding yourself? Walls around your heart? Never letting yourself get in that situation again? You see, when we don't recognize what our lies, lenses, deficits, and hurts have done to us, we will often make vows about them. A vow is a commitment, a solemn promise. Through these solemn promises and assertions, a person *binds* him or herself to "a person, act, service, or condition."[1] It is essentially swearing, asserting, or covenanting to some position, action, or belief.

Obviously, vows take on many forms. For instance, in the Old Testament, any time a vow was made, it was basically in the context of a prayer. Many present-day vows reflect this aspect through the phrase "so help me God." A marriage vow is a promise "in the sight of God and these witnesses" to be with someone until death. Even when we make vows outside the will of God, they nevertheless are still prayer-like in their thrust. When we make vows in response to hurt, it is then an unwitting prayer outside the will of God. For example, "I will never allow anybody to do that to me again" is a vow. It's definitely an internal commitment, but one that does not line up with God's rightful place as sovereign, creator, protector, and curator of justice. His word is clear about what He has designed for us in terms of relationship, so who do you think will "honor" that vow made out of alignment with God's desire? Indeed, all manner of evil will come along and scoop up any vow opposed to God's ways.

Vows can be insidious and when left intact create deeply embedded perspectives. Remember, vows most often come in response to unresolved hurt and are designed to keep out further pain. As an aside, I think we all would agree that nothing ever really works to keep us from experiencing further pain. It's amazing (read "stupid") that we keep trying. Nevertheless, common vows people make include:

I will never let anyone have my heart again.

I must always stay in control.

I will not allow myself to need.

I'd rather die than be like my father.

I will never be taken advantage of again.

I will never give without getting back.

I cannot let my deepest sins be known, or I'll be rejected.

I must always be strong.

I will never completely trust.

I will never again show weakness.

I won't date again.

I'll never pray in public again.

I will not allow myself to hope.

When we make these, there is an evil one who hears that "prayer" and dispatches fallen companions alongside you in unholy allegiance to support any vow made outside of the will of God.

Because such vows are antithetical to God's way, whenever you start to go against them, there is an evil companion alongside you, gladly reminding you of your commitment. For instance, if you've made a vow never to get close to anybody ever again, God's Spirit inside you will press in you to live opposite of that. It's because we were designed for relationship. He will woo us to be in free, giving and receiving friendships, marriages, and families. So, when you inevitably begin to take risks to be close, you will undoubtedly sense the pause. Out of nowhere, you feel it: "Whoa! Remember your vow. Remember the last time you did this? Don't forget your vow!" This happened to Dawn, whom had vowed that she would never "need anyone – especially a man." When the person she secretly admired for years finally asked her out, she declined because the onslaught of fear and doubt came. Powers of darkness are more than ready to help you uphold a promise that will ultimately result in your destruction.

Vows are voluntarily made. Therefore, they can always be unmade, thank the Lord! And a vow, once made, carries with it the weight that it must always be kept. That's why it's a vow instead of merely a flippant statement. Vows that we make from our woundedness are self-protective. They are dangerous things that act as major pacts with the enemy. So, childhood vows are especially difficult and especially dangerous because, like the lie, they grow along with us. (Remember the lens concept from chapter four?) Vows are what we use to keep the lie intact. If the lie is, "I must not be lovable because my mother rejected me," the vow is, "I will never get close again so no one can reject me." The vow serves as placeholder for the lie. If I can make the vow to never get close to someone again, then no one can ever get close enough to me to reject me for feeling unlovable.

It's important to notice we actually *make* the vow. It's not just the lie that slipped in there and you accidentally agreed with it. It's yours now and it came about because of some sort of denial, hiding, or pretending to cover up your true inner world. So if your vow is, "I will never allow myself to be vulnerable," you go on interacting that way. In doing so, you are going against the revealed will of God (1 John 4:16-18).

Every time you begin to jeopardize this or any other self-protective vow through developing healthy, holy intimacy, there is one whispering in your ear, saying, "Remember, you promised to never let this happen the day you made this vow." Vows are dangerous things. They act as major agreements with the enemy, giving him permission to enter some part of our lives. Remember, the enemy cannot take anything from us unless we offer him a place to land. Vows provide such a place. It becomes a dangerous place of resistance to God's way. Proverbs 28:14 says, "Blessed is the man who always fears the Lord, but he who hardens his heart falls into trouble."

Although admittedly a minor point, I must comment about the insidious and dangerous nature of vows. Many, many people make vows that begin with "I will never." What we don't realize is that attempting to live in opposition to something or someone is just as constricting, hurtful, and limiting as that which we are trying to avoid. The energy it takes to live within the confines of a vow and to maintain it binds us up equally as much as living without the vow would. Mary swore, "I will never be like my mother." Imagine the reason Mary probably said such a thing. She could have been hurt by, disappointed in, disgusted by, or controlled by her mother. It certainly wouldn't be because she believed her mother a person worthy of emulating. However, what if Mary had an incredible gift of working with children, and because her mother had been a schoolteacher, Mary completely veered away from teaching? Or, how about if Mary looked fantastic in bright red lipstick, but never allowed herself to try it because it was what her mother wore? *Living in opposition to someone gives them just as much power over you as if they controlled you.* Although in a different direction, it is constricting your life just as much as the reason for the vow in the first place. In fact, because of how you are monitoring your life so closely, you have lost the very freedom you hoped to garner by making the vow in the first place. Indeed, I know a "Mary" who has vowed to never be like her mother, and as a result, fades into the background at social events (because her mother always made herself the center of attention), doesn't wear a stitch of makeup (because her mother was always very made up), and is lonely in her independent personality (because her mother was so extremely codependent). Is her vow working? Is she freed up from her mother's influence? On the contrary, her mother's impact continues to greatly affect her present-day life.

The wounds that have shaped our lives fuel our vow making. It's as though the messages we have received form a sort of "unholy alliance with our fallen nature."[2] For Stasi, the process of realizing the message she received helped her identify the vow. Her mother was overwhelmed with the thought of having another child. That child was Stasi. She describes, "The message that landed in my heart was that I was overwhelming; my presence alone caused sorrow and pain."[3] So, like many of us, she made a vow. She describes, "Somewhere in my young heart, without even knowing I was doing it or putting words to it, I vowed to protect myself by never causing pain, never requiring attention."[4] Unless we are willing to strive for greater clarity, understanding, and healing, our vows remain implanted, poisoning our hopes for a future of freedom, peace, and joy.

Masks

Wounds are hurtful. Implanted lies distort our perspective. Deficits that pull on us feel shameful, and vows are internally dangerous. Instinctively, we want to hide such things. "I can't let that be out there for others to see" is barely even a conscious thought, but somehow it prevails. Vows, exposed, often lose their power, so we wear masks in order to keep them intact. The ways we shelter others from seeing our deepest issues are through hiding relational styles. Said differently, we put on masks to deflect people from seeing what is actually going on inside. Long-time Christian influencer Chuck Swindoll queries:

> What mask are you hiding behind? There's a mask for every occasion – have you noticed? No matter how you really feel, regardless of the truth, if you become skilled at hiding behind your guard, you don't have to hassle all the things that come with full disclosure. You feel safe. There is just one major difficulty – it isn't real. What's worse, as we hide the truth behind a veneer polished to a high gloss, we become lonely instead of understood and loved for who we are. And the most tragic part of all is that the longer we do it, the better we get at it…and the more alone we remain in our hidden world of fear, pain, anger, insecurity, and grief – all those normal and natural emotions we hesitate to admit but that prove we are only human.[5]

The purpose of a mask is to cover and confuse. While physical masks disguise true identity, emotional ones deflect penetration. How do these masks work? Have you ever been part of a conversation or a small group that's going in a really good direction, and somebody cracks a joke? The joke is funny – it's a good one – but what happens to the conversation? It's derailed. Or how about when somebody looks in your eyes and says, "No, really, how are you?" Instead of taking advantage of a sincere friend's concern, instead you respond with your typical, "I'm doing good. I'm fine. Thanks for asking." Rather than moving toward authenticity, you whipped out your "I have it all together" mask. There's also the person who so wants to be included. He gets an invitation, however, and declines. His mask is isolation, and his M.O. of being a loner remains intact. Others have a way of spiritualizing everything. While Biblical knowledge is good, the way this person uses it is actually a way to keep people from knowing *him*. Who would even try to come back to someone who has just quoted Scripture after a penetrating question? Masks are any device or mechanism that we use to keep people from getting close. Do you know yours?

What are some of these cover-ups?

humor	super spiritual	constantly busy
lone ranger	aloof	depressed
quiet	know-it-all	turn-it-back-on-you
the "yes" person	have it all-together	sarcasm
always serving	tough guy/girl	devil's advocate

It's important to note that masks come out of our God-given personalities, so they're not all bad! God has given you humor. God's given you that perky personality. God's given you the ability to complete a lot of tasks in a short amount of time. God's enabled you to retain information well. These abilities and characteristics only become masks when we use them to hide, to keep our vows in place, and to keep our woundedness hidden. In many ways, what ends up as a mask is simply a God-given corner of our personality that got refined and polished through repeated use. Have you ever thought about how you deflect penetration? What is the way you keep people from seeing your stuff?

Masks are only negative when they become a way to hide. When they endure over time, they become quite problematic. Perhaps you don't want to hide that way any more, but now that's all you know how to do. The danger of these relational veiling styles is that they paralyze us from those who would love us the most. Our masks keep out the very people with whom we were designed to have closeness. Picture someone moving in to kiss another person. At just the split second prior to contact, the other half of the duo whips up a mask and the person plants one on a piece of cardboard. That is the effect of our subtle ways to hide. We're shooting ourselves in the foot when we do that, because we all actually long for relationship, closeness, and loving exchanges with others (whether we presently realize this about ourselves or not!). These vows and masks result from damage and are themselves further damaging because they keep us from the very love and closeness we long to have, both from others and more importantly, from God.

We usually don a number of masks throughout our lifetime, or even over the course of a day. We tend to use a variety of hiding patterns depending upon the situation. For example, some people find that they have one defense at work and another at home. At work, it might be the "high performance" veneer, while at home, the fear of failing relationally leads to withdrawal and isolation. Many relational hiding styles exist to disguise certain situations so that whatever vulnerability we have won't be "found out." The overdeveloped self-sufficient person, for example, unconsciously pretends not to have inadequate, frightened feelings. She reacts oppositely to what she feels. The aggressive, opinionated person is compensating for fearful insecurities of being devalued and left out.

The worst-case scenario for mask wearers is when others just begin to describe you by your mask… "Oh, that's just how John is." If we haven't challenged them, most of our own personal hiding styles have existed for the much of our lives. Over time, and without intervention of some sort, they take on a fixed, rigid quality. If the injury being protected by the relational pattern is deep enough and damaging enough, the defensive mask will be so much a part of the person's everyday life that it seems like a part of the soul. "Steve's had that quirk as long as I've known him." When others become so used to us functioning in the manner of a mask, we are successful at deflecting them, and our vows remain snugly in place. At what cost, however?

That self-protective way of relating to others has nothing to do with real loving, and nothing to do with deeply trusting God. It is our gut-level response to a dangerous world. Basically, we're trying to live as though a legitimate, God-ordained part of ourselves doesn't exist. We deny some truth about ourselves. The hiding style results in our living as if that lie were true. Harmful hiding patterns keep us from the very resources God has provided for our healing: grace, love (relationship), and truth.

Shhhh....

Isn't it overwhelming to consider all the depths inside us? Isn't it intense to delve into it? Yes, it is, and I am so proud of you for hanging in there!! You are indeed pressing on to the goal with endurance (Philippians 3:14), when it could be much easier to bail out and settle for something less than true victory and healing. In fact, the choice to take the easy way out is characteristic of our instant-gratification, on-demand, faster-is-better society. Soul *reflection*, staying in the *process* of healing, and *stilling* oneself to hear God's truth are all antithetical to twentieth-century life in America. However, what is deepest and most true will always tug on us from within. Therefore, the murkiness lifts, and two alternatives are left: deal with it or tell it to shut up.

The internal noise created by wounds, lies, vows, and masks is excessive. Therefore, if we have not done the corrective work of acceptance and grief, we are left with a lot of intensity inside. At that point, people almost universally numb out. Think of how we treat prolonged physical wounds. Medication management. The longer the wound hangs around and isn't given proper treatment, the more pain management will become a part of our lives. Again, the parallel with emotional hurts is striking. As a result, anesthetizing oneself is practically an art today, at least in America. Because the wounds we receive cause so much pain, whether from a lie or deficit, unless we face them head-on and deal with them, we then resort to numbing ourselves.

Anesthetizing oneself has reached epic proportions. We do this any time we don't want to "hear" or face reality. What do you look to for pain relief? Do you desire the next "atta boy" from the person in charge to take away your pain? Instead of struggling with some issue in your life, do you stay up all night and work on a proposal which would get you the "good job" to make you feel better? Some of us, sadly, are living for the next Starbucks in the morning. The Eldredges describe our machinations well:

> "We buy ourselves something nice when we aren't feeling appreciated. We "allow" ourselves a second helping of ice cream or a super-sized something when we are lonely. We move into a fantasy world to find some water for our thirsty hearts. Romance novels (a billion-dollar industry), soap operas, talk shows, gossip, the myriads of women's magazine all feed an inner life of relational dreams and voyeurism that substitutes – for a while – for the real thing. But none of these really satisfy, and so we find ourselves trying to fill the remaining emptiness with our little indulgences (we call them "bad habits")…They are what we give our hearts away to instead of giving them to the heart of God."[6]

Take a moment and consider yourself. Where do you go and what do you do when the ache of your heart surfaces? Surf the web, go shopping, drink, binge, purge, masturbate, work, clean, watch a sitcom, grab a magazine, turn on a talk show, play a computer game, exercise? It is quite unfortunate, but the difficult truth is that the ways we anesthetize do indeed make us feel better…for a while. They seem to "work," but the hideous reality is that they really only increase our need to indulge again. We "numb out" only to have our drug of choice wear off. Our longings cease to ache and the loudness within quiets for a minute, but later we find ourselves empty once more, needing to be filled again and again.

The harsh reality is that no matter what you use to anesthetize yourself, *it will never be enough.* It will never meet all of your needs. It doesn't take away the pain of your deficits. It doesn't take away the pain of living through a lie. It doesn't take away the pain of living in untruth about yourself. It won't take away the reason for your vow, or the exhaustion of wearing masks. It will never be enough because you're looking to the wrong thing for the wrong job. This is the nightmare of addiction, and also explains how we can become addicted to virtually anything. These ways we find to numb our aches, our longings, and our lies are not benign. They wrap themselves in our souls like a cancer and become cruel and relentless masters. Just try to go without your "vice" for a week, and see what happens. Psychologist Ernest Becker wrote, "Modern man is drugging himself out of awareness, or he spends his time shopping, which is the same thing."[7]

How can we tell if we are utilizing alternative ways to take our pain away and hush the bedlam inside? A clue is the feeling that something's "got" you. If you find yourself absorbed in or by something, most likely it has an anesthetizing effect. We become engrossed in the thing we are looking to for removing the edge off the ache. Just yesterday, a wonderful client told me about her Ebay usage. What started out as innocent email checking became obsessive streaming which then lead to Ebay watching, which lead to compulsive Ebay searching. She herself was incredulous at how this happened, saying, "I am embarrassed, but I am completely obsessed." How does a physician on a cancer ward become obsessed with Ebay? To the point – it can happen to anyone and with anything. She realized her computer compulsion was permitting her to flee from her marital troubles, the spiritual battles she knows she must fight, and her loneliness for friendships. Whatever is filling you up in the short-term will never compensate for your pain/vow/insecurity/fear, and therefore damage you further in the long-term. If you spend your life looking to "get," you need to know it will never be enough. It won't take away the pain. It won't give you significance. It won't undo the wound. And it will be necessary in larger and larger doses to anesthetize your pain.

The point here is that when we leave our internal condition unchecked, then we start to go toward anesthetizing. If we don't let the Lord do His work there by shining the precious light of His Holy Spirit in those dark places, then our lives will reek of the results. It's the Biblical principle that every good tree bears good fruit, but the bad tree bears bad fruit. According to Matthew 7:17-18, a good tree cannot produce bad fruit, nor can a bad tree produce good fruit. Said differently, results always point to causes. Common indicators of emotional avoidance and suppression include: compulsive behaviors (can't not do it), obsessive thoughts (can't not think it), and symptoms like anxiety, shame, overeating, substance abuse, overspending, depression, guilt feelings and physical ailments. What are some patterns that have developed in you? When my parents split up in my pre-teen years, my mother moved into a trailer. Every Friday night, I would visit, and we would sit on the floor eating buttered popcorn, peanut M&Ms, and playing Boggle. Can you guess what my number one way to escape and anesthetize myself is today? Whenever I desire to check out, food is my primary temptation.

Larry Crabb has also brought to light our propensity to try to fill voids and cover pain through false means. He points out that we attempt to meet crucial longings which cause our "thirsty souls to pant after satisfaction" with shallow coping mechanisms. His commentary on their effectiveness is poignant: "In moments of deep pain, most encouragements and pleasures mean no more than a bucket of sand to a thirsty traveler."[8] While this is true, and many of us have experienced it of our anesthetizing agent, we still go back for more. Think of how you have felt after an evening of TV watching, promising yourself that you won't waste that amount of time again, only to have a repeat performance the very next night. Or how about overeating, and the fact that the food didn't even taste good anymore, but you kept consuming? You swear you won't do that again, but... The drunken binge, the shopping spree, or the sexual exploit – they all have their palpable aftertaste for a reason. Scripture speaks of this cycle of foolish sinfulness starkly: "As a dog returns to its vomit, so a fool repeats his folly." (Proverbs 26:11).

Not only is it foolish to be a party to anesthetizing ourselves through worldly means, it is also sinful. Doing so actually involves an unwillingness to trust God with our thirst, our pain, and our internal condition. We don't want to give up control and power to God, which was the very sin of our foresister, Eve. Instead of taking it all openly and vulnerably to our living, active, involved, faithful Father, we move about as ones "determined to satisfy the longings of their hearts by picking up a shovel, looking for a likely spot to dig, and then searching for a fulfillment they can generate."[9] Anytime we take matters into our own hands, we are in dangerous province. It is the area of idolatry, and communicates to a perfect God that we just don't think He's handling things well. Sure, none of us would dare say such a thing outright, but when we attach our hopes for fulfillment, our needs for comfort, and our longing for healing to worldly things, the underlying assumption is God's insufficiency.

Modern-day idolatry is not about golden calves and graven images. Instead, *anything* we hope in for life, significance, value, meaning or fulfillment is evidence of idolatry. Yes, even our anesthetizing agent can become an idol, as can our children, our jobs, our success, and certainly, our money. In Jeremiah 2:13, our Lord is gracious to explain: "My people have committed two sins: They have forsaken me, the spring of living water, and have dug their own cisterns, broken cisterns that cannot hold water." Whatever we look to instead of our Creator to hold us, to affirm us, to comfort us, to give us meaning, or to provide value is a broken jug into which are trying to pour very precious water. As with "numbing out," it will not work. There is only one place of true comfort, meaning, and value. His eternal plea is "Come unto Me" (Matthew 11:28). Saint Augustine said it best: "Our hearts are restless until they find their rest in Thee."[10] We will never find true peace until we understand we're looking in the wrong places.

The bigger idea here is that healing will never come under anesthesia. Healing involves awareness, knowledge, proactivity, and intentionality. Trying to hush the inner noise will only prolong and further complicate our issues. If you placate your insecurity through your put-together attractive appearance, it will not solve the problem and provide deeper security. If you numb out through computer games, you will never heal from being betrayed. If you make lots of money, your feelings of inadequacy will not go away, even if successfully muted for a time. And in the meantime, we develop addictions, become idolators, and unknowingly reject God, not to mention losing the pleasure found in

162

our initial enjoyments. C.S. Lewis said, "Whenever we try to put second things into the first-place position, we lose the joy of both God and whatever we are trying to replace Him with."[11] Deadening our inner pain does not make it go away. Instead, the ache goes underground where it can't be dealt with effectively, and presses for relief with greater intensity until we find ourselves in some pretty predictable patterns.

Patterns

All told, the aforementioned facets form destructive and ungodly life patterns. Unhealed wounds and the effects thereof combine to create patterns that characterize our lives and our relating. Such blueprints for functioning result when we don't open it all up, accept and grieve, and renounce vows and masks in the presence of a loving God. Until we *face* our disappointment, pain, and internal struggles, we cannot clearly identify the strategies we've adopted to insulate ourselves from further hurt. This is how we come to live in consistently negative patterns. Instead of living the purposeful, peaceful lives purchased for us by the blood of Christ, something inside of us shifts because we have embraced the messages of our wounds. Whenever we accept a twisted view of ourselves, there is an ensuing way of relating to the world. We vow never to be in that situation again. We adopt strategies to protect ourselves from being hurt again. Many, many of us who don't know we're living out of a broken, wounded heart are living self-protective lives. We may not be aware of it, but it is true. Our patterns are a result of how we try to "save" ourselves.

If you're having trouble connecting with this, consider the following series of questions that I find particularly enjoyable:

> Take your little phobias. Why are you afraid of heights or
> intimacy or public speaking? All the discipline in the world

wouldn't get you to go skydiving, share something really personal in a small group, or take the pulpit next Sunday. Why do you hate it when people touch you or criticize you? And what about those little "idiosyncrasies" you can't give up to save your life? Why do you bite your nails? Why do you work so many hours? Why do you get irritated at these questions? You won't go out unless your makeup is perfect – why is that?... Something in you "freezes" when your dad calls – what's that all about? You clean and organize; you demand perfection – did you ever wonder why?[12]

Asking ourselves why we do what we do is extremely helpful. To help see what your personal patterns are, complete the thought: "I'm most likely to…" or "I'm the type of person who…" I wish I could actually stop you from reading any further and have you drill down on this point. Why *do* you screen all your phone calls? Why *do* you keep your house so perfect? Why *do* you spend money on everyone but yourself? Why *do* you not have any close friends? Why *do* you loathe Sundays? Why *do* you do what you do? Take a look at some of these common patterns, and ask God to reveal if any befit you:

- Getting close and pulling away
- Never letting anyone know too much about you (sharing only select parts of yourself with people)
- Distrusting everyone until they pass your little tests
- Drinking after work
- Sharing everything with everyone you know in an attempt to get someone to really care
- Gossiping about others (which usually takes the edge off one's own internal bitterness)
- Smiling a lot
- Being over-busy so as not to disappoint anyone
- Constantly apologizing
- Codependency: only liking yourself if others like you

Another frequent pattern involves passive-aggressive behaviors. What this means is that I'm feeling aggression, but I let it out passively instead of aggressively. It's still coming out, mind you, but just not in an "out front" kind of way. Passive-aggressive behaviors come into play when someone has hurt or angered us. If we don't deal with it straight up, in a forthright and godly fashion, then it's going to come out some other way. A truism we can all wager on is this: *if it doesn't come out the right way, it will come out the wrong way.* A classic example of passive-aggressive behavior is the wife whose husband calls and says he will be home late again for dinner. Instead of expressing her feelings directly to him, she "accidentally" charcoals his food. When I explained passive-aggressive behavior patterns to a group of college students, one of them excitedly volunteered that she knew what I was talking about. She explained that instead of telling her boss how upset with him she was, she just began to give away free stuff from the office to everyone she knew. She was "getting him back" instead of getting things cleared up.

Seeing the patterns we live in can be a simultaneously painful and freeing mirror. What are the consistencies in your life that you cannot provide a reasonable explanation for? Why does a 35-year-old woman I know collect teddy bears obsessively? She has a past of heinous sexual abuse. Her actions aren't those of an adult woman, but they are the cries of a little girl's heart that was broken when she was five, and that part of her remains young, afraid, and desperate for someone to protect and restore her. I stood next to an adult male pouring over the matchbox cars in a store the other day. When I said that I couldn't ever remember which ones my boys had, he sheepishly said, "These are for me. I just need a few more to have the entire collection." Our tendency is to keep the hurt parts of ourselves forever under wraps, with the hope that in time they will go away and not cause us more pain. Our patterns reveal if this is true for us.

Again, look in the mirror of your life. What does it show you? Those of you unable to resist a cream-filled donut – you can be certain it is a hunger for more than sweets. Love, perhaps? Comfort? The drive that keeps you late at the office – what is it you are hoping for? Approval? For someone to finally say, "We're so very proud of you?" What of the lure of the website you've sworn never to revisit? Is that the cry of a seven-year-old wanting his emotional innocence back? Wanting what he felt like before shame came? Have you ever met a man who has a distinct childlike, playful spirit? While it is a good thing, it might also be the cry of a little boy who never got to be playful. Sometimes it's the unspoken plea: "Will you accept me for who I am because I wasn't back then?" It's not *just* "I don't do small groups" or "I just don't like crowds" or "I simply don't prefer outspoken people." It's not that simple. Such patterns exist as faithful sentries, set in position by our souls.[13] We need to remember that *they're there for a reason*. They're usually there because there was, and is, an injury to protect or something to hide. Our patterns didn't pop out of thin air.

The clues are here. Our patterns bespeak volumes about our internal coping devices, emotional health, and unearthed pain. Francesca didn't passionately love animals because she just loved animals. She became involved in rescue efforts, had a house full of animals, and spent large amounts of money on all manner of creatures. When she slowed to reflect on these patterns, it was a sober realization that she was afraid to give all the love she had to humans because of how she had been hurt in the past. Animals were safe. While there are many responses to being wounded, it is a truism that all of us to some degree live two lives. We have an external life, in which we determine the feelings, attitudes, and behaviors that are "safe" to express and an internal one, in which we lock away our "unsafe" traits.

Will you wisely examine yourself so that He can set you free rather than holding on to some foul lie, anger-based vow, false sense of comfort, or inaccurate mask? Much of what we think of as "our personalities" is actually just a composite of our choices for self-protection, responses to woundedness, and coping tools we have discovered to keep us safe. While this "works," especially for a time, there will come a day when we hit some trip wire which calls it out of us. Instead of waiting for this trigger, let's "lay aside every encumbrance, and the sin which so easily entangles us, and let us run with endurance the race that is set before us" (Hebrews 12:1). Our bigger point is getting rid of those encumbrances to our growth: where they come from, how they operate, what they tell us, and what we can do about them. Why? Because God's glory is obfuscated when we are given over to lying, hiding, covering, or self-protection in any form. Jesus paid too high a price for us to live dimly behind sinfully erected barriers.

8

MENTAL HEALTHING (The Intellectual Pathway)

> *What comes to our mind when we think about God*
> *is the most important thing about us.*
> A..W. TOZER

> *Do not conform any longer to the pattern of this world, but be transformed by the*
> *renewing of your mind. Then you will be able to test and approve what God's will is –*
> *his good, pleasing and perfect will.*
> ROMANS 12:2

The journey of healing is anything but simple enough to capture in twelve steps. Healing is poorly portrayed by the picture of a ladder whereby one crawls out of a pit rung by rung, and progresses to a higher plane only after completely departing the rung prior. Instead, real change occurs more like the effective playing of a drum set. For the instrument to be utilized to its full capacity, one must hit all the various elements of it repetitively, and in different patterns, *consistently over time.* Great drum playing involves not only keeping a steady bass beat going, but also rapping on all the other parts of the set.

You and I are multifaceted creatures. Becoming healed to live fervently for the Lord will mean we "tap" many different components over and over. The foundation is belief in God, His goodness, and His plan. This bedrock must be revisited every day, multiple times a day, over and over again, a la our bass drum. The other aspects of healing (discussed in the following chapters) will be regularly stimulated as well. For instance, grieving doesn't happen once, and then we forever move on from it. Identifying a lie doesn't preclude us from having to go back and identify more. Walking in freedom and victory will come through revisiting many components over and over again. Let's press in and ask God to cement in us the aspects that must comprise our personal path to true healing in Him.

As we come to the point of opening up, and no longer holding all our grief at bay, we will actually have energy to do the work of healing. People are amazed at how much more "space" they have inside when they simply accept what their wounds are, rather than deny, hide, or fight against them. It's true that simply *knowing* our patterns, vows, masks, deficits, lies, and resulting symptoms isn't enough for spiritual maturity to take place. "Knowledge makes arrogant, but love edifies" (1 Corinthians 8:1). We need more than understanding for real change. In fact, one of the legitimate complaints about counseling is that some professionals seem to see diagnosis as the cure. It's as if people in therapy are supposed to get healed automatically when their deepest issues have been pointed out. The kind of internal change that provides a richer life with God is wonderfully possible, but it requires commitment to the process. Because you are still reading on in this book, this is a good sign you are committed! Too often, though, we try to take shortcuts to healing – we pick and choose among the resources for true change instead of drawing on all of them. Because we are multifaceted beings, healing requires a multifaceted approach.

The "drum set" of living beyond the pain of your past is spelled out in the next few chapters under categories reflective of our composition as human beings: intellectual, spiritual, emotional, and behavioral. Attention to all aspects of our complex nature as humans is critical to deep healing. Many Christians have emphasized the application

of discipline and doctrine, which is certainly necessary and crucial.
However, why are there so many people who know vast amounts of
Scripture and yet still have suicidal thoughts, depression that keeps them
in bed, or panic attacks? Why is there this discrepancy? It is because our
emotional wounding cannot be solved by the *mere* application of
discipline and doctrine. Rigorous attention to God's Word and self-
discipline in one's life will reap great reward, but even Pharisees who
ultimately betrayed Jesus knew God's Word. Holistic, real, lasting healing
must also include routine and intentional attention to the other facets of
being a human. We must allow God to wholly sanctify and meet us,
spirit, soul, and body, where He invades our entire system.

While there is no magic formula, I have seen that when we spend
time attending to our hearts, and paying attention to all aspects of
ourselves, healing is accelerated. The key emphasis here is intentionality.
If we, *on purpose*, begin to do many of the items suggested in these
chapters, we will see change. Doing one by itself, however, will not bring
about the freedom we seek. Instead, we must deliberately give attention
to the emotional as well as the intellectual and the spiritual as well as the
behavioral. Expending effort towards change in any of these areas is
productive, and necessary. It's a must for lasting effects. Even the most
gifted musician still has to practice and the ablest of athletes must stay in
training. Proverbs 4:23 admonishes, "Above all else, guard your heart,
for it is the wellspring of life." Let us intentionally, with great hope, take
risks all for the sake of providing a willing and open vessel for the Lord
to freely display His glory.

The Battleground

If you recall from chapter two, one of the overriding truths of
our day is that we are at war. We are in a battle, and Scripture is quite

clear about where the truest battleground in the Christian life is. The warring ground between evil and truth is squarely in our minds. The power of our thought life is critical to grasp. With this in mind, consider these verses: "And you shall *know* the truth and the truth shall set you free." (John 8:32), not "and you shall *feel* the truth and it shall set you free." "Be *transformed* by the renewing of your mind" (Romans 12:2). I love that it says "be transformed," not just "get a little better or feel a bit different." Fully apprehending God's truth by the force of our mind's will permits us to be completely altered. Second Corinthians 10:5 admonishes us to "take every thought captive to make it obedient to Christ." Philippians 4:8 says, "Whatever is true, whatever is noble, whatever is right, whatever is pure, whatever is lovely, whatever is admirable – if anything is excellent or praiseworthy – *think* about such things." Again, it does not say *feel* such things. In the same vein, a familiar verse also supports Scripture's emphasis on the power of the mind: "And we *know* that all things work together for the good of those who love God and are called according to His purpose" (Romans 8:28). Certainly, there are plenty of times we don't *feel* as though all things are working for good.

The point here is that Scripture is replete with references to the power of the mind. The battleground for spiritual warfare is the mind, and the will is our central weapon for fighting. The will refers to one's innermost core. In biblical language, the will is usually referred to as "heart." One author describes the will as that which "organizes all the dimensions of personal reality to form a life or a person. The will, or heart, is the executive center of the self."[1] To us, this means that a central point of our spiritual aspect is linked with self-determination, or the power of the will to choose, to fight, to change, to act. While this point will be revisited again, it cannot be overemphasized how important our will is in fighting the battle, and in our level of true change.

A Critical Movement

<u>Recognition</u>

In the arena of the intellectual, a primary tool for soul healing is captured in the concepts of recognizing, rejecting/rebuking/renouncing, and replacing. To replace a lie that has taken root, we must first recognize what has happened. We have to see how we perceive all of life through some distorted lens of a lie-based perspective. We must recognize our vows, masks, patterns, and ways we seek to anesthetize. We must identify how our unfilled vats from the past are pulling on us in the present. Uncovering, or recognition, has been a large part of our earlier chapters.

This all-important recognition is essentially Scripture's admonition to "take captive every thought to make it obedient to Christ" (2 Corinthians 10:5). As such, it means that we must actually *think* about what we are thinking about. It implies a vigilance about our own thoughts, which makes sense when considering that the battleground in spiritual warfare is the mind. To this point, it is revelatory why the curse of this age seems to be busyness coupled with noise. When we are running from here to there, we have no time to actually "hear" the stream of thoughts running around our heads. Just yesterday a friend synopsized her view of hell's plan to me: "If you can't make 'em sin, make 'em busy." Similarly, the plea to "be still and know that I am God" is further occluded by the constant noise of our time (Psalm 46:10). TIVO, mini Ipods, cell phones, 24/7 radio streaming, DVD players in the car, voice mail, and satellite dishes coalesce in a cacophony of ceaseless audio and visual input. The resulting effect is that we have lost our ability to hear ourselves, much less the Spirit of God within. I know people who actually fear turning off their music, because they don't like how they feel when they start thinking. Could there be any more evidence that we should be doing so?

People who are serious about their soul's condition and intent on living victoriously in Christ make wise choices in this arena. They turn off the radio in the car, watch minimal TV, and say no to many societal pulls that are touted as "musts" in today's world. If you desire soul healing, be smart about what you are putting into your head. Chances are you'll be surprised what happens if you silence the CD player in the car. I guarantee you'll feel something deeper than just, "I can't stand that driver in front of me." You'll not only hear your own thoughts more clearly, after awhile you'll start to sense Him speaking. This is because He longs for us to hear His voice -- He's constantly speaking. Even though we don't have cable, our family recently unplugged the television for three months. Anyone who's ever taken such a challenge has never regretted it, for the tangible and intangible benefits it brings. The thrust here is that true recognition occurs as we slow down and clear out enough to be able to track what is really running around between our two ears. Attending to our thought life allows us to see how the true battle is progressing. Making good choices concerning noise and busyness provides time and space for us to recognize the lies that have taken root.

Rejection

While it is a crucial "must" for healing, understanding alone doesn't work. With the force of our will, the next active movement for change is to reject that which is causing the damage. We have to say "no" to the vow or the mask, to say "stop" to the pattern, and to put a halt to the plethora of coping mechanisms we have. To stop perceiving life through a lie, we have to reject the lie. The first step to fighting an addiction is to admit its hold and then to *decide* to stop. After we've become aware of how we anesthetize or stuff our pain, the next step is to reject those as alternatives any longer. When there is a cancerous growth affecting the rest of our system, we remove it surgically. When we realize someone or something is bulldozing us, we speak up and cry, "You must stop." After God reveals something to us about our inner condition, ours is the job of discarding and eliminating whatever untruth or ungodliness we uncover. How it got there is irrelevant at this point. It's ours to deal with now, and change will not happen without this movement.

Replace

Once the lie, vow, mask, pattern, or false comfort has been rejected, it must be replaced. Through a decision made by the force of your will, you must choose truth (not *feel good about* truth, but select it). Reinsert truth in the places where untruths were ruling. So, the person who realizes his or her soul is being damaged by the lie "it's not okay to fail" needs to actively reject that falsehood and replace it with the truth that failure is a normal part of life, growth, and can even provide future success. I recall sitting behind a chair in my living room under the weight of the idea that children are to be seen and not heard. As an adult, it's been challenging to believe my opinion will be heard, even when I'm at a meeting where my input is what is desired. The stance that took root was that "I don't have anything valuable to offer" and I have since replaced that with God's truths about His purposes for His children on this earth. It's definitely through a series of choices to say "no" to the darkened perspective and to actively don the truth. It doesn't just immediately change.

So, what has gone way deep in you that is disparate to the glory of God? What has a diabolical schemer unleashed upon you in the form of a lie, which you have believed and it has grown with you to the point where now you think it is *just you*? "I don't know. I just turn people off." "People just don't listen to me." "I won't succeed." You think that is your reality. Is there a possibility that there was a wound that happened, a lie came rushing in, and you've been living out that lie ever since? To do so means we perceive everybody and everything through the lens of the lie. If I believe I'm second-rate, have nothing to offer, am here to meet the needs of other people, and should just keep my mouth shut, I will interpret the way people interact with me through that lens.

Ask the Lord to reveal any lies that came into existence at a time of great hurt. This takes some time, thought, and reflection. It's helpful to think about the most significant events shaping your life. If they were hurtful in nature, ask yourself, "What are some lies that could have entered, that I am now living my life acting out?" Another excellent prompter is to bring to mind *any* memory that stands out as vivid in your mind. It's vivid for a reason. I've found through working with people that usually a memory stands out as vivid because it holds clues to something (and those are not always negative). The younger a lie took root, the more it will seem like "That's just me." Remember, though, everything has a beginning source and an origin. The present is a reflection of the past.

This "insert a lie" plan is, as we discussed earlier, a major satanic initiative. As the father of lies (John 8:44), his very first attack against the human race was to do what? Tell a boldfaced lie to Adam and Eve about where life was to be found and about what the consequences of certain actions would and would not be. While we'll add to this discussion below in the "spiritual" aspects of change, the pattern of recognizing, rejecting, and replacing is akin to what John Eldredge calls "agreements." He purports that evil suggests to us some sort of idea or impression, and what is being sought is sort of an "agreement" on our part.[2] The powers of hell are hoping that we'll buy into whatever is being insinuated. Consider, what do you believe about yourself that is against God's truth about His chosen? That you're not worth anybody's time? That you can't trust a soul? That you'll never measure up? That you're bad? These accusations that you heard, unless you disagree with them and reject them, will remain there until they are dislodged. Eldredge says,

> It becomes a kind of permission we give the enemy, sort of like a contract. The bronze gates start clanging shut around us. I'm serious—maybe half the stuff people are trying to "work through" in counseling offices, or pray about in their quiet times, is simply agreements they've made with the enemy. Some foul spirit whispers, "I'm such a stupid idiot," and they agree with it; then they spend months and years trying to sort through feelings of insignificance.[3]

In this realm of rejecting untruth and replacing it with truth, I feel it necessary to point out an often-complicating factor. It seems people have a hard time rejecting a lie because they feel a portion or part of it is true. For instance, a person might not be able to reject the lie that they are a failure because they did indeed fail a time or two. The difference is subtle, but vital. A woman might have a hard time rejecting the lie that she's fat, dumb, and ugly (the universal premenstrual saga) because she is somewhat overweight. However, the deeper lie is that she is somehow defective, and therefore ineffective. That is what needs to be rejected and dismissed. As well, carrying a little weight doesn't make one dumb and ugly. Just because a fundamentally lie-based assertion holds a smidgeon of truth does not mean we can let it alone. The person who failed a time or two is not a blanket failure as a human being.

After we are clued in that a lie is being offered up to us, rejecting it and replacing it with accurate truth is paramount. When Mike and I had a troubled interchange awhile back, I can recall thinking, "He always does that." As that thought took hold, then domino-like other "downers" came quickly… "If he still does that after we have talked about it, then he must not care enough about me to try to change." And deeper still…"I wonder if he even really loves me or just tolerates me." By the Lord's grace, I was able to catch what was happening, and quickly rejected the lie. It was a bit challenging because of the fact that a spoonful of truth was in the thought. However, it is absolutely untrue that Mike always does that. He *sometimes* does that. He has done that in the past, but by no means does he always do that. As a matter of fact, he does that much less than he ever used to. And it is never on purpose or because of not caring about me. If left unchallenged, it's not hard to see what damage such a sneaky little thought could do to a relationship. (Remember how relationships are attacked because they are a screen on which God's glory is to be projected?) However, when I rejected it and replaced it with the truth, my emotions were significantly different.

To replace with truth is twofold. Always, we must find an opposing Scriptural truth or principle straight from the Word of God. Consider these starting places: "He rewards those who earnestly seek Him" (Hebrews 11:6), "He will never leave you nor forsake you" (Deuteronomy 31:6), "All the ways of the Lord are loving and faithful" (Psalm 25:10), "His love endures forever" (Psalm 136), "He who began a good work in you will carry it on to completion until the day of Christ Jesus" (Philippians 1:6), "And my God will meet all your needs according to His glorious riches in Christ Jesus" (Philippians 4:19), "No weapon forged against you will prevail" (Isaiah 54:17), "Greater is He who is in you than he who is in the world" (1 John 4:4). We can be confident that for every satanic lie there is an applicable Biblical truth that must hold sway instead. God's truth is our final authority as we face life in this world, and also for our internal world. We do not always think or see clearly; else we wouldn't need the variety of mirrors we have been given (our children, the faces of others, storefront windows, compacts). If you were committed to this one facet alone (finding a countering Biblical truth for every hellish whisper), you would be overwhelmed at your increased level of peace and joy.

In addition to substituting God's truth, we will also need to exchange hellish ideas about a particular situation with general truth about it. For example, there is a common struggle that children from divorced families face. They often believe it was their fault. A general truth that applies is that it is never the fault of a child when two adults choose to divorce. No child has the capability to overrun an adult's will, no matter how challenging he or she might be. To fully root out the destruction evil wants to do, we need to find the opposing Biblical truth as well as any other general or specific truth. Some approaches of healing prayer, spiritual direction, and Christian counseling do a good job of leading people to learn to listen well to God through His Holy Spirit, and in that posture, they then receive more specific awareness about a situation. Sometimes, although a human could tell us something over and over, it won't sink in until we know that Lord has told us the truth.

So for those who have wounds from which you are struggling to be healed, be sure you are replacing lies with truth from God's word, and also truth about the situation in particular. Bring it to Him, in the manner of the Psalmists who provide us a great model for consistently crying out to the Lord about the details of life, and allow Him to continue to speak truth to you. For those on the helper side, especially you with a little bit of the prophet nature, sometimes it's good to just harness your own mouth for a little while and instead pray. Occasionally, while it might be plain as day for us to see, the truth can't come from us. It has to come from Him. We can always speak truths from His Word about who they are to Him. Do this always. Don't ever be afraid or timid to speak the Word of God. Ever. However, make sure you do it judiciously and appropriately and with massive amounts of mercy, grace, and love. If your motivation is anything else but love, healing, and victory in Jesus for that person, then don't dare speak it. It is excellent to bring God's Word in, and to also pray for the specific truth that He would reveal to someone so that the deeper healing and the deeper freedom can come.

Oh, and one final note about rejecting and replacing lies with truth. If you've been around a dirty diaper before, you know how just a small little diaper can stink up an entire house!! It's true that our lies, if left in place, can be like the rotten apple that spoils the whole bunch. That's why it's so important we go after these with vigilance and effort! When we get rid of the dirty diaper, though, does the smell immediately go away? No. In fact, it usually takes some time before the stench is gone, even when the diaper itself has been removed. Such is the same with our lies. We must realize that when we recognize, reject, and then replace a damaging lie with truth, we are probably not going to sense much of anything different right away. As a matter of fact, it might seem like it didn't even do any good, all that recognizing and replacing. Don't fall for it! Stand firm that you have sent the dirty lie a-packing, and that after a little while, the unpleasant feeling accompanying it will go away.

So, if you reject and replace some lie feeding your depression ("I don't matter to anyone," for instance), don't freak out if you awake the next morning and still feel some depression. Remind yourself that you took the trash out the day before, and that the stench will eventually dissipate if you are vigilant about keeping it out. Whatever you do, be sure not to run back out and get the disgusting thing out of the trash! While our emotions may not change at the moment we apprehend by faith the truth of Christ, we can be confident that over time, the general aura surrounding where the lie used to be will become different.

The Word of God, Seriously

For the astute thinker, there is an obvious implication if we are to become adept at recognizing, rejecting, and replacing. It is that we must *know* the Word of God if we are to replace lies with truth. We cannot hope to traffic in the truth if we are not familiar with it. Stated simply, we will not change unless we are serious about the Word of God. If you want to be serious about being more like Jesus and getting rid of the damage done by the wounds and the power the scars have over you, then you've got to intentionally be in the Bible. It has been a necessary part of any real change I've ever seen. In pursuing a degree in psychology, I sat in many types of non-Christian counseling endeavors. I never saw anybody truly change. I saw them make small changes. I saw them adjust. I saw them learn new ways to talk about things. But did I ever see the kind of transformation we're talking about that's reflected in the eyes of the soul? I never saw it. And by God's grace, I get to routinely see it now! It's Him. There is no healing without Him and His primary modality of communication to humans who use language – the authoritative and complete Word of God.

As such, we must be committed to making God's Word a priority in our lives. The question for us if we desire lasting change is whether the living and active Word of God is a regular part of our lives (Hebrews 4:12). So many people today, when they don't see immediate change from their reading of the Bible, fall prey to thoughts like, "It just doesn't do much for me; I don't really connect with it." The principle in Isaiah 55 is that no word of God will return void, and while we normally think of that in relation to sharing the gospel, it is also true that when we place God's Word inside of us, neither will it return void. Jesus fought lies offered up to Himself with God's Word. It is indeed the sword of the Spirit (Ephesians 6:17). We are in a battle, and our primary piercing weapon is the flawless Word of God given to humanity.

When we are committed to the rigorous exploration and application of His Word, that Word begins to do things that change us. To this end, I am overwhelmed at Romans 10:17 which explains, "Faith comes by hearing and hearing by the Word of God." What good news for all of us who desire more faith, that it doesn't come by a massive, strenuous, straining on our part, but simply by putting ourselves in situations where we hear God's Word. Yes, every time you read another verse, hear another sermon, peruse a Biblical commentary, meditate on a devotional, or listen to your friend tell what Scripture impacted her through last week's study; your faith is automatically increasing! What a wonderful God we have. Surely, He does help us in our weakness (Romans 8:26).

Larry Crabb aptly describes the intellectual strengthening necessary for a believer:

> As you walk this path, keep a few things in mind. First, don't let the confusing parts of life rob you of confidence in the central truths of Christianity. Cling to what you know is true. There is a God. He loves you. He sent His Son to die for your sins. He's promised to never leave you, and one day He'll return to make everything right. Remind yourself of these truths. In moments of soul-wrenching confusion, ponder the importance of these unchanging truths until they become burning realities in your soul. Increase your faith by regularly reading the Scriptures.[4]

Dallas Willard, who writes extensively on the path of becoming a disciple of Christ, says that if we read the Gospels through as much as we could over a few weeks time, that alone would allow us to see Jesus with a clarity that would be life altering. Of Jesus, he says we can rely on Him to meet us as we struggle with healing, changing, and becoming more like Him, "for he is far more interested in it than we can ever be. He always sees clearly what is at issue. We rarely do."[5] Our ability to have full understanding and to craft authentic change is impossible without the words of the One who made us, loves us, speaks to us, and died for us. Let these precious words "dwell richly within you" (Colossians 3:16) and watch how you change.

Releasing Someone Back to God

In the journey of healing and into freedom, there is almost always another space we must enter into; another domino must fall. Forgiveness is a word fraught with misconception, and heavy-laden with preconceived notions. Incredible works have been written on this most important topic by amazing authors like Charles Stanley, Ken Sande, John Eldredge, and Joyce Meyer.[6] My desire here is to not address the entire concept, but instead to offer three specific aspects pertinent to you and me. First, forgiveness is more crucial for our own sake than for or about the person we are forgiving. Often, the other person is not hurt or even bothered by your unforgiveness of him or her. However, the toll it is taking on your soul, the internal energy it is consuming, the vileness it is letting come into your heart – this is a major danger. When forgiveness is not extended, it is not long before bitterness takes root. Once bitterness takes root, you've given up ground that is very hard to regain. You've probably witnessed the hold it can have on someone and how poisonous it becomes, contaminating everything about a person's life.

My second point is that forgiveness and feelings are distinct from each other and must be handled as such. If we use one to validate the other, then we are mistaken. Said differently, if I think I will not hurt any more after I've forgiven or conversely, that I have to be rid of all hurt and anger before I can forgive, I am in error. Such misconceptions just serve to prolong forgiveness, thereby increasing the chance for bitterness to enter. A diabolical ploy, wouldn't you say?

Forgiveness is a decision. My third point: it is an act of the will. That is why I have included it under the "intellectual" section of healing aspects. When trying to explain the distinct nature of forgiveness, I often hold up my left hand and reveal the wedding band on my ring finger. Just like getting married was something I thought about doing ahead of time, made a commitment to do it regardless of how I felt at that particular moment, and then actually married, forgiveness is a very similar process. If you choose to forgive, you must decide to do it, "go through with it," and then remind yourself daily that you've done it, akin to wearing a wedding ring. A little piece of precious metal serves as a grave reminder that there was forethought, decision, and completion -- that "the deed was done." There are certainly times I don't feel like being married, and early on had times where I forgot I was married…until glancing at my left hand. That glance can serve as a prompt to make a different decision. The "Oh, that's right, I'm married" idea is similar to how we must remind ourselves that we have indeed chosen forgiveness. It could be something like, "I can let this thought go right now, because I chose to release that person back to God."

The best definition I've ever encountered of forgiveness is that it is laying down the *right* I have to hold something over someone's head. It is an active decision to release consequence and punishment for a wrong done to me to God. I quite specifically tell Jesus, "Because of how much you have forgiven me for (even this very day and hour!), I now choose to release _____ for doing _____ to me. I now entrust you for whatever resolution of this situation you deem best. I know that vengeance is Yours alone and that every person will have to give account for his or her actions. I will now choose to extend grace to _____, and my forgiveness of them is not impingent upon whether they ask for it" (Romans 12:19, Matthew 12:16). (He died for our sins before we asked His forgiveness and even for those who have not yet asked. This reminder can help us in our weakness.)

Forgiveness is definitely a choice – you'll never feel forgiving. If you wait to forgive until you feel like it, you will never get there. Feelings heal with time after the choice to forgive is made. We have to acknowledge the hurt from the past, because forgiveness will be incomplete if it doesn't "visit the emotional core of your life."[7] Forgiveness is not admitting "It really didn't matter" or "I probably deserved what I got." As a matter of fact, it actually validates that what happened was wrong and hurt you deeply, but that the one(s) who inflicted the pain are released to God.

However, if we don't forgive, bitterness and unforgiveness can sink deep in our hearts and become chains that hold us captive to our wounds and the messages of those wounds. Unless we forgive, *we* remain imprisoned in a web of lies, not the one who wronged us. God warned us through Paul that unforgiveness and bitterness can ruin our lives and the lives of those around us (Ephesians 4:31; Hebrews 12:15). "Forgive as the Lord forgave you," God's word implores (Colossians 3:13).

This instruction – to forgive following Christ's example – helps us sort through several misconceptions about forgiveness. The first one is "If I forgive, it means that I'm condoning the act." No. Forgiveness is spurred on with a righteous anger that the offense was wrong and that it did damage to you. Another false idea is that "If I forgive, that means I must forget." Anyone who has been deeply hurt knows you can never forget. Forgiveness does not mean you forget anything. I like the way Clinton and Sibcy put it, "You just give up the right to replay the event, and you stop wishing for revenge."[8]   Another common misconception is that if we forgive, then we become a doormat to be walked over, and must put ourselves right back in relationship with the one who wronged us. Certainly, a holy, almighty God never condones sin and certainly isn't a doormat to be trampled. We can forgive as He forgave because He lives in us.

It can be helpful when choosing forgiveness to remember two things. The first is that the person or people who aggrieved you are also broken people who were hurt or deeply wounded themselves. *Hurt people hurt people.* (Which is why we are working so hard on healing – in order that we not walk around unknowingly wounding people who are also designed to reflect God's glory!!) An enemy who hates them, lies to them, and wants to play them as pawns to sideline God's children is scheming against them. While it doesn't absolve them of the decisions they made, it can help us to let them go, and release them back to God's justice.

Secondly, it is very helpful to think of the ways you have sinned against God this very hour. Really. Think of your self-focused thoughts and your manipulative desires. Think of the snap judgments you make, the things you turn to for comfort, how you speak of the driver in front of you, and what you watch on TV regularly. We are sinners to the core, and yet have been forgiven completely. If you would make a list of the ways in which you have hurt your beloved Maker in the 24 hours prior to forgiving another, I guarantee you will find it much easier. This is the principle captured in Luke 7:47: "For this reason I say to you, her sins, which are many, have been forgiven, for she loved much; but he who is forgiven little, loves little." I am advocating that a concentrated realization on the degree and depth of the forgiveness we believers have can keep us for taking it for granted in our daily lives.

It's okay if it takes some time to work through emotional feelings involved in forgiving someone what they did to you whether once, or even if they continue to do it to you today. It's not okay, though, to wait any longer to forgive. While we cannot instantly dismiss the feelings, we can immediately forgive. It will take time to reprogram the computer when those old, familiar thoughts about a person come rushing in, or our worn-out anger suit knocks at our door. However, while we won't ever erase all recall, if we apply our wills and surrender someone to God, we will begin to see a new perspective arise before long.

There is a corollary with forgiveness that arises here. Thinking about forgiving others is actually easier for some people than what they refer to as "forgiving themselves." Many people will even go so far as to say that they know God has forgiven them, but that they just can't forgive themselves. People who accept Christ's blood sacrifice on behalf of their abortion, the cycle of web porn and masturbation, gossiping at work, the lie, the indiscretion, the anger outburst...such ones who accept a holy God's forgiveness but who can't cross a self-condemnation threshold are actually in grave danger. While certainly not on purpose, if one carries this thinking pattern ("I know God forgives me but I can't forgive myself.") to its furthest conclusion, it's as if the person is saying, "I'm a better God than you."

Stay with me here – because it's relatively recent at the writing of this book -- picture yourself in *The Passion of the Christ* movie. You're looking up at Jesus who bleeds in agony on the cross. He's pouring Himself out for all humanity; He's pouring Himself out *for you*. To not be able to forgive yourself is like looking at Him, saying, "That's amazing. Thank you for such love. You're up there on the cross dying for me. However, while it satisfies God's standards, and I appreciate it and all, it's just not quite good enough for me." That's essentially what we're doing when we do not forgive ourselves. Are your standards higher than a holy, perfect God? Oh, that we would never believe we need more guilt, hotter shame, or a more painful punishment, for it is the ultimate affront to a brutal death died on our behalf by a sweet, beautiful, strong, incredible human Savior. Do not uphold higher standards than God one minute more. Let's not do that to our precious Savior. Accept his free and unending gift fully and completely. "If the Son sets you free, you shall be free indeed" (John 8:36).

Playing Catch

The foregoing discussion has been to parse out some of the helpful healing actions we can do through the force of our minds, and we have referred to these loosely as "intellectual" elements to healing. Forgiveness is a choice; recognizing, rejecting, and replacing is a series of thought-filled actions; and inculcating the Word of God is a decision to be enacted. At this point, it is important to realize that "catching" what is happening is often a decisive hurdle as we seek to change and be different. In other words, we need to sharpen our minds to distinguish when we're seeing through lenses, acting out of our wounds, or wanting people to fill voids they can't. Catching a number error in a bank statement saves hours of trying to figure out what went wrong later. It's the same with us. If we can catch some of what we're doing in the moment, we can stop potentially disastrous effects and make a small change that brings about an entirely different outcome. What follows are examples of some things we need to catch.

Little Tests

It's as if we have little tests that we put others through. We'll lob some small, mildly vulnerable disclosure out there and watch the reaction of the person we're talking to like a hawk. If they handle it well, and don't seem to have judged us, we'll share a little something else. Again, if received and processed in a manner pleasing to us, we'll share more. If not, we shut down and in a notebook in a corner of our brain, we write them off to some degree. Teens are notorious for this. I believe the only reason adults are not notorious for it is that they have become adept at being subtle.

For instance, one of the many protective reactions we develop can come in the "I'll reject you before you reject me" type of mode. Kate really wanted to go for a walk with her friend. They did so frequently, and when doing so, enjoyed sweet, authentic connection. When she realized recently that her friend would be unable to go for a walk with her, she could feel the reaction "I didn't want to go for a walk with you, anyway" rising up in her. There is a sense of vulnerability when we get our hopes up. We feel as though we are putting ourselves "out there," because we're letting a little "I want" show. If it goes awry, we can quickly pull back and hide our hopes for connection. People do it all the time.

Many hurt people will often show the ones closest to them the most ugliness. It's as if we "save" the worst in us (and often wrongly think it is the "real" us) and put it out there for someone who says they love us and will be with us. When they are still there, then we bombard them with more, like, "Okay, can you take this?" Then, "Still here? Then take this. I'll prove you'll leave me like everyone else has." Of course, none of us do this in our conscious, rational minds. But, when we have unhealed pain and do not understand the inner forces that drive us, we will often sabotage the very intimacy, closeness, and love we long for by doing things we don't even realize we're doing. Disbelieving their words, minimizing their efforts, disappointing them again…these are some ways in which we push away the very people who have drawn close, and whom we want close. Learning to "catch" when we are putting others through tests is a huge step towards stopping that knee jerk reaction, and instead replacing it with free, unhindered, loving interaction with others of God's children.

Getting "Plucked"

As described earlier in chapter four, if we are not aware of what we are doing, we can often act out of our wounds, especially out of our deficits. Do you yet know when you're taking your empty dad vat to your boss, or father-in-law, or friend to fill? The indices for these are the "too much" gauges. Wanting approval from your boss is normal and natural, but there is a place of "too much" approval wanted. While our thoughts naturally wonder how others perceive us, there is a line that's crossed when we do so "too much." If we're engaged in a conversation with someone in front of us, but are locked on what someone across the room is doing, this might be an instance of the "too much" meter. You're obsessing about if they notice you. Additionally, consider the effect on the valuable person right in front of you to whom you are sending a subtle, yet perceptible message about their worth. It could be wounding them in the very process of you acting out of your wounds. Remember, we are working so hard at healing because hurt people hurt people.

The point cannot be overemphasized that we've got to "catch" when we're acting out of our wounds. The picture of taking the bait and getting hooked on a line is effective at describing what happens when we look for others to fill voids they cannot. Can you feel when the fishhook has gotten you? It's what happens when you're enjoying your friend, but then cross the line into obsessing. It goes from "Thank you, Lord, for bringing her into my life" to "I wonder why she won't get coffee with me sooner? Maybe I should call her and ask to get together tonight." You can just feel it; you've been baited and opened your mouth. It can happen when someone doesn't respond to us in just the way we wanted him or her to. They might have been celebratory and positive about your achievement, but it somehow left you unsatiated. You were waiting for the "I'm so proud of you" and as a result overlooked the "Great job! What a blessing and I'm happy for you." The woman who says, "Look, I got a new outfit! What do you think?" and hears the response "Oh, that's nice!" is plucked when she thinks "He didn't like it" rather than, "He thought it was nice." Not truly hearing or choosing to believe others is a neon indicator that "my issues are breaking through here!"

Just the other day, someone told me she and one of our pastors were conversing. Of it, she said, "I think he was trying to tell me he doesn't think I'm coming to church enough when he said, 'I hope you'll join us.'" I replied, without sarcasm, "I think he was saying, 'I hope you'll join us.'" How often do we do that? When we start reading things into other people's comments and actions, that's *our* stuff. Do you recognize when you're plucked? Another surefire example of our issues breaking through is when we have major emotional reactions to minor events. When I sang for our Christmas Eve service and played one wrong note, the huge reaction I had wasn't merited by one errant tone. It tapped on a sensitive area. If you stub your toe and get so mad that you want to kill the person who installed the floor in the first place, that could be an issue! Road rage isn't just for funny jokes. Whenever you have a huge reaction to something, which, when you step back and look at it in recognition that it isn't that big, what does that signify? Whenever your emotional reaction is disproportionate to the actual event, that's your clue. Something's being plucked. Pray, "Lord, help me see it." He will.

Hit Me Baby One More Time

Our relationships are a gift from God given to us for His glorification, for mutual edification, and for our enjoyment. However, we can put too much into these relationships, looking to them for what only God can fill. We can use them as idols, as our drug of choice, and to try to compensate for past hurt. As mentioned earlier, we are permitted to enjoy those relationships to a 10, on a scale of one to 10! Don't settle for an eight in that friendship, that budding romance, or that sibling connection. However, something we need to catch is when we begin to look to that relationship for too much, for a 13 or 18. To do so reminds me of those fountain drink machines where you dispense your own choice of drink. Nowadays you are provided the cup, and you are free to choose what type of soda you want. I think of how I like to fill my cup up to the very brim and get every penny's worth of drink, even being happy to fill that cup up again if refills are permissible. Our relationships are some of the best things in life we will ever enjoy. Fill it up, and get all you can out of it! A new feature has arrived on the scene in these dispensers, though, that reminds me of just how we can want more, more, more for all sorts of unconscious and ungodly reasons. There is a "shot" machine whereby you can squirt a shot of lime, vanilla, or cherry into your already sweet drink, for even more flavor intensity. Really – think of how very indulgent it is to add a shot of flavor into a Coke, for goodness' sake. While certainly not wrong, it is akin to what we can do in relationships. That fantastic taste is not quite enough; I want more! Trying to squeeze more into an already full relational cup can indicate to us that our issues are winning the day. Intellectual acuity to catch when this is happening will facilitate deeper emotional potency.

At this point, a related aside must be addressed. For those of you who do not relate to much of this discussion because you were blessed to have mostly full vats, thank the Lord!! Truly, give thanks daily for the gift that your parents were able to give love freely and unconditionally in abundance to you. Undoubtedly, they are sinners also having experienced their own hurts in life, but they didn't live out of their own hurt. Your potential present-day challenge is different. For those who did not experience deprivation, you come to life with a sense of fullness or security many others do not. Whereas the majority of people come to relationships in adulthood out of a sense of need and desire for filling, you come with a sense of "already full" at best or "not insecure and needy" at worst. Believe it or not, in addition to the myriad ways you are blessed and benefited by your upbringing, there is a downside to this. In this way, you, too, must "catch" what is happening at times.

When one comes from an atmosphere of *assumed* love ("of course I am lovable" and "no question that my parents love me"), you may be a little spoiled in some ways. Consider the person who came from an insecure and unsure environment. They do not assume people love them. Therefore, they often *work* for other's love (through performance or manipulation) and are deeply impacted (and often surprised) when someone expresses love for them. One who comes from abundance might assume people do love them. Therefore, they can be seen as aloof, cocky, or insensitive to the needs of others. While others are busy grappling for love from others as a result of their deficits or lies, you are oblivious, thinking everyone's okay with you and them.

The point to this discussion is simply to warn the one who was blessed with unconditional love in large doses to (1) not forget that most people don't assume you love them, so you need to tell them, (2) be careful if you are taking for granted the people in your life and make sure you express your appreciation for them, (3) not judge others who "just seem so insecure" and (4) watch for any other way you might be acting a bit under-aware in relational give-and-take.

Maneuvering Wisely in the Dark

To summarize the foregoing section, we need to "catch" little tests, when we're acting out of our wounds, wanting too much, or simply plucked in a situation by keeping our minds sharp. This reminds me of how I have bruised my leg in one place so many times that I flinch whenever anything gets close to that spot. That's what it's like with our emotional wounds. Whenever we have been repeatedly hurt, we develop our own emotional "flinching" response whenever anyone gets near our wound. You might have seen an abused animal duck or whine when someone raises a hand near it. We are much the same emotionally. If someone I trusted let me down, I'm probably going to freak out a little on the inside when a friend forgets our lunch appointment.

The repetitive bruise has come from hitting my thigh on the corner of my bed in the dark. You see, the trek from my side of the bed to the toilet is actually rather long, and somehow becomes elongated in darkness. Since the birth of my two children, my bladder seems to have rebelled, and likely enjoys some sinister pleasure at the number of times I am called to make the long journey in the wee hours. Because I have hit that same corner so often, I now have a new habit. Every night when I go to the bathroom – if once or ten times – on the way back I put out my left hand anticipating the footboard of the bed. As I make contact with it, I slide my hand the entire distance to and around the corner, so that I will know where the corner is and avoid it. I have developed a strategy for "when I'm groping around in the dark bumping into things."

The changes and awarenesses we are exploring are similar. I am aware that many of these ideas, while apparently helpful, might seem awfully hard to put into practice. Essentially, though, this picture is what we need to do. While we do not know all of our internal reactions and triggers, we do know how we've been hurt. Part of what we need to do to not "flinch" or be oversensitive to ways in which we have been hurt prior is to develop a proactive strategy, akin to my left-hand feel in the dark. In that maneuver, I anticipate what's coming, and guide myself around the potential hurt. This is such a good picture for us. What are the lies, feelings, thoughts, triggers that you have come to see trip you up for the reasons we have discussed thus far? Can you now begin to get a sense of anticipating what situations are likely to cause you to downward spiral?

For instance, I know that because of my deficits and how it played out in formative years, I have tended to overreact, overread, and overemphasize the opinion of all "head honchos" in my life. I realized early on that I was an approval addict, focused on whoever the "alpha dog" was. There have been plenty of times I have overanalyzed a comment made by my pastor, fretted over why my academic advisor didn't do something, and lost sleep over whether my boss was pleased or not. Knowing this as a past pattern and temptation for anxiety, I now have a strategy for how I handle my own weakness in this area.

Whenever I know I have a meeting with the person in charge, or will be getting a phone call, I figuratively put my hand on the bed board in preparation – I pray. I try to be specifically aware of my own propensity towards over-sensitivity and be in conversation with Jesus about it. Then I think about how a middle-aged employee would interact with her middle-aged boss, or how a mature female would interact with the person to whom she directly reports. It helps to envision a conversation between a 39-year-old woman and a whatever-age-the-person in charge is, as opposed to one with an 11-year-old girl. From there, I choose wisely when my instances for interacting with these folks will be. In other words, if I'm having a particularly insecure day, if I've just experienced rejection of some sort, or even if it is a hormonally challenging date on the calendar, I talk myself through how I need to proceed. And, you know what? Whenever I do that, I find that my interactions with the same person that sent me spiraling last time, are wonderful. The times when I proactively think through what I need to be sure to do and not do, it always turns out well. I turn the corner without bruising the old bruise! What's even better is that, just as my nighttime navigational endeavor has become a pattern, so does my emotional attentiveness. Whenever I choose to vigilantly act like a loving, mature, caring, confident adult instead of a needy, insecure, passive, self-focused child, it begins to actually "stick" after awhile!!

For such growth, I'm basically saying we need to know our own over-sensitivities to people and situations.   I react to people who can be moody because I was really hurt by someone with that characteristic in my past. So if I get even a whiff that a person is quite labile in their moods, I will automatically begin to put distance between us if I'm not paying attention. I have to reject the thought that this person will hurt me because a similar type of person did me wrong and replace it with the truth that God orders my steps, works all things for good, and urges deep love for all people (Proverbs 16:9, Romans 8:28, Mark 12:31, John 13:34). Do you know your own sensitivities? Who are you on eggshells around? Are you over attentive to the person with striking brown eyes? Why is that? What situations are terrible for you to be in? Is it at a party? Why is it so bad for you? How about the church lobby? Where in your life do you find evil having a heyday with you? Be wise about your own sensitivities and areas of potential sin. Christian "A" can go to a bar and evangelize or hang out just fine, while Christian "B" can't ever be near a bottle of alcohol again. God's guidance to us is that "all things are possible, but not all things are profitable" (1 Corinthians 10:23).

Reminders to Remember

Acceptance

Just as knowledge of one's over-sensitivities is an important intellectual task, so is the concept of acceptance introduced in chapter six. It is recalled here because it also falls under the rubric of what a healing mentality looks like. An example provides reference: Taylor realized that every time she started to develop a new friendship, she got her hopes very high. Unknowingly, it was as if she was saying internally, "Maybe *this* will be the one." (The one person who will neither leave nor disappoint nor hurt her.) After deep processing and exploration, she was able to realize this pattern and finally accept it about herself. As discussed in chapter six, such acceptance is crucial. Recently she has begun a new friendship and described it thus: "All the obsessive thoughts kicked into gear early, as usual. Although frustrating, I got through that and can feel like I'm not a freak of nature again. Thank the Lord, I feel normal. That whole thing, though -- It's a little painful." While she did (and does) not like this initial relational roller coaster, she uses her own self-knowledge to stay appropriate and have realistic expectations early on in budding friendships. If she were still hating and shaming herself for her initial obsessions, she couldn't move on. Acceptance (not being happy about something, but merely giving it permission to exist) opens the door for maturity.

<u>A House is Not Our Home</u>

Another fundamental of healing thought patterns is to remember that this earth is not supposed to be our home. We weren't created to be fully and completely content in human bodies on earthly soil. As such, while we long for ease and comfort on this earth, such a pursuit is fruitless. We will never experience complete at-home-ness here because this is not our true home. Just like we can spruce up and put enjoyable items in someone else's house, it will never totally feel like our own haven. Because our citizenship is in heaven, there will always exist a measure of discomfort as we move about on planet Earth. Perhaps this answers the restlessness question for some of us.

Whatever the case, reminding oneself of this reality is paramount for two reasons: the world we live in today exalts and emphasizes our comfort. Such a focus is in direct opposition to our Lord's promise of heaven and a hereafter where there will be no mourning or crying or pain (Revelation 21:4). Immature or struggling Christians can often wrongly think that because they feel an inner discomfort, even when times are good, that means something is wrong. In actuality, it *can* mean that something is right – our citizenship really is in heaven (Philippians 3:20). Secondly, living in this reality is helpful for normalizing our inner longings. In other words, we are helped when we have an "Oh, yeah, I won't ever totally feel comfortable in this life" perspective. Such a vantage point can free us from falling prey to thinking we have to keep pursuing stuff, activities, and people until this internal desire for deep comfort wears off. Learning to live amicably with some inherent uneasiness is not a bad thing.

The Power of Choice

Perhaps one of the most important of the intellectual thrusts is the reminder that we can never underestimate the power of choice. People who understand this fundamental truth are radically different than those who do not. We always have the power of choice in every situation. Viktor Frankl was a man who waited in the gas chambers of Auschwitz, surrounded by death on every side. In that horrific situation, he learned that while people could take away much, they could never take away the capacity to choose a person's thoughts and focus. He even discovered how to find a measure of calm in the hell of his surroundings.[9] In like manner, another author explains:

> God has placed the only key to the innermost parts of the human
> soul in its own hands and will never take it back to himself, or

198

give it to another. You may even be able to destroy the soul of another, but you will never unlock it against his or her will.[10]

I reference such intense examples to drive home the truth that the power of our will is huge, and can transform our entire existence. Notice I didn't say it could change our circumstances or the people around us. However, the extreme power of our will in submission to God for His plan and purposes is a life-altering truth.

Psychologists have referred to people who possess this as having an "internal locus of control." Such people are secure, take responsibility for their lives, and know the decisions they make affect it. Even though they can't keep difficult situations from happening to them, they choose their reactions, and generally don't feel like victims (even if they sometimes are). Those who don't grasp the power of choice or the strength of one's will have an external locus of control.[11] In other words, what is outside of them controls them. They feel life happens *to* them. They don't understand how much choice they have in their reaction to events, and seem to think their own feelings and thoughts are outside of their jurisdiction. When facing something challenging, such folk aren't likely to do much to problem-solve. If they try something and fail, it's time to go to Starbucks. True healing is quite challenging for someone who doesn't understand the power and force of one's own will exercising choice.

We've already discussed some choices vital for change. For instance, when we discover we are viewing life through some lie-based perspective, we must ***choose to take off the lens***. To walk in freedom from the effects of our wounds, we must ask the Lord to reveal His truthful perspective to us, and then actively grab onto it with the force of our will. If your life thus far has been filtered through the "I'm a failure" grid, you can't just wish it off. You must select, grip, and squeeze the truth instead of the familiar lie.

Such grace was given me concerning one of the lenses I described of myself in chapter four. While in college, I continued to operate from the understanding that I was homely. Any achievement or popularity, I concluded, was a result of just having a "great personality." My senior year, I found myself once again at the helm for counting Homecoming Court votes, along with a committee of five others. It was quite literally a surreal experience as I heard my name read many times. I felt the room spinning as my inner reality clashed with the outer one unfolding before my eyes. When the names were read, mine was among the top five, and I knew deep inside that no matter how much of a "great personality" someone had, the reality of our harsh world was that a truly homely person would not be selected to be on the court.

From that point I had a choice. I could either accept God's gracious revelation that my lenses were faulty or hold onto my long-term self-loathing. Almost 20 years hence, I can now see why evil would want to keep my perspective of myself as essentially "ugly." I can only describe the process whereby the change occurred as effortful. If you can picture yourself as shoving something in your mouth, pushing it down your throat, and muscling it fist-first into your belly, that's what the process of inculcating the truth can sometimes look like. It's a choice from beginning to end.

Because I lived for so long feeling unattractive, if you wake me from a dead sleep even today, my unconscious answer to "What do you look like?" would probably be "I'm homely." However, God has in His grace given evidence to the contrary. I can live life based upon His truth of me, or continue to stay in my little-girl, incorrect perception. Are you running around with some childish pair of glasses on your eyes distorting your picture of reality today? You need the right prescription! God will reveal it and you must reach out and grab it with the force of your will. It grieves me to think of how many of us live life in some condemning falsehood rather than embracing a new reality God is offering to us. Indeed, it is a reprogramming, act-like-it-even-though-I-don't-feel-like-it *effort*. The way we must change will be through the consistent choice of truth over lie *over time*.

Similarly, another choice emphasized thus far is that to change we must **choose to reject the lies**. We can recognize, talk about, identify, and explain internal lies, but unless we apply our will to saying "no" to them, we will not change. Sometimes a lie has to be jackhammered out of us, and a person with an external locus of control struggles to possess the internal fortitude for the strain of such a process. Some lies have become cemented in us, and breaking up that emotional concrete will take effort over time to stay at it in belief it will eventually be broken up enough to be cleared. Seriously, if you're fighting a lie, it's like reprogramming. Keep at it, give it time, and understand it's been there awhile, but if you keep at it, your efforts will have an effect. Choosing over and over the truth of God will always defeat the lie and transform His child.

Another effective choice in the process of change is to be what I think of as a "quick turner." Such a decision means one will **choose to turn to God first**. For instance, if you receive bad news, to whom do you talk first? If you are "plucked" and having a reaction to someone, who do you inform? What do you do when you are struggling? Who do you ask for wisdom when you don't know what to do? In most situations, our automatic response is not to turn to God first. However, we can train ourselves – by the force of our will over time – to begin to pray. We can stop ourselves from picking up the phone and calling the friend, even our spouse or parent, and speak with the One who loves us most first. At that point, then talking with another is a good choice, but learning to quickly turn to our Lord can change our lives. It merely takes determination.

Another example of a reminder to ourselves that will abet a healthy perspective in our lives is to **choose to stay in today**. So many of us lose the joy of both today and tomorrow by worrying about tomorrow. Jesus was pretty clear about the only way to handle life on this earth by telling us to "not worry about tomorrow" (Matthew 6:34). Two of the most dangerous words in the English language are "what if." People can completely become incapacitated by the "what ifs" of life. "What if I lose my job?" "What if something happens to my kids or spouse?" "What if I have another anxiety attack?" "What if my presentation doesn't go well?" Such trouble-borrowing sabotages the life of peace and purpose purchased for us. Reminding ourselves to stay in today will augment the pace at which our healing commences.

These few examples of the power of choice provide us a picture of the how much difference it can make in our lives if we grasp the potential of our own minds. We *can* change. Many people who now crave beer or cigarettes or even coffee did not enjoy their first encounters with these, but instead describe having to "acquire" a taste for them. Now they feel they can't live without them. How much more will our souls "lap up" mental habits we acquire through familiarity and choice, since these types of thought patterns help us live in truths for which our hearts were designed! In other words, reminding ourselves to embrace truth, reject lies, stay in today, turn to God first, and take off false lenses

202

will become habits we can't live without in a very short time. Consistently bringing to mind godly perspectives allows us to experience true peace: "You will keep in perfect peace him whose mind is steadfast, because he trusts in you" (Isaiah 26:3).

This entire section concerning the intellectual or mind-driven part of ourselves can be encapsulated through a picture Scripture gives us. In Psalm 42:11, the psalmist asks "Why so downcast, oh my soul? Put your hope in God." In Psalm 103:1, 2, "Praise the Lord, O my soul; all my inmost being, praise his holy name. Praise the Lord, O my soul, and forget not all his benefits." If you notice, the writer is having a conversation of sorts with his soul. He is actually commanding his soul to bless the Lord. What we can glean is the idea of "speaking" to your soul, almost as if it is an entity distinct from you. On a day when your feelings run wild, do you command your own soul to bless the Lord? The concept of willing yourself into God's truth is huge – we must *choose* to recognize, reject, and replace lies with truth; we must *decide* to pour God's Word into us; we must *remind* ourselves on purpose to stay in today, turn to God quickly, and remove inaccurate lenses. These are all ways in which we instruct ourselves into change. In this way we will have "taken off the old self with its practice, and have put on the new self, which is being renewed in knowledge in the image of its Creator" (Colossians 3:10). No verse better captures the "getting-rid-of-and-putting-on" picture advocated in this entire section.

9

BATTLING POWERFULLY (The Spiritual Pathway)

> *To live in ignorance of spiritual warfare is the most naïve and*
> *dangerous thing a believer can do.*
> JOHN ELDREDGE

> *You, dear children, are from God and have overcome them, because the One*
> *who is in you is greater than the one who is in the world.*
> 1JOHN 4:4

As you can see, the intent of this chapters eight through 11 is to provide practical, effective means for change and healing. These steps are being given in broad categories reflective of all the aspects of being a human, because a truly effective approach will be multifaceted. While the preceding section focused on the power of one's will enacted by the force of his or her mind, we now turn to the spiritual aspect. First Thessalonians 5:23 provides our guideline for delineating such a category: "May God himself, the God of peace, sanctify you through and through. May your whole spirit, soul and body be kept blameless at the coming of our Lord Jesus Christ." In the quest for being healed through and through, attention to the spiritual as well as the intellectual is necessary. In other words, here are some more things you need to know to live beyond the pain of your past.

Swim in the Ocean

In the last section, we discussed being a "quick turner," or a person who is able to realize that turning to Christ is a necessary discipline one must develop to make it in life. If Christ is our life (Colossians 3:4), then the wise person knows that looking to Christ is the only means to finding anything substantial. *Anything.* The wise person also knows this doesn't come naturally. If you want a clue to why, look again at the Garden of Eden with me. The temptation was to focus on something other than God's abundant provision. They were enticed with desire for the only thing that wasn't accessible. Think of it – they had the perfect biological, spiritual, emotional, and intellectual system. Instead of rejoicing in all that they had been given in such lavish measures, evil asked the question that brought discontentment into the life of every believer henceforth. "Did God really say, 'You must not eat from any tree in the garden?'" (Genesis 3:1)

Mature, whole people distinguish themselves from others by their ability to focus on what *is* versus what *is not.* Myriad marriages are being decimated because one spouse is zeroing in on the other's faults rather than his or her strengths, or even what attracted them in the first place. (Many authors have said that if the grass looks green on the other side of the fence, it's time to water your own grass!) Some believers are wasting their lives bemoaning their financial struggles or harsh bosses, all the while missing that they have a car that *does* run, and a job that *does* pay. While this point seems obvious, it actually runs deep. We wonder why God isn't speaking, answering, or changing something, and we become locked onto that. Our prayer life becomes focused around that thing. We bring it up first when others ask how we are doing, and the more we think about it, the greater our discontent with God grows. It's an echo of that first diabolical ploy!

To apply this to our healing journey, recall the significant challenge for any person who has past deficits in life. The temptation is to place others in the position of the void created, for example, by the emotionally absent daddy or deceased mother, and to be disappointed with them. As well, we can become quite disillusioned with God when we realize He has no intention of filling voids made by humans. Instead, He offers love, security, comfort, peace, and joy in measures actually beyond finite comprehension. However, we will never seize these assurances unless we turn our eyes from the thing that *isn't* to all that *is*. It is a critical movement to look away from what isn't happening to really meditate on who He is. Turning our attention away from God's hand and placing it on God's face will work to transform us every time.

Think about this truth: There is never a wasted experience for those who claim Him as Savior (Romans 8:28). There is nothing beyond His touch (Psalm 139:7). The problem, however, is that many reading these words simply do not believe this reality for themselves. The reason? Because when our past wounds are not yet recognized and healed, we *miss* His deliverance. We are *missing* His love, uniquely for us in a particular situation. Just like those who missed the Messiah, we can overlook Him because of our own preconceptions. As He initially came, He often enters our lives gently, quietly, humbly, and with a fanfare-less message of peace. Many of us today are missing how He *is* providing for us, how He *is* delivering us, how He *is* so very close to us, and how He *is* strengthening us, all because our pasts have predisposed us to look for something else. Healing will commence every time we unlock our mind's gaze from those things that irritate, disrupt, and bring anxiety and force ourselves to look at where God is at work, what He is doing, and how He most certainly reigns.

In other words, it's as if we have an ocean (really, picture an ocean) – of all that we desire – of love, of affection, of longing fulfilled, of security, of meaningful purpose, of joy, of contentment, of freedom from lust or envy or jealousy. And instead of drenching our whole body in that ocean, we walk around with an empty little Coke can on the beach, asking other people and things to fill it up with what we want. The contrast is indeed that stark, and the choice, that clear. Will you turn yourself to run toward that ocean and swim in Jesus and all He purchased for you, or will you simply keep walking around asking this person and the next, "Will you like me? Will you fill me up? Can you give me love? Fix me, please." This is what it is to turn our eyes from earthly things.

Christ promised to supply us with living water, by saying springs would flow from our "innermost being" (John 7:38). In some places, that phrase is translated as "belly," and seems to refer to a hollow place inside of us. Another meaning of that very word is appetite. So, when Jesus told us He would provide living water from deep inside us, He was referencing a work to include our soul's desires, longings, and hopes.[1] The answer will not be found, however, in looking anywhere else but to Him. This emphasis on spiritual focus – turning what Scripture calls the eyes of our hearts to Jesus – is a key discipline for any believer, but especially those of us seeking to "get over" past hurts. Dallas Willard eloquently addresses the profound necessity of choosing to focus Christ-ward if we want fulfilling, abundant lives:

> You must find the goodness of God and the fellowship of Jesus in who you are, or your love for the Father and his unique Son cannot become the foundation for a life of abundance/obedience. They desire to dwell with you in your life and make

glorious of it every aspect of it in the light of the whole that God has planned (John 14)… Today many will say that this simply does not do justice to the bitter facts of life. What of victims of sexual abuse or of dreadful diseases, birth defects, war, and other terrible things? But if we have suffered terribly, we must not choose to let that be our life focus. We must, if we can, focus on God, God's world, and ourselves as included in it with a glorious destiny of our own. And when we cannot, we should seek out those who bring or can help us find the power of the kingdom to do so. Gratitude then focuses forward on redemption, and on the future that is given to us in God's future, come what may. In light of that, we return to receive, to even welcome, our life as it actually has been and is.[2]

"All right, already!" some of you are probably saying. "I get the whole turning to Jesus concept, but don't know how that looks in my everyday life." Fixing your gaze on Jesus might involve a verse that becomes a daily meditation for you. During a lonely time of life, Kayla kept a poster over her bed that read, "Oh, Lord, you understand my thoughts from afar" (Psalm 139:2). As she walked back and forth between classes and her apartment, she would remind herself that God knew and empathized with her sense of isolation. The frequent mental images of God as an ally and support in her need helped Kayla to act positively towards developing new relationships.

We can redirect our focus towards Christ through practicing gratitude. Jim came to know Christ under the pressure of a failing marriage. When his wife left and took their three-year-old son with her, his level of frustration peaked. He wanted to win back his wife and be a father to his young son, but she refused to talk to him. Jim faced plenty of temptations to use physical force against her, run wild with other women, withhold needed financial support, and be angry with God for not "fixing" the problem. Over and over, he told Jesus his frustrations and then tried thanking God for all the positives in his life: a healthy body and mind, the musical talents he possessed, friends who were supporting him in his newfound faith, his son, and the beautiful setting of the mountain cabin his mother loaned him to live in. Though his business failed, he found another job elsewhere. Jim's habit of thankfulness for God's kindness and provision slowly transformed him and ultimately, his life.

So very much is accomplished through the adjustment of one's gaze. Tomorrow morning when you awake, place Jesus at the center of your vision, then do it again mid-morning when you are busy with life, and again in the afternoon when that lull hits, and again before you go to bed. Placing Him at the center means just to meditate on Him, what He did, and who He was and is. Do this again the following day, and again the following, and I guarantee you will begin to see a vast difference in yourself.

Seeing the Unseen

As is obvious, understanding the spiritual realm has much to do with developing spiritual eyes to see what is unseen. That's why the first section focused on seeing Christ and all the fullness of His completed work for you and me. At this juncture, we'll deal with the ongoing assault that will sabotage fully focusing on Jesus. We're talking about a levelheaded, clear-minded, understanding of spiritual warfare. Chapter two laid the foundation, and now we'll look to how this works itself out in our daily lives. I appreciate John Eldredge's admonition on this: "You don't escape spiritual warfare simply because you choose not to believe it exists or because you refuse to fight it."[3]

Some people reading these words become uncomfortable because they have observed abuses of spiritual practices, and associate spiritual warfare with television preachers and B movies. While this is indeed troubling, we cannot dilute Biblical admonitions. For instance, the elders of our church anoint with oil people who have serious sickness. Their reasoning is simple. It's because the Bible says to (James 5:14). It's not because they fully apprehend or understand it, but that God's Word commands it. Whether or not your particular church setting emphasizes spiritual warfare or not is irrelevant. It is not a Catholic practice, Presbyterian practice, or a charismatic one – it's a *biblical* practice. The Word of God instructs us to battle in the spiritual realm. If you want the life and freedom Jesus offers, then you're going to have to do the work of spiritual warfare.

Evil spreads the lie that "there is no war" in whatever way it can. This includes fears of being fanatical or feelings of being uncomfortable. In this way, many a person is kept from breaking free. Take a frank look at the number of Christians engaging in spiritual battle as a normal part of their walk of faith. Scripture is clear that it is a necessary, daily part of life, but instead:

> The alarm goes off, and they hit the snooze button, catch a few extra winks, gulp down a cup of coffee on their way to work, wonder why there are so many hassles, grab some lunch, work some more, come home under a sort of cloud, look at the mail, have dinner, watch a little TV, feed the cat, and fall into bed – without once even wondering how the Enemy might be attacking them. All they know is, they sure aren't enjoying that abundant life Christ talked about.[4]

If we buy into lies about spiritual warfare, we won't routinely break strongholds, rebuke oppressive harassers, and claim truth in Christ. If we agree with whatever stigmas others might have about warfare, we might never experience what it feels like to be set free from captivity. Battling in spiritual realms to bring release from "oppression might seem really weird to our modern, scientific world, but it has been a normal part of Christian ministry ever since Jesus modeled it for us. The disciples made it an essential part of their ministry, too."[5]

If this is challenging for you, think about how quickly you will begin to tell yourself what a jerk you are over the littlest thing. Or, think of how you can't say no, immediately see yourself as a failure, or spew bitterness at yourself for the slightest social miscue. Now think about it. Would you really want to treat yourself this way? Do you honestly think any person would want to constantly disparage him or herself? You wouldn't ever think of saying to a friend what you do to yourself on a regular basis. Can you begin to see what becomes clear through spiritual lenses? You know the source of such condemnation is certainly not God, and it is also not *just* you. Consider what entity would take the most pleasure in pummeling you, creation of God that you are. All hell will attempt to use the effects of your past hurts to pin you to the mat. The assault is intended to cement the message of your wounds deep into your heart. The shame, the accusation, the self-hatred, the doubt and mistrust are all hurled at you and unless you fend them off, they will land. If not promptly dealt with, they will begin to take root and result in a spiritual stronghold. *Does this make you want to begin doing battle?!*

While the concept of spiritual warfare does not strike one as rational or even logical, it is actually very much like the "recognize, reject, replace" blueprint suggested above. Handling malevolent forces involves rebuking, renouncing, and just plain disagreeing with them. If you remember from earlier, evil agreements are offered up to us to take or reject. For instance, "People can't be trusted," "You're dirty," "You're an addict, and you'll never break free," are examples of such agreements. Simply put, whenever we discover any such hellish handshake, we need to immediately withdraw from it, renouncing those agreements, and appealing to God through Christ for forgiveness and freedom once again.

A Truth Encounter

The spiritual reality is that Satan was thrown to earth and his angels with him (Revelation 12:9). This means that there are fallen angels, or foul spirits, seeking to destroy you and me, even this very minute. Just like holy angels often have distinct assignments, so do fallen ones (Revelation 12:7, Daniel 8:16, 10:13, 21; Luke 1:19, 26; Mark 9:25; Mark 5:1-13; Acts 16:16-18). There are spirits of betrayal, abandonment, disillusionment, some with specific names, and they're all found in scripture. Their barrage is constant. Think of how you do something that is normal for human life, like lose your keys, trip on the carpet, or misunderstand something someone said. If we take the bait to believe what some accusatory or hopeless spirit is hurling at us, we are filled with self-hatred, frustration, or hopelessness in seconds flat. Rather than realizing losing one's keys is normal, we instead get caught in a satanic snare and end up in a funk for the rest of the day. To take us out, evil merely needs to get us to move from "I did something wrong" to "I am wrong," or "I made a mistake" to "I am a mistake," or "I failed" to "I am a failure."

It's important to understand clearly that these entities are not in your head, although it may seem like it. If you have accepted Christ, you are a temple of the Holy Spirit and pure evil cannot take up residence there. Then why does it seem like our minds are being read at times? As a person who has been intently watching and listening to humans in close proximity for years now, I can tell a great deal about someone. Sometimes people are shocked at what I've perceived about them. I've only been watching human behavior this closely for a relatively short time compared to spiritual entities. They've been watching humans for years. They were observing on the playground in third grade when you were taunted, they were peering on in that dark bedroom, and they are waiting even now to use the information they have against you by watching your nonverbal cues. They were there then and know how to feed just the right thought to you to make you think it's in your own head.

The assault doesn't manifest as apparent. Seriously, if we saw some demon standing in front of us, we'd certainly cast it to hell. Instead, it's just usually a sense, an impression, or a vague feeling that comes over us. If we don't live believing spiritual warfare needs to be a part of our lives, we dismiss the uneasiness as "just a bad day" or our own feelings. We've got to tune in, and realize the self-hatred that washes over us, the gloominess that takes hold, or the bad mood that seems to come out of the blue are assisted in their depth by suggestions from outside of us. "Yes, you are a loser. This is just the like the time last year when you disappointed your boss." "Yes, you should be mad at her. She isn't even thinking about your feelings. She's selfish." "What makes you think they're going to be glad to see you? As a matter of fact, you don't even fit in. You never have."

To stand against the barrage, we must recognize lie-based thoughts, and reject the untruths. There are myriad ways to do this – as different as the number of denominations and types of Christians. My primary suggestion is that, while there is no "formula," we must do it. Because they are not in our head, per se, it is good to rebuke hellish ideas out loud. Plus, appealing to Jesus by referencing His blood is also crucial. Christ's blood is the believer's authority, and the enemy's defeat. At His name, every knee will bow. Therefore, our victory is assured every time we call out to our Savior, the king of all. Calling out can be as simple as just saying "no," or as complex as prolonged renouncing of specific demonic harassers. You can say, "In the name of Jesus, I stand against the lie that..." or "Jesus, please deliver me from the harassment of Satan" or "No, I don't agree that God isn't good" or "By the blood of Christ, I renounce a demon of lust" or "I rebuke any evil spirit and ask you, Jesus, to deal with it as you wish" or "No! I'm not going to go along with that lie. That's not true."

It's not a power encounter. Spiritual warfare is a truth encounter. There's no need to shout or use a theatrical voice. The only requirements are that we acknowledge the demonic as real and stand against evil. There's no formula or way to do it "right." Many believers fall prey to the thought "I'm not a mature enough Christian to really do spiritual battle." Don't agree with that lie. Any time we sense oppressive forces and appeal to Jesus, we are battling the unseen enemies. "Jesus, save me!" is enough. It's crying out, "Father, deliver me!" or "Whatever evil thing is trying to do whatever destructive evil to me, I say no in the name of Jesus because He died for things such as these, and I receive it." Catching assaults and fighting back are an essential and effective part of living the victorious Christian life.

A clear instruction regarding battling darkness is to put on the armor of God. Ephesians 6:11 tell us to "put on the full armor of God so that you can take your stand against the devil's schemes." The armor of God includes the belt of truth, the breastplate of righteousness, feet fitted with readiness that comes from peace, the shield of faith, the helmet of salvation, and the sword of the Spirit, which is the Word of God (Ephesians 6:14-17). Figuratively donning the armor is a helpful way to prepare for whatever battle may ensue in the night. When I was doing missionary work, and had to sleep three feet away from a Buddhist house temple, I was disturbed in my spirit to the point where I was concerned about my sleep. God brought to mind a full-time Christian worker who had shared about putting on the full armor prior to bedtime. I pulled out my Bible, rebuked any evil force seeking to invoke fear or doubt, and envisioned myself putting on every piece of the armor. I slept soundly, praise be to God. To be wise about warfare is to realize we can claim protection even in an involuntary altered state of consciousness. Last year, I prayed such a prayer for an abuse survivor who was going under full anesthesia for surgery. While I'm certainly not overboard in searching for a demon in every corner, I do want to be wise in battling for God's glory and freedom in my life.

In addition to wearing the Lord's armor, we must fight spiritual battles by refusing to allow any strongholds in our lives. In Ephesians, Paul discusses how a believer can allow a stronghold in his or her life by allowing the sun to go down on one's anger. If we willingly permit something to remain inside us that is unhealed or ungodly, it's as if we open the door to evil to take over a part of us. Psalm 66:18 says, "If I had cherished sin in my heart, the Lord would not have listened." The principle here is that if we are holding on to something sinful – an attitude, a habit, a secret, a lie – we are in essence holding the door open, inviting an enemy to come in and wreak havoc on a room of our heart. Part of spiritual warfare involves assuring that there are no open doors for evil to enter.

Battling unseen enemies also involves anticipating opposition. Whenever you make movement toward God in any form, it will be met with resistance. If you step up your devotional life, open up more to your Bible study group, begin being vocal about your faith at work, seek to forgive your unfaithful spouse, volunteer to lead a new church ministry, or pursue healing from an addiction, you will be attacked. Any steps towards intimacy with God will receive pushback. The attuned believer will learn to anticipate and adjust for it. I received an email from a woman who has been getting set free, layer-by-layer, for the past year. She said, "I'm going down. I'm bitter. I'm down. I'm mad. I don't like the world. As a matter of fact, I'm suicidal." Why this, now, after such progress? All because she's on the threshold of a huge breakthrough, beginning to invite people to her home, starting to let people into her closed-off heart after fifteen long years, and making a wholehearted commitment to Christ.

Even as I write, I am in the throes of Christmas program preparation, wherein we ask people to authentically share about God's movement in their lives. The testimonies that people give are real, raw, unpolished, and very honest. Because of their steps to share, they are experiencing tremendous opposition. The previous sex addict is feeling shame he hasn't in years and a young man recently out of rehab has a family all down with the flu, as well as dealing with a car that overheated and ended up in the repair shop. Part of asking people to share their stories of God's intervention in their lives involves making them aware of the opposition that will come. Just today I sat with a woman who, along with her husband, said "yes" to taking on a significant leadership role in their church. She told me that since that moment, the bombardment of circumstantial and emotional challenge has been fierce. If you've walked with Christ for any length of time, you know this is to be expected. Don't ever forget, though, that you need not fear it.

For every believer, there is no need to be intimidated by anything, because of the blood of Christ. It is the final word in any discussion concerning spiritual warfare. If we have claimed Christ as

Savior and Lord, because of His Spirit that now resides in us, the power that raised Him from the dead is in us. Evil does all it can to convince us otherwise, but the undeniable fact is found in this verse: "Greater is He that is in you than He that is in the world" (1 John 4:4). A.W. Tozer synopsizes it this way:

> "He knows that the believer and justified Christian has been raised up out of the grave of his sins and trespasses. From that point on, Satan works that much harder to keep us bound and gagged, actually imprisoned in our own grave clothes. He knows that if we continue in this kind of bondage, we are not much better off than when we were spiritually dead."[6]

Fear, depression, self-condemnation, anxiety, flashbacks, addictions, jealousy, or bitterness need not hold you. They may bite at your heels, irritate you, threaten you, and bother you, but because of Christ, they do not rule you. You will only feel as though they do if you are not taking the action steps listed in this chapter. The fact that they trouble you is a normal part of human life on this earth, but freedom comes through Christ by applying our will to bring His truths into our hearts. This is not a one-time event. Neither does it mean that you won't struggle. However, doing so will indeed allow you to experience freedom from that which used to imprison you.

Fighting the assault is crucial, and we must do this actively, daily, even minute-by-minute. Seriously, stop and ask what type of spiritual attack or harassment you are under even now. Just an hour ago, I could feel my emotions plummeting, so prayerfully discovered some unspoken lies I was sliding into. I said "no" out loud. As I write this moment, I must be vigilant, saying "no" to accusations that "you're not a good enough writer," "your words won't effectively communicate truth," "you're not being clear enough," "you really should just stop trying to write this book." A reasonable goal for us is to become adept at *quick* recognition of lies. To think we can have a life without struggle or free from battle is unrealistic. Being aware of how we're being attacked and then turning those thoughts is so much of the victory in the spiritual battle process.

Powerful Practices

Another practice which will promote healing through the spiritual realm is setting aside time and space to **experience God's presence**. Said differently, you will not overcome that which trips you up without actually sort of "soaking" in the presence of the Lord. What's important to know, though, is that experiencing God's presence is a skill that must be developed and then sharpened, just like carpentry or sewing. You'll have to start somewhere, and realize it's not going to necessarily come naturally right away. We must literally "practice" the presence of the Lord. In this way, it's just like anything else that develops and gets better over time and with greater familiarity. Again, to do this, you and I will need to work against our natural inclination to give up on something when it doesn't "work" right away. Keep turning your gaze to Christ, battling lies, recognizing demonic subtleties and enticements, and spending consistent time with the Lord, and you *will* walk with greater joy, peace, purpose, and freedom.

Practicing thankfulness – cultivating a grateful, positive, look-for-God-in-it perspective – has changed my life. While not typically listed under the heading of spiritual practices, I do know this action is commanded by the Bible and blessed of God (Ephesians 5:20). If you've ever traveled to a foreign country not as affluent as America and given a gift, you will see a stark difference in the level of gratitude of the recipient. We Americans will routinely return gifts, re-gift presents, or put them in a white elephant exchange two years later, whereas a Honduran, Haitian, or Hungarian will cherish a gift forever, it seems. You and I are simply not very thankful because we have been fashioned in an environment that promotes us to be fat, dumb, and happy. We are surrounded with messages to take it easy, give ourselves the best, and pursue pleasure. Exercising a thankfulness muscle will strengthen us in ways that will deepen us and fight worldliness.

The verse "I will enter His gates with thanksgiving and His courts with praise" (Psalm 100:4) has reflected my experience of choosing an appreciative attitude. While certainly not the contextual understanding of the verse, one could see thanksgiving as a key to the gates, which permits a person to get closer to Him. Through thanksgiving and praise, you get closer into the space where others who do not use their keys can't. Next time you are grumpy, begin by making a list of the most basic of things to be thankful for: start with the fact that you are wearing clothes, had food to eat for breakfast, and are taking another breath. Think of your home, your friends, your car. Don't assess whether you are happy with them, just say "thank you" for them. Thank Him for saving you and for the fact that it is a free gift. Thank Him for the last vacation you had, last compliment someone gave you, and last beautiful day. Say thank you for the health you've enjoyed, for being in a country where you can openly worship Him, and for someone in your life that loves you. Think of others' difficulties, and thank Him that you have not had that job loss, cancer, death of a loved one, depression, or whatever you've been spared thus far. You won't be able to do this but for a few minutes, before your perspective and maybe even your feelings begin to change.

How much more will this attitude transform troublesome times? When difficulty comes, praise Him for the fact that He won't leave you, that He is steadfast, and that He is a shield for you in times of trouble (Hebrews 13:5, 13:8, Deuteronomy 31:6, 2 Thessalonians 3:5, Psalm 3:3, 28:7). Praise Him for listening to you, and for the inestimable privilege of speaking clearly to a holy God. Praise Him that His ways are not our ways, and that He is loving, merciful, and gracious (Psalm 3:4, 25:4, 25:10, 86:5, 145:17, Isaiah 55:8). Praise Him that even though you are financially struggling, you still have your health, or while you are feeling betrayed by a friend, your family is very close, or …you get the picture. If you've been hurt, evil will want you to focus in on that pain to the exclusion of seeing all that is good and right and blessed about your life. Willard asserts that true discipleship and spiritual maturity occur when one is able to, at the deepest level, be thankful for who they are and what they have.[7] It is at this point that the believer has "learned how to be content whatever the circumstances" and "can do everything through him who gives me strength" (Philippians 4:11, 13). Developing a thankful heart and choosing an attitude of praise heals.

A subpoint here is to **hold death closely**. What was the one thing everyone said after the terrorist attacks of 9/11? The world was different for a time. People were kind to each other. There was no road rage. Citizens were suddenly patient in postal lines. Why? At once, death came close to us all. When it does, it shifts perspectives, and people's petty concerns with one another melt away. The person is valued above the issue. When we realize an imminent loss of someone or something is possible, our minds will move us to consider potential regret. The result is to adjust the situation so as to alleviate the prospect of remorse. A common marital therapeutic intervention is to ask how one's life would be worse without the other spouse, and to inquire as to what he or she would regret were the other to die that day. There are no guarantees, and we are unwise if we do not keep close the lessons that sudden death brings. Yesterday I sat at the funeral of a 57-year-old man who died unexpectedly. I watched as the adult children wept with joy and incredible relief, for he had just accepted Christ six months prior. It's not hard to imagine how horrific their grief would be had he died last year. It's true that we should never save for tomorrow that which we need to do, say, or forgive, today.

Along these lines, another spiritually mature mindset is to **_give when and what you would like to receive_**. Our reasons for not giving freely to others are many: we are needy and wanting very much ourselves, we protect ourselves from potential hurt, we feel inadequate and disqualified because of our own sin. Whatever the case, a person who is committed to focusing on Christ will take seriously Luke 9:24: "For whoever wants to save his life will lose it, but whoever loses his life for me will save it." This principle has also turned my life around -- to give away that which I want to get. When I want some affirmation, God enables me to give it. When you want a hug, give a hug. When you wish someone would call and initiate interaction with you, make the call first. By such paradoxical movements, the promise in Luke begins to appear. You will have a deeper joy, purposefulness, and sense of power. So, whatever it is, do it. Make a meal for a sick friend, say hi to someone new at church, cut your neighbor's lawn, do something nice for your spouse. I list this under the "spiritual" category even though it involves your behavior, because you will not be enabled to do this except by the deepest belief and communion with the Lord Jesus, and His life surging within you.

Finally, it is a spiritually healing act whenever we search for God. Learn to go on a ***God hunt***. Scripture tells us to see that which is unseen instead of that which is seen, because that which is unseen is eternal, but that which is seen is temporal (2 Corinthians 4:18). The idea of a God hunt is built on the belief that God does make Himself known, is involved in human affairs, and is working out the progressive plan of His Kingdom on the earth. However, because His ways are not our ways (Isaiah 55:8), we cannot often see His movement because of our human perspective. Going on a God hunt is to look for signs and activities that align with God's character and Word, and magnify those in your perspective.

I will never forget a woman whose marriage, and probably her life, were saved by hunting fervently for any vestige of God. You see, both she and her husband worked in hospital administration, which was like a small community. He had an affair with another woman in the same area, and rejected his wife with unconscionable meanness. She was a believer in Jesus, and believed God had given her a promise straight from His Word that her marriage would be restored. Things became so ugly, that even her Bible study friends said she should divorce him, as those outside the church called her crazy to her face. Even after he divorced her, she held on to the promise.

Because of her faith, she determined to find God, and we called such searching "God hunts." It was so bad at points that she would say, "Well, Dan only referred to me with a lesser swearword today than he has for the last five weeks. That's God." "He didn't rip any more pages out of my Bible this time when he stopped by the house. That's God." "He didn't take every cent out of the account that he drained. That's God." In other words, there wasn't anything in this situation that a person not looking for God could possibly see as hopeful. Maximizing the smallest positive and putting it in the tally column for God is what she held onto. Well, eight years after it all began, her husband came back to her, they have remarried, and God was faithful to His faithful daughter and the promise He gave her. Being committed to searching for God kept whatever sanity she could hold onto.

Building these five entities into your life will help effect deep change: experiencing God's presence, an attitude of thankfulness, holding death close, giving what we'd like to receive, and God hunting. Which area is God prompting you to pursue? Determine now to make it a personal reality. One way to do this is by building it into your daily life. Set a watch for the alarm to go off at predetermined times. When it does, stop and thank God for something, or look for where God is present in your life at that moment. Don't get out of bed until you have acknowledged God in the morning. Don't allow your feet to hit the floor until you have said hi to the lover of your soul. For whatever reason, the simplistic saying "Good morning, Lord, this is your day. I am your servant. Show me your way," has stuck with my mind since hearing it 20 years ago.

Do anything to help yourself mold these spiritual perceptions. In this vein, something is always better than nothing. Put a note on the steering wheel which asks how your day would be different today were you to die tomorrow. Wear something around your neck so notable that others will see it and comment. Every time they do, use it to prompt you to pray, give to others, or praise God. Put a prompting question like "Where is God right now?" on your screen saver. Make it a habit to travel to work or class with no noise first thing in the morning, and pray. The point is this – these perspectives will come about in you over time and with consistency. So, if you make something a purposeful habit for awhile, it will actually become that – a habit. My kids and I pray every day on the way to school. Is it some deeply moving, spiritual experience? No. Do I want the boys to have that as their only prayer model? No. However, it is to the point now where one of my sons will comment if we don't pray, simply because we've programmed that into our routine.

10

MAKING CHANGE (The Behavioral Pathway)

Life is either a daring adventure or nothing.
HELEN KELLER

*His divine power has given us everything we need for life and godliness through our
knowledge of him who called us by his own glory and goodness.*
2 PETER 1:3

The third major category of suggestions to bring about change in
your life concerns your actions and behaviors. Encompassed here are
more alterations we can make to our patterns of living to promote
healing. Behavioral actions involve doing things intentionally, like the
Biblical admonitions to *put on* love, *clothe* yourself with the Lord Jesus, and
don the full armor of God (Colossians 3:14, Romans 13:14, Ephesians
6:11). Suggestions in this section involve ways to catalyze change from
the outside in through new behaviors. One caution exists, however.
*Never would I encourage anyone to fast forward to behavioral adjustments who hasn't
first undergone the very important aspects of accepting and grieving.* Oftentimes
people do indeed adopt new behaviors, like having a quiet time, or
speaking up for oneself, or joining a small group, or confronting hurtful
people only to say, "It didn't work." In many of those cases, the person
tried to shortcut his or her way to external change. External change is
not real and will not "stick" unless the internal attitudes, postures, and
perceptions we've been discussing thus far are in place.

What's That You Say?

For instance, Maureen, whose healing process was described in chapter six, benefited tremendously from the challenges of moving forward through acceptance and grief. Although she says she'd never want to go through it again, she also admits she wouldn't trade the benefits of having done so for the world. You see, as Maureen moved into facing, accepting, and grieving her losses, she found herself in a different place than ever before. Memories of seeing her father sell her doll collection in a garage sale, of hearing her mother engaging in intercourse with a stranger through the thin panel walls of the mobile home, of looking into the empty stands at the track meet they promised to attend, none of these held the power over her they previously had. Acceptance and grief were what paved the way for her to aggressively deal with the outworkings of her difficult past and begin to put on new behaviors.

Identifying lies and choosing forgiveness came as Maureen took the difficult step of embracing her past reality and present condition. For instance, she identified a lens of "I'm not worth it" which came from her dad's unwillingness to stop his endless drinking. She realized the "I'm not worth it" lie was pervasive. It was the reason she didn't share her struggles, the reason she didn't voice her opinion in staff meetings. Believing she was powerless to change her father caused her to think she was unimpactful and impotent in other situations. Our lies affect our behaviors, and in her case, they produced a nonassertive, insecure, quiet woman. Being rendered speechless or insecure to speak up is a violation of one's voice and is a common effect of wounds. Our voice is part of God's image within us, and is intended to be a powerful force for His work.[1] No surprise that evil would seek to silence God's image-bearers.

Many people experience "losing their voice" like Maureen did. At best, this means operating from a basis of insecurity and doubt as to whether one adds anything valuable to situations. At worst, this means a complete unawareness that one even has a voice – a right to speak, to say "no," draw boundaries, have a different opinion, express desires or even wants. "When God created human beings, He gave us a voice, a means of expressing ourselves out in the world."[2] Losing one's voice is one of the many devastating effects of abuse. In the extreme example, it's easy to see how the rape victim who said "no" concludes her words mean nothing. On a lesser level, one who was wronged in other ways might believe he or she has no voice or no choice. That person may respond to "Hey, what do you want to do for your birthday?" with "I don't care. Whatever you want." As for Maureen, not only did she need to rebuke the lie "I'm not worth it" and replace it with truth, she also had to learn to use her voice. This is indeed something many people need to do. Have your wounds handicapped you when it comes to knowing what your needs are and how to appropriately express them?

As an example, when I asked Maureen one day what she needed from me, she looked shocked. As her face flushed and she stammered, in that moment she saw how she never even considered what her needs were. When her friends would ask her preference, she would say, "It doesn't matter." When ill, never did she think of going to a doctor until someone told her she should. These are evidences of a lost or nonexistent voice. To learn to identify one's needs is a step towards living beyond abuse. Pull your life apart in categories, and think about what you need in that area. Physically, what do I need right now? Emotionally, what would benefit me? What is missing in my spiritual life? Intellectually, what do I need?

Then, express those needs. It doesn't mean to demand that they be met, or to manipulate others until they meet them. Rather, it means we believe we have a voice, and learn to make requests as we determine our particular needs. No person can be whole when significant desires are perpetually hidden. It is immature to think, "I'd rather do without than ask" and unrealistic to want others to be able to read our minds or just sense our feelings. Dropping hints is not expressing needs appropriately. ("It's hot in here.") Neither is question asking, nor is any other indirect form of communication ("Isn't it getting hot in here?") A crash course on verbalizing legitimate desires is to speak straightforwardly. Just a few phrases you need to become comfortable with as you learn to exercise your voice are:

- "Would you please _____?"
- "I'd really like if _____."
- "I like _____."
- "I wish _____."
- "I don't like _____."
- "Would you be willing to _____?"
- "Can you help me _____?"

Can't you just sense how relationships lived on that level are much healthier than ones based on passive, indirect, meta-communications? An action you can take to move towards more holistic functioning is to begin to express your needs.

A silenced voice is one outworking of abuse; a thundering voice is another. It is seen in a person who, because of being hurt, came to believe that he or she must be extra strong, ultra assertive and constantly standing up for self. The unconscious underpinning of this behavior is the same as that of a sexually abused male who becomes a body builder:

"No one will ever do that to me again." The overcompensation of a victim through physical strength, controlling behavior or a thundering voice is yet another mechanism of protection, which might have helped in childhood, but is a hindrance in adulthood. Especially for the Christian, having a voice and using it wisely is critical. Jesus was certainly not voiceless, a doormat, or a wimp, but He also did not feel it necessary to dominate, correct, and protect Himself in every situation. His trust was in the Father.

Changing Direction

Probably the most obvious behavioral changes we must make for healing in our lives involve actively renouncing vows, interrupting our patterns, removing masks, and ceasing to numb ourselves. The definition of repentance means to change direction. Repenting, or refusing to continue doing the same sin, is a significant action necessary for living a life of freedom. Scripture is robust on this point. To fully renounce any vows we have identified, we must disagree with any hellish agreements, while asking God to cleanse us by the blood of Christ and commanding our enemy to flee (James 4:7). If, in your reading of the vows listed in chapter seven, you've identified any that you've made, please don't let it go on for another second without revoking it. Say "No! I renounce the vow that I made outside the will of God. I take it back for the sake of Jesus, and will no longer live my life in that self-protecting manner."

Self-protective behavior in any form is hurtful. Upholding vows, anesthetizing oneself, wearing masks, and living in hiding relational patterns all stem from agreeing with evil that you have to take care of yourself. It's important to consider why this action is so very damaging. Ultimately, to do so is to say to God, "You cannot be trusted." Sure, we trust Him in many areas, but when it comes to the hurt in our hearts, and how desperately we don't want to feel that again, many of us take matters into our own hands. Seriously now, how many of us, even as Christians, live with our hearts barricaded? It just hurts too much to put ourselves out there again – to share insecure thoughts with a friend, to disclose an ugly habit to a mentor, to hope that our new friend will be loyal. Instead we serve and love and give...up to a point. Living free from the effects of our wounds also means demolishing this brick wall and refusing to keep our hearts hidden.

Besides, has it worked? Are we really better off living protectively? Have we been able to stave off having hurt feelings, being disappointed by another, or experiencing the thud of fallen hopes? Any honest person must admit the tactic as unsuccessful. Like Jesus, the only way we can negotiate earthly relational life is by putting our trust squarely in God alone. When I trust my friends or spouse or boss to handle me correctly all of the time and to never hurt me, I am setting myself up for disappointment. I can't hope that by interacting with sinners in a sinful world being sinful myself, I'll escape pain. It won't happen. It's unwise at best and stupid at worst, to place my tender heart with its bruises and scars fully in the hands of any human. Again, I'm not advocating self-protection. Hurt people hurt people. Do you know anyone who has no hurts? I am merely straightforwardly saying that there is only *One* we can trust fully, totally, completely – God our Father.

As a side note, I will continue to counsel against extremism in any form. Just like the practice of regaining one's voice must not swing the other way to overbearing, we must also not become extreme in laying our hearts out nakedly for everyone to see. In other words, while I trust God for my emotional state, I still need to be wise with whom I choose to be vulnerable. I'll still share secrets with safe people and tender feelings with empathetic ones. The point is that I am thwarting God's plan for me to be a blessing if I keep my heart walled up to try to not get hurt. It's ineffective at best and sinful at worst. "Why sinful?" you ask, "I'm just reacting to what someone else did to me." Well, if you think about it, when we "take over" a part of our own protection, even if we trust Him with everything else, we are in essence demonstrating, "I think I'm a better God than you."

This is especially hard for ones who have had deep trauma. They are unconsciously thinking, "You let me be hurt in this area before, so I'm just going to have to take matters into my own hands so it doesn't happen again." In the same way that He will not violate your free will to speak harshly with Him, He did not violate the free will of the person or people who wounded you so terribly. However, to uphold vows, wear masks, and live a self-protected life is ultimately saying that God, while good and worthy of worship, is not quite up to the task of protecting you in a manner that you deem acceptable. You and I must repent of self-protection in any form – we must change direction and live more trustworthy lives.

Ebenezer

When we do make the decision to stop a sinful behavior, to revoke a vow, to choose forgiveness, or to lay down a self-protective mask, it is a significant event. I have found that having a physical reminder of an important spiritual act is often helpful. It's also Scriptural. A review of the Old Testament shows that many times when people experienced an act of God, they set up altars or some memorial as a remembrance of what He did. When Samuel cried out to God and then watched Him deliver the Israelites from the hand of the Philistines, he took a stone and set it up. Calling it "Ebenezer" (stone of help), he said, "Thus far the Lord has helped us" (1 Samuel 7:12).

I gave our Easter choir small glass stones one year as a type of Ebenezer, because we needed the Lord, and He delivered in miraculous measure. Over the next years, individuals who participated in that event would show me the ways in which they continued to carry with them that reminder of God's faithfulness and provision. They'd pull it out of their pocket or purse. One saint came and slipped one into my hand during a challenging portion of a Christmas program preparation, and indeed it encouraged me to remember all the myriad times God had shown Himself faithful. I have a miniature wooden shoe and leather sandal on my key chain to remind me of the miraculous work God did on trips I took to Amsterdam and Venezuela. Tokens of remembrance can take many forms.

The practice of providing ourselves a reminder counteracts our natural tendency to forget all that God has done, sometimes even in our immediate past! It's why we wear wedding rings – to serve as a reminder to self and the world that a significant decision has been made. One of my friends now has a picture that hangs on her living room wall, signifying the day she trusted God to completely free her husband from his addiction. Another wears a ring that symbolizes the day she forgave her mother and gave her bitterness over, committed to laying it down forever. We all need to have "mark it down" days where we *make a decision* and no matter what happens, we remind ourselves, "Oh, yes, I almost forgot. I have already done this or given this up or made this commitment or forgiven so and so." One client and I last week agreed that is was time to deal with a lie and make a decision to cross the threshold and live in a new truth. I joked and said, "It's time to put it to bed." She once and for all decided to choose to live in God's perspective of her – regardless of her feelings on the matter. She now wears a ring that testifies to her choice.

Is there something you know is time for you to "put to bed" forever? Is there a lie that has so gripped you that you have felt powerless under it? Is there bitterness you know lives on in your heart? Do you know that you won't ever experience the freedom you so desire until you stop your addiction? Perhaps today is a mark-it-down day where you burn the date in your mind because of a decision you make. Be it a lie that you are tired of, forgiveness you need to extend, an addiction that has gripped you – whatever it is – by committing an act of your will, you can decide to live in that new freedom today. Repenting is an action worth memorializing.

Community

An important action step if we want to be healed in Jesus is that we must be in community. Chances are, we were wounded in relationship. No matter what, we cannot be healed apart from people. If you're not in contact with others, there's no hope for the kind of healing God wants to give you. Our basic need for one another's love is emphasized throughout Scripture. Paul urges believers to "consider how to stimulate one another to love and good deeds, not forsaking our own assembling together, as is the habit of some, but encouraging one another" (Hebrews 10:24-25). Secular psychiatrists like Harry Stack Sullivan have done extensive research on interpersonal relationships and found that "lack of intimacy with others is definitely a major source of emotional pain.[3] The point is this – you cannot be someone who isolates and minimizes contact with other people if you want to experience a full, free, and healthy life.

Try as we may, we cannot rid ourselves of our desire for meaningful connections with other humans. We are dependent by nature. God intended that we warmly respond to the love of others, and what we were made to enjoy, we deeply desire. God gave Himself first to Adam and Eve for them to depend on and then He gave them each other to enjoy. In short, God's plan for humans involves other humans. We need people to show us God, help us live our lives for His glory, and serve as mirrors for us.

In earlier sections of this book, we have discussed how we cannot put people in the place of God, although it is something we often unintentionally try to do. However, God does give us others through whom His love touches us. Because the living Christ takes up residence in believers, God will minister to His injured children through them. A hug, a kind word, a faithful friendship...God's fingerprints are on all good interactions between people. We see glimpses of Him in one another, for we are all image bearers. One author noted how a schoolteacher helped restore what his parents couldn't do.[4] Oh, how powerful it is when we realize we can be healing agents in each other's lives. Larry Crabb encourages:

> We need a safe place for weary pilgrims. It's time that we dive into the unmanageable, messy world of relationships, to admit our failure, to identify our tensions, and to explore our shortcomings. It's time we turned our chairs toward one another and learned how to talk in ways that stir anorexics to eat...sexual addicts to indulge nobler appetites, and tired Christians to press on through dark valleys toward green pastures and onto the very throne room of heaven.[5]

In addition to providing each other pictures of God, being in community provides us accountability. Accountability is a word that can have heavy or negative vibes associated with it. In fact, it is a beautiful concept. It is one of the nicest, most comforting things I have in my life. Accountability among believers has to do with encouraging one another towards love and good deeds (Hebrews 10:24), but is also the sense of sharing with people who will pray for you about what you believe God wants for your life. People who love each other will look together to see if their lives line up with Scripture, and then help each other stay on the path to where they feel God wants them to go. Accountability is not another person looking at your life offering random critique and criticism, but instead assuming the posture, "How can I help you press on toward the goal for which Jesus has called you? Show me your vision of what God has given you. Be vulnerable with me. Open your heart to me. Share with me what God is doing in you, and then I'll help you get there." When two people prayerfully do that for each other, that's godly accountability.

Finally, being in ongoing relationships with others provides us a chance to see ourselves. If we will let them, people reflect to us how we impact them. Issues of our character will become evident as we live, work, and play with other people. Are others generally glad to see you? Do they constantly defer to you, perhaps too much? Are you the one everyone just assumes will say "yes"? Without rubbing shoulders with other Christ-followers, we will not be given the opportunity for character refinement. For those of you serious about growing, do you have someone in your life that you regularly ask, "What's it generally like to be around me?" "What might be a blind spot I have?" It's a real show of maturity to have loving mirrors in our life who kindly show us things about ourselves. This will not happen lest we are in community.

The whole concept of Christian community is to openly live life together with other believers similar in heart and purpose, where you come together around the Word of God as your standard and the grace of God as your climate. Such places of prayer, love, inclusion, and acceptance are possible only as we keep our own sinfulness ever before us, and realize that it's only by God's mercy that we live at all. A quote from Dietrich Bonhoeffer provides the clue to the attitude that will facilitate such an environment: "Our community with one another consists solely on what Christ has done for both of us."[6] Are you in community? Is there at least one person who really knows your heart, goals, dreams, struggles, and joys? The bottom line is that we can't be fully healed outside of community.

Wearing the Pink Jacket

Making behavioral changes is like transitioning to a style of clothing you've always wanted to wear. In other words, for years you've window-shopped, perused magazines, and eyed others in admiration of a certain natural, put-together, crisp, cool look. You now have the resources to make the changes – the money, support, and even perhaps someone to help you put it all together. Whether you do it all at once by going out and buying a new wardrobe or just start with one new piece, the reality is that it will take some getting used to. Yes, even as much as you've wanted it, it probably won't feel completely comfortable the first few times you put it on. Not only will you need to be ready to endure your own initial discomfort, you'll also need to be prepped to endure other's comments, whether good or bad.

For some of you, the behaviors being described here are what you've wanted for a long time – to have a voice, to be in real community, to walk in freedom, to hold on to God's faithfulness, and to stop depending on that damaging addiction. You've ogled others who live that kind of life. With this book in your hands, you now have the opportunity to enact change. To make behavioral adjustments, though, is a lot like putting on those new clothes. While this is what you've wanted all your life, the first time you share vulnerably with another will feel uncomfortable. When you begin to exercise your voice, it's not going to feel as good as you thought. And not depending on that "crutch" you've had for so long? Well, it's surprising, but even after 30 days of non-dependence; you'll probably not be walking around thrilled with life.

Lest this seem discouraging, I want to be sure you know it so you don't make the wrong conclusions when the discomfort from trying new, godly ways of being happens. It's just a part of the natural transition from one type of wardrobe to another! We have to break in the new shoes, which will later be your favorites. We have to adjust to the new fabric, which we'll soon love more than our old flannel shirt. In other words, we can't be enticed to give up when our first stabs at new ways of operating don't come naturally, don't seem well-received, and don't feel all that great. Over time, though, it will come to pass. Being in community will feel like your true home. Replacing lies with truth will bring quick release. Fight against our cultural tendency to judge something as ineffective if it doesn't cause immediate change. Keep praying, seeking God, being in His Word, making the steps He is leading in you for your healing, and there will come a day in the not-so-distant future when you indeed feel like you are a radically different person.

I have a light pink duster jacket. One of my clients said she really liked it, but could never see herself wearing it because she was more of a khaki, black, and white girl. After spending many months recognizing lies from wounds, replacing internal untruth with God's Word, and grieving over legitimate losses, she was excited about making some external changes in the way she interacted with others. God guided the two of us to think of her changes like that doggone pink jacket. She realized that one day, she would simply need to wake up and put it on, no matter how self-conscious and even uncomfortable she might feel in it. She did just that. She began to share prayer requests in her small group, affirm others in her workplace, and be humorous with her close friends. In all of these, she kept envisioning putting on that pink jacket. The first times she "wore" her new ways of interacting, she did have to tolerate other's comments and fight the urge to take it off (to just stop trying because this was too hard!). However, it wasn't very long when she began to beam as she donned her pink jacket behaviors, and person after person would ask her what was going on because she seemed really different.

To make changes in our behavior means we will need to "try on" these new actions. Many of us have been wearing a worn, fairly unattractive brown jacket that we know is overdue for retirement. At this point in our journey, you have that new blazer hanging in your closet. It's time to make the change. Two helpful hints to do this might sound cheesy, but they really work: (1) fake it 'til you make it, and (2) act "as if." Being so committed to authenticity, even I'm shocked to write a suggestion with the word "fake" in it, but the principle is sound. Listen, we don't always feel like being cheerful, but we know that our children can't have a grumpy dad in the morning, so we force ourselves to be something we're not. We're technically faking. However, before long, our own mood has lifted. It's been proven that merely raising one's eyebrows or squinching one's cheek muscles upward stimulates the part of the brain that affects mood. If you are out of sorts, try activating your smiling muscles and see how long you can stay unhappy. Oftentimes, I am not feeling patient with my children, but I will constrain myself to remain calm. Before long, I truly do have a more forbearing attitude towards them. Similarly, on the days when I feel unattractive, I will often dress in my nicest outfits to try to adjust my perspective from the outside in.

In some psychological paradigms, acting "as if" is a very effective tool. The suggestion is to act "as if" you weren't insecure, or "as if" you were a person who knew they were smart, or "as if" you weren't concerned about getting someone else's approval. Again, it can be a helpful mindset for us to act "as if" we truly know we are forgiven, changed, set free, or victorious. The reality is we are, and acting as if what is true is actually true can help dislodge those old thoughts and feelings that are still hanging around. Again, it reminds me of how Scripture urges that we "clothe" ourselves with compassion, humility, and the Lord Jesus (Colossians 3:12, 1 Peter 5:5, Romans 13:14). A great way to assist in this change process is by purposefully choosing to be around people who truly apprentice themselves to Jesus. It is human nature to pick up the behaviors and actions of the people we are around.

All Systems Go

The fact that we are multifaceted, multidimensional creatures has been mentioned many times in this book. I raise it again here because of an obvious, yet neglected reality. To be healthy and whole, we must pay attention to all aspects of ourselves. Our healing is hindered when we fail to recognize we are fully emotional, physical, sexual, psychological, intellectual, and relational beings. We've got to attend to all these parts. Assessments like "Where am I weak? What's God doing in each of these areas? Where am I doing well, by God's grace?" are beneficial.

Some of us are really good at focusing on the physical aspect. Questions like, "Am I getting enough sleep? Am I energized?" are helpful. Perhaps fitness and healthy eating are a part of your life, but what about your emotional health? Are you numb? Do you look around the room and see others weeping and think, "Why are they crying? I can't relate because I'm feeling nothing." Others of us are really good at indulging the emotional aspect and letting the physical go. How about the spiritual component? Do you spend as much time in the Word of God daily as you do in front of the mirror? Are you experiencing what it is to have God be your daily bread? How about the sexual aspect? Are you gauging, "Am I out of control? Am I ignoring this all together?" If you're married, are you learning about yourself in this area, and not over- or under-valuing this facet of yourself? What does it mean to pay attention to the sexual aspect of yourself when you're trying to maintain purity with the Lord? It probably doesn't mean to push it down, but certainly involves dialoguing with the Lord about it. The reality is, we are multi-faceted beings. If we're paying attention to one area more than the others, it gives the opportunity for evil to exploit the weaker part. Most often the area that is ignored is the emotional aspect.

Carry the Toolbox

Perhaps the most practical encouragement for making active changes in your life is to really *use* the tools you've been given. In Western Christianity, the amount of information we have at our fingertips is massive. It is indeed a blessing. However, we are in danger of being more consumptive than productive in our spiritual climate. The number of Bible studies we can attend, books we can read, and strategies we can be exposed to is wonderful, but we are compelled to *use* what God has given. In this book alone, you have been given multiple suggestions for how to better apprehend and live the abundant life purchased for you by Jesus. Don't just *know* you should read the Word more, actually *read the Word more*. More than realizing you need to identify lies and rebuke demonic influences, *sit down and journal* about some lies and *renounce evil* in prayer. Actually *do* what you know.

Will you use this as a tool in the toolbox for your journey? Will you, when stuck, pull out this or some other resource God has given you to go after whatever is getting in between you and true, close communion with your Father? This is, in a nutshell, the entire vision God gave me for this work. That true disciples of the living Christ would so want to allow His life to pulsate through them that they will work hard at clearing out, protecting, and presenting the vessel He's given them.

11

FEELING YOUR WAY (The Emotional Pathway)

*And the day came when the risk [it took] to remain tight in the bud
was more painful than the risk it took to blossom.*
ANAIS NIN

*Let us then approach the throne of grace with confidence, so that we may receive mercy
and find grace to help us in our time of need.*
HEBREWS 4:16

The fourth category of healing concerns aspects of our
emotional selves. Before we embark on this discussion, it is helpful to
establish a few clear insights. First, **emotions are neither good nor
bad.** They just *are*. They have a distinct purpose in the human being to
act as signals for our fluctuating condition, conduits for deep expression,
and indices for internal functioning. Many people veer one direction and
indulge their emotions as the final arbiter of truth, as well as the grid
through which decisions are made. Their emotions are their barometer
for life. In contrast, others deny, avoid, or downgrade emotions as
juvenile and unnecessary. They attempt to disallow the reality and power
of emotions. Neither way of handling our emotions is helpful or mature.

To categorize some emotions as "good" and others as "bad" is
inevitable, but not particularly useful. For instance, anger is usually
considered a bad emotion, but it helps us in that it signals we have been
hurt, and that we have had a goal of ours that has been thwarted. Think
about the last time you got really ticked. What was it that you wanted to

have happen that didn't? Anger often indicates a thwarted or unfulfilled goal or desire. Likewise, anxious emotions signal to us that something we hope for is in jeopardy. You're hoping something will happen, but have no guarantee that it will. The fuel of anxiety is any form of "what if." These two words are like poison, and lead the believer off a path of trust every time. Determine now to remove them from your vocabulary. Depression is an emotion signaling to us that something is impossible. It's what we feel when we base our future success on something that can never happen. Emotions have purposes, so even the challenging ones can be seen as positive for providing us internal insight.

Just as we respond to the warning signals of physical pain, we also must learn to respond to our emotional indicators. Here is a truism worth repeating many times over: ***If it doesn't come out the right way, it will come out the wrong way.*** In other words, if we do not learn the appropriate expression of emotion, we are in jeopardy of having it seep out and contaminate other areas of our lives. The woman whose husband has expressed a desire for sexual intimacy in a certain evening, who then "accidentally" falls asleep on the couch after he didn't help with the dishes is being passive-aggressive. She was upset, and instead of expressing it to him, it came out in a passive manifestation. The person who feels wronged at work and says nothing might not realize that his irritation with his wife and kids is actually being fueled by his sense of injustice and hurt from the office rather than their performances. Be assured, God gave us our emotions, and they must be given their due. If not, they will eek out in ways palpable to others, even though you think they may be hidden down deep. Feelings will be expressed eventually. I am urging that you learn to express them appropriately; else in their press for expression, they sabotage some excellent goal or relationship you have in your life.

While I don't typically speak in overarching generalizations or stereotypes, for just a moment think with me about what most males in our society have been socialized to do with their emotions. Many men actually think they are emotionless. In general, men have been given two options when it comes to their emotions. The first is to be angry. Spiteful football play, tough guy movies, cold-hearted executive decisions all convey acceptance of the angry man. Really, when is the last time we saw a TV show or movie where a man came through the door and said, "Hey, honey, my boss hasn't given my any feedback for awhile, so I'm feeling a little insecure. Will you just hold me?" Can you envision a guy calling up a buddy and saying, "Hey, let's go play racquetball, but before we do, I just want you to know I'm not in a very good place right now. I'm kind of struggling with this whole mid-life crisis thing, and need you to remind me of some good things I've done in my life." The fact that these scenarios are so far out of the norm as to be laughable should prove to us the limited examples of emotional expression men have been given.

The second "sanctioned" emotional outlet modeled for men is to sexualize their emotions. If a man is happy, what does he want to do? Have sex. If he is lonely, what does he want? Sex. Sad? Sex. Upset? Hungry? We laugh, but it's true. If a male is disappointed, there aren't many healthy models and examples of reaching out to another for prayer, affirmation, and comfort. Instead, when laden with a strong emotion, the two options of becoming angry or sexualizing those feelings seem to come first. By sexualizing, I mean taking the emotion and channeling it through a sexual medium such as pornography, fantasy, intercourse, masturbation, etc. Doing so is an unconscious attempt to provide a pressure release valve for some emotional buildup. Because it is a counterfeit mode of expression, the effects do not last.

My recommendation for handling emotions is this: imagine them like waves. They come and they go. Our job is to ride them out. If we spend time trying to fight the waves, we become exhausted. Instead, if we simply hold on and let the emotion exist, when it has been "ridden," it then dissipates. "Riding" an emotion means neither ignoring it nor indulging it. Fighting it doesn't work. A clearer picture might be that of a pushy person who shows up at your door while you are in the middle of something very important. You're assuming it's a salesperson, but don't take the time to find out. Imagine that if you slam the door in the face of that person, he or she goes and gets someone to help. When you shut the door on the two of them, picture that they go and get a supervisor who then appears with them. They just keep pounding on the door until you open it and listen. Strong emotions can be like that when we attempt to ignore them.

The best way to handle our emotions as we imagine them knocking on our doors when we are quite busy is to let them in. However, you don't let them take over your agenda or take you completely off course. Instead, visualize letting the person in with the caveat that they are welcome to sit in the corner of an adjacent room and talk all they want, but that you will need to continue on cooking dinner as you were (or whatever example befits you.) It's the same with our emotions. They need to be let in and heard. However, they cannot take completely over, take us off course, or dominate. They need to be acknowledged as part of you, but not the central point. Following the analogy, it's easy to see how someone sitting and speaking from a corner chair would impact your functioning, but not overtake the household.

Plus, when finished, the person would then probably leave peaceably. Indeed, they might have been a pushy salesperson, but they also might have been a neighbor coming to offer something kind or valuable. You wouldn't know unless you had allowed them in.

So, the next time sadness knocks at your door, imagine an inner dialogue: "I'm not really thrilled you're here right now, but I'm not going to ignore you or pretend you're not here. Instead, I'll let you be a part of me, but you are not permitted to control me, take me out of the path I believe God wants me walking, or be used as a means for injecting a lie into me. So, I'll feel sad for awhile, and that's okay. But I will not lie down and roll over until it goes away. I'll continue on, and listen to whatever you're trying to tell me." Because your emotions are a legitimate force God has given you, you cannot fight them.

So sometimes it's good to pull back and ask yourself, for example, "Why am I going down this fantasy path in my mind? Why? What am I dealing with? What am I feeling?" Try and put it together rather than just fighting the whole thing. It never works to tell yourself, "Stop thinking that. Stop it. Stop thinking about that!" Obsessive thoughts and pervasive feelings will not exit on demand. Some counselors suggest that people take rubber bands and snap themselves every time they have the bad thought. It doesn't work to tell yourself to just stop thinking something or even to associate a physical punishment with it. Instead, I recommend learning to cry out, "Lord Jesus, you're the Light of Truth. You're the Living and Active Word. By your Word, by your Spirit, would You reveal to me what's going on here?" And He'll do that.

Dallas Willard provides an excellent maxim – "Feelings are...good servants. But they are disastrous masters."[1] Exactly.

Pondering what is happening with ourselves emotionally can deepen our relationships, draw us to God, confirm His presence, and be an impetus to help us change direction. Emotions are like dashboard light indicators. They light up when something underneath the hood is not right, and urge further exploration. "I think I want to cry. Why do I think I want to cry right now?" "Oh, I feel happy. Why? That conversation with Tyler really felt good." Feelings tell us much about our relationships, especially our closest ones. They help us see ourselves, our needs, and our sin. Sometimes they will be extremely beneficial and others not so much. Whatever the case, it remains that learning about our emotions is fundamental for our healing and future well-being.

Tolerate Me

An emotional skill that we must develop on the trek for maturity is to learn to tolerate ourselves. No, you didn't misread that statement. Consider how a wise woman will track her hormonal cycle so she can try to anticipate when those two or three days of pure irritation hit. She knows herself. She knows this is part of life. She learns to sort of put up with herself when those times come. She tolerates having to endure PMS. In much the same way, our issues will flare up in our lives as we grow. Instead of being completely shocked and dismayed when this happens ("I thought I was over this!!"), you will do much better if you learn to tolerate yourself. This involves holding on as your issues flame up. Instead of surprise, a better internal response is, "Oh, yes, this again. That's right. I'll be tempted to fall prey to this issue all my life, but it doesn't mean I haven't grown or that it controls me. I can handle this, because I know it won't stick around forever. In the meantime, I'll hold on to truth and choose to be okay with how bothersome this can be."

Sheila, for instance, knew she had multiple deficits. What she hadn't been aware of, though, was how significantly they impacted her adult life. She felt stupid and ashamed many times because whenever she had to say goodbye, or depart from significant others, she decompensated into insecurity and tears. She would cry and become mute. The Lord revealed to her that this pattern was deeply tied to the entire question of whether anyone really *wanted* her in her life. Her mother had been consumed with various boyfriends and working to make ends meet, often leaving Sheila alone for long periods of time. She would be "shipped" to her father's house for various stints. Recalling this reality, Sheila had a distinct memory of being in an airplane by herself on the way home from a visit with her dad. She was barely a young girl, alone, weeping at over 30,000 feet next to strangers. The feeling she remembers had no word to describe it. To this day, she merely calls it "umph," like her insides are falling.

In only ways our souls can do, this feeling has become associated with saying goodbye to people. Having become familiar with it over time, Sheila is not caught off guard by it any more. However, she still doesn't enjoy her reactions in those times. Describing a recent episode that provoked the "umph," she said, "Same old, same old. I know this feeling of wishing I were being given more, but being deprived. I wish things were different, but they're not." Sheila has fully come to realize present reactions have past roots. She also fully embraces how her longing for more from people today (and her disappointment that she doesn't get more) is rooted in past void. Ed Smith calls these "echoes" and speaks of us being "triggered."[2] In other words, the same emotional pain we experienced in an earlier time of wounding comes rushing back to us today whenever something about a present situation is strangely similar. The familiarity evokes the old feelings, like an echo of what was. Becoming tolerant of the fact that certain issues will flare up occasionally does not mean you are not healed. It merely validates that we have a schemer who knows our hurts and seeks to use those against us on a regular basis.

Bring Them Out

Indeed, emotions that are not expressed the right way will come out the wrong way. This begs the question of what it means to correctly express feelings. Essentially, conveying emotion maturely is to name or articulate whatever one is feeling in contexts appropriate to such expression. It is to choose to reveal what you're feeling; whether through word, deed, tears, facial expressions, touch, or writing at the time you're feeling it. The consonance of conveying an emotion *when* you are feeling it is a key to true emotional expression. While it is certainly fine to report having felt a certain way yesterday or to write a note about how you were feeling during the meeting last week, the healed and mature person will be able convey an emotion that they are feeling in the moment they are feeling it. True vulnerability is concurrence between feelings and expression.

To say, "I'm so glad we're friends" while feeling gratitude is sincere and vulnerable. Admitting, "I'm struggling a bit with my reaction to our last conversation" while feeling nervous is mature. To say the same thing with a harsh presentation is dissonant, and therefore, inauthentic. Manifesting a long face when you are discouraged is acceptable. To mask sadness with a smile is immature. Certainly, a person has to choose the environment wisely. Telling others you are angry during a bridal shower wouldn't be prudent. Sharing, "I'm hurt that you seemed more concerned about her than me in that interaction we had" in a heart-to-heart conversation is good for the soul. Inappropriate expression would be "I'm furious with you and don't think I can forgive you" while raising your voice. Conveying that you are feeling lonely when a good friend asks how you're doing is healthy.

These are just a few examples of emotional expressions – to show what it looks like for them to come out the "right way." If it were possible to give a blanket formulation of maturity with one's emotions (and it's not because it's such a complex topic), it would probably be something like "I feel _____ because _____." Examples are: "I feel sad because Drew moved away" and "I feel hurt because I wasn't invited." To say "You made me feel _____" is not accurate because another person cannot *make* us feel an emotion. They might do something that evokes a feeling in us, but we do the feeling. In addition, whenever articulating an emotion, we need to own it with "I." To speak in third person is not true expression.

As well, stating "I feel *that* _____" is not expressing an emotion, but actually a thought. "I feel that there's not enough collaboration here." The emotion is probably frustration or anger, so even though the sentence begins with "I feel," it doesn't actually include a feeling. Start being emotionally attentive and mature today by sharing at least one emotion with someone every day. If that's too big a step for you, before you go to bed at night, complete these three statements, "Right now I feel _____," "Today I felt mostly _____," "The strongest emotion I've had lately was _____." Adding such a dimension to your life is healing in that doing so acknowledges the validity and reality that you are just as much an emotional being as a physical one.

We're also going to have emotions specifically related to our previous hurts. Learning to communicate those is likewise important for us. Just like physical wounds leave scars, we'll have emotional scars, too. These usually express themselves as over-sensitivities. Some people will feel rejection coming a mile away; others will be oversensitive to perceived betrayal. Just like a person with a large scar in his or her chest might wince whenever someone tries to give him or her a big hug, so you might overreact to certain people or situations because of an emotional scar. Identifying our feelings related to past hurts, and being able to discuss these with others is critical to forward progress.

For instance, I have a propensity towards feeling insecure when I discuss my hopes for the future. As a result, I am unwise if I do not let others know when we are approaching my vulnerable area. Especially because I help other people in these areas, if I don't express my needs to my friends, they might miss them. Just recently I was sharing some seemingly innocuous information that just so happened to be vulnerable for me. I had to tell my good friends, "Hey, time out. I need to tell you that even though I might not look like this is nerve-wracking for me, I'm feeling really vulnerable right now." We have to learn who we are and be able to then get our needs met in appropriate ways. If I had just blundered forward with no expression of my true emotion, they might not have responded to me with the tenderness I actually needed. How devastated would I have been if they had uttered, "Oh, that's great. So anyhow, what did you think about the soup?" Instead, they thanked me deeply for sharing it. If I hadn't flagged them up front, they wouldn't have known it was a scar for me and might have unwittingly further injured that already tender area.

Expressing emotion appropriately to others is just one facet of healing. The other is to learn to pour out your feelings to God. It's actually surprising how few people really do talk with the Lord about their emotions. They'll tell a coworker they're ticked, a girlfriend that their spouse hurt them, or a hairdresser they're insecure. But to bring your strongest emotions to God sounds practically sacrilegious to some. Dan Allender has done fantastic work in this regard, and has brought out with clarity an enlightening truth.[3] Dwell on the Psalms for a minute, and think specifically what some of the Psalmists speak to God. If you pay attention, some of these words (mainly in the Psalms of lament) are less than flattering to God about Himself! Now think how these same expressions might be worded in today's vernacular. Whew! Think of how 20th century folk might say, "Why, Oh, Lord, do you stand far off? Why do you hide yourself in times of trouble?" (Psalm 10:1) or "How long, O Lord? Will you forget me forever? How long will you hide your face from me?" (Psalm 13:1).

Considering this, it is a stunning point made by Allender that all the Psalms were used in *worship*.[4] Slow that down and really think about that – even the Psalms of lament were songs used in worship services. What does that say about our God? Could it be that He prefers us to be up close and personal – fully human – interacting with Him even with great emotion rather than distant and "together"? God considers *worship* even when we express our frustration with Him?! Allender suggests that this is indicative of the truth that we only yell at people we really trust.[5] Think of it – our strongest emotional expressions are usually reserved for the safest people in our lives. I know there's only one human on the face of the earth I've raised my voice to – Mike. It's because he's committed his life to me, and will not leave. What does this say about the amazing nature of our confusing and terrifying and wonderful God? It just might be that He would rather have us "in His face" interacting with Him, perhaps even shouting at Him, because that's reserved for people we really trust, instead of far away, getting it all together, working it out, then becoming disciplined and doctrine-filled until we feel like we can come back feeling, "Okay, I've gotten it all together now"? Our almighty Father "gets it" that when we bring Him ourselves full force, that bespeaks and begets a deeper level of real trust.

However we receive this information, the principle is profound and pervasive in Scripture: the Lord desires intimacy and nearness with us (Psalm 51:6, Ephesians 2:13, James 4:8). Closeness is his heart for each of us ("Oh Jerusalem...how often I have longed to gather your children together, as a hen gathers her chicks under her wings" Matthew 23:37) and the heartfelt expression of emotions indicate closeness. We'll only tell true confidants our hurt feelings, insecurities, and hopes for the future. Because our Lord completely knows the plight of the small-minded human, in His unfathomable graciousness, He will take the smallest little turning we offer to Him and accept it as worship. When humankind in miniscule effort will draw near to God, He will draw near to them (James 4:7). So, when it comes to hurts, pain, joys, anger, sadness, even bitterness, are you interacting with your Father about it? Do you lay your raw self out to Jesus – is He the primary One that you're interacting with about what is in your heart and on your mind? How many of us will call a friend first before we even think to talk to the Lord about something, or worse yet, talk with myriad others without ever praying about it? Do you allow Him to be the intimate companion He so wants to be? Expressing our true emotions to the Lord is part of how we are transformed. The Psalmists model this well.

Broken and Real

Coming to God in the manner just described, in the intimacy of the Psalmists, demonstrates Psalm 51:17: "The sacrifices of God are a broken spirit; a broken and contrite heart, O God, you will not despise." The most mature and healing emotional movements we can make are when we intentionally pursue brokenness and authenticity. One of today's popular Christian songs repeats the phrase "I'm desperate for you. I'm lost without you." We would do well to allow this refrain to be in our head continually, because it is the deepest truth that we *are* desperate for God's intervention. If He does not offer another breath, we will not live another moment. If the cycle of food production that He has set up is taken away, we cannot survive. If He does not give His grace, we will self-destruct. Brokenness is realizing He is all we have.

To be broken is to die to self. Brokenness is a state of mind that recognizes who one is before God, and lives daily with this perspective. To advocate dying to self in a book about healing might be surprising to some, but the Bible is full of such counter-intuitive direction. Jesus told us if we wanted to save our life, to lose it; that only those who humble themselves will be exalted; that if you put yourself last, you'll be first; to rule, then serve; and if you want to live, then put to death the deeds of the body (Luke 9:24; Matthew 23:12; Matthew 20:16, Mark 10:44; Luke 22:26-27, Romans 8:13). The apostle Paul highlights the uncanny connection of strength coming through weakness (2 Corinthians 11:30, 12:9-10). To live out such admonitions is to move toward brokenness.

True healing cannot come without emptying oneself of the natural and insidious pride every human has. Wounded or not, every one of us has a significant regard for self – think of how we gauge every situation through the lens of how it will affect us, how well we keep ourselves fed and clothed, and how we somehow find the time to watch the shows we want. The point is that our natural bent is not towards brokenness and authenticity. We must exert our will to put ourselves in that posture intentionally, lest we be forced there. The Lord Jesus is unable to live in us completely and reveal himself through us until our proud self is broken. This means the part of us that justifies itself, wants to get its way, stands up for itself, and works for its own glory must bow to God's will, admit its total dependence, give up its own way, and agree that a complete surrender to the ways of Jesus are best. The broken person fully believes that without Him, he or she is nothing.

Such brokenness can come one of two ways – we can either pursue it on our own or be taken there, so let us make a practice to cry out from the bottom of our hearts that we are desperate for our God in every way, at every minute. When we come thirsty, we get filled. The word confirms: "If anyone is thirsty, let him come to me and drink. Whoever believes in me, as the Scripture has said, streams of living water will flow from within him" (John 7:37-38). The emptier the cup you bring, the more you can experience His filling. Without knowing the reality of our deep thirst, our pursuit of God will be disciplined at best. If reading the Bible is a matter of duty to complete a "good Christian" checklist, we may or may not sense God. When we come to God in touch with our deep thirst and need for Him, it impassions our pursuit, and in those times so often the Bible is alive, and His comfort is palpable. When we come like that, grace meets us. "Grace is not God's reward for the faithful, it's His gift for the empty and the feeble and the failing."[6]

Accepting an attitude of brokenness by being willing to die to self demonstrates full belief that "in Him we live and move and have our being" (Acts 17:28). The broken soul is a humble one who acknowledges: "I have been crucified with Christ; it is no longer I who live, but Christ lives in me" (Galatians 2:20). Has your "I" been crucified with Christ? Moving toward your brokenness, rather than trying to hide it behind masks or anesthetizing it through illegitimate means is a truly healing step. Jim Petersen says, "Healing, according to Jesus, is for those who are broken and admit it."[7]

Managing Memories

The promise of restoration to Israel in Jeremiah 30:16-17 encourages, "But all who devour you will be devoured; all your enemies will go into exile. Those who plunder you will be plundered; all who make spoil of you I will despoil. But I will restore you to health and heal your wounds,' declares the Lord." What beautiful news this is for all of us who have been hurt. Certainly, it is understood that health and healing will come to those who are seeking after the Lord, desiring to walk in His ways, and trusting Him as the only source. Sometimes as we follow the Spirit and allow Him to do His work, He will lead us to places of pain in addition to those of peace and joy.

Deep restoration comes from asking God to come to those painful places. Often, they are certain memories we have. Have you ever considered asking God to enter in to those two or three vivid scenarios from your past that are emblazoned in your memory? Your strongest recollections hold keys to when lies became implanted, vows were made, or schemes were unleashed. Some excellent research and writings have been done by Christian authors about deep healing through memory exploration in the presence of Christ.[8]

A helpful way to handle your clearest memories is to ask God to reveal His truth. Write a memory down, in as much detail as you can, or speak it out in prayer. Listen, watch, and attend to God's movement.

Think, "What Scriptures come to mind?" Ask, "What else, Lord?" and pay attention. Many times the revelation involves one of three general things: (1) solid, general truth, (2) situation-specific, intimate truth, or (3) His presence. You can be certain there is always a Scriptural truth that applies to your hurtful memory. Keep after it until you find it. For instance, "He heals the brokenhearted and binds up their wounds" (Psalm 147:3) would apply to someone whose memory involves trusting someone who hurt them. That God is a "Father to the fatherless" (Psalm 68:5) can minister healing to someone who lost a parent. General truths from Scripture offer healing to any hurtful memory.

Sometimes, though, as we bring our past events to God, He will reveal more specific truth. For the child hurt badly by a friend, the Father might provide the perspective that the offending youngster's parents were going through a divorce and he took it out on you because yours weren't. For the sexual abuse survivor, He might whisper that you are not dirty because your body responded to that inappropriate touch – it is supposed to respond. At times, even though this more situational truth might be obvious to others who don't carry the memory like you do, it does no good to hear it from anybody else. We need to hear it from our Savior before we will believe it. For instance, Tina's best friend of many years shocked her with the news that she was leaving her husband. It was a devastating blow to all who knew them, and Tina couldn't shake the feeling that there was more she could have done to prevent it. She ruminated about how she should have asked more questions, watched her friend's kids more, and prayed with her more. Others, including me, assured her (to no avail) that doing more couldn't have prevented the divorce. We went into prayer and she poured out her heart to the Lord about this event. As we sat in listening prayer, after some time she raised her head with her eyes full of tears. "He told me there was nothing I could have done! I feel peaceful now." There are specific healing truths you need to hear about something in your life that can only come from the One who knows.

Because He is indeed all-knowing, as you enter your memories in His presence, you just might have your eyes opened to how He was there with you. It has been a source of profound healing for some to picture Jesus in that bedroom, weeping next to your bed; to visualize Him there in the closet with you as you hid from your father's alcoholic rage; or to realize He was close to you as you lay on your bed, feeling the loneliness of high-school rejection. There are visions you have of past events that simply knowing God's presence in the situation would help heal. Sometimes you can even see how He sheltered you from even further hurt.

The point here is that in our healing journey, there are some marked memories that hold power over us. To enter into that recollection with the intention of dispelling a lie that became implanted at that time, to see it now for what it actually was instead of what it seemed like at the time, to ask the Lord to reveal to you where He was at the time – these are just a few ways such powerful memories can be emptied of their destruction and pain. Essentially, the Lord's truth is not removed from *any* aspect of our lives. Handling those flashbacks, those unpleasant feelings when you think about a former time in your life, and those pictures indelibly etched on your mind are possible through interacting with our living, active, involved God.

12

A Better Life

Everywhere a greater joy is preceded by a greater suffering.
ST. AUGUSTINE

He has sent me to bind up the brokenhearted, to proclaim freedom for the captives and release for the prisoners...to bestow on them a crown of beauty instead of ashes.
ISAIAH 61:1,3

As we press deeper than acceptance and *embrace* our past and present reality, wounds, and grief, and do the work of a healing journey, a new work can begin to occur. Our experience can indeed be one of God's paradoxical "beauty-for-ashes" (Isaiah 61:3) miracles. So much of His word contains paradoxical, irrational equations - life through death, strength through weakness, least as greatest, last as first, highest praise from infants, meek inheriting earth (Mark 8:35, 1 Corinthians 12:9-10, Mark 10:43-44, Matthew 21:16, Matthew 10:39, 2 Corinthians 12:20, Luke 9:48, Matthew 19:30, 18:4, 5:5). We shouldn't be surprised, then, that His plan is to relentlessly turn our hurtful woundings around. In other words, God can take our place of greatest hurt and use it to be the place of our greatest strength and effectiveness.

After a life of abuse, betrayal, and unjust treatment, Joseph said, "What Satan meant for evil, God meant for good" (Genesis 50:20). A client, Jordan, admitted this week: "What I'm going through is the most painful thing I've ever gone through, and I'm so glad it happened." Liz said it, too, just recently, "Well, if it can be used by God, then I'm glad.

Yeah, I'm okay with that." She is a sexual abuse survivor just now reckoning with her losses. Glad for sexual abuse? Can you come close yet to saying such a thing about your own hurts? If we allow God in, to have our pain, and if we believe He is for our good, we can then start to see Him use it and transform us through it.

I have consistently believed that my parents' divorce was one of the most productively shaping events of my life. No, it's not because they had an outwardly poor marriage that I would be relieved to escape. In fact, just the opposite was the case. The reason I can say with such freedom that I am glad it happened is merely because of how much I have seen God do in and through me as a result of it.

Beth Moore does an amazing job of discussing God's desire for us in this area.[1] She points to Psalm 130:7, which says, "for with the Lord is unfailing love and with Him is full redemption." Focus on the word "full" in front of "redemption." Her point is that most of us will "deal with our stuff" until just the point at which the edge is taken off our pain. She says this is not far enough; it is not full redemption. In her framework of "deal with your stuff or it will deal with you," she has rightly identified that we must go the whole way through this healing process; we can't stop when we feel a bit better.

Asking, "Am I bowing down to my past, or is it bowing down to me for the advancement of the gospel?" is where Beth takes the concept of full redemption. She says it is fully captured in Paul's words in Philippians 1:12: "Now I want you to know, brothers, that whatever has happened has really served to advance the gospel."[2] Did Paul *really* say "whatever has happened?" Do you remember even just a bit of what he endured? Betrayed, beaten, left for dead, imprisoned, shipwrecked…for the advancement of the gospel? We can either take responsibility for and deal with all that our past has wrought, or we go further and allow it to become something God can use for His glory and our good.

I'll never forget a day that, with my mother's permission, I now share. When I was 11 years old, she told me that she would be leaving dad and our family three months later. What was actually harder was that I was asked not to tell anyone. Three months to any junior high female is, in actuality, an eternity. It was awful, and my mother, who is now committed to Christ, acknowledges that as a mistake. Both she and I, however, now see in many, many ways how God has taken the pain of that situation and used it for His glory and my good. One such way in the manner of Philippians 1:12 is that I, as a counselor, now am an excellent secret keeper. I keep secrets for the glory of God. Daily, I get to help people bare their inner darkness and confidentially keep it so that they may be set free from its hold, having grown in the "dark" lo these many years. A place of deep wounding has become a place of true effectiveness and strength. Whenever I think of the damage done to souls by wounds, I am often excited to see how God will do as only He can, which is to "restore the years the locusts have eaten" (Joel 2:25).

Julie's life testifies to this reality. She and her husband have served as a foster family for 187 children over the past 22 years. They have two biological children and two adopted children, one of whom was found in a brown paper bag five days after she was born. In addition to such unconditional love and care, they've also done something unprecedented. They adopted four babies found dead and abandoned, gave them names, funerals and arranged for their burials. A secular magazine article written about them describes that they have a "strength in their vulnerability" and "a sense of mission born from reconciliation."[3] You see, when Julie was 17, she found herself pregnant and unwed. It was the 70's, and she believed the information given her that said it wasn't a baby until after the third month, so she had an abortion. Julie testifies that she hasn't been driven to "make up" for her abortion. Instead, she simply asked God to use her and in doing so, He once again took a place of deep pain and made it a force for the advancement of His perfect purposes.

How might God be fulfilling the promise in your life to restore that which has been stolen so that all things truly do work together for good (Romans 8:28)? Do you believe He can take that rejection you experienced and turn it around to a place of blessing for you? Can you see your betrayal scars as contributing to a depth of loyalty others don't know? Can He take your terribly dysfunctional upbringing and use it in your own life to make you a parent among parents? Do you have a unique message to others because of your awful sexual abuse? Are you more sensitive to outcasts because of your own experience? Do you have a "dog-sniffing-meat" instinctual discernment about people forged from previous wrongdoings? How might God use that? I imagine that because you're still reading this book, you are, but I must ask outright – *Do you embrace the thought that your past hurts, challenges, and difficulties are actually a pathway to a more intimate walk with God and a more effective life?*

One author spoke about his experience this way:

> "Although I still carry with me (and I imagine I always will) a font of sadness and worry from my childhood, I think even my connections to the hard parts of my past sustain me now, and help me understand other people's suffering better. Most of us, after all, have suffered through some bad times. The bad times can actually become useful…"[4]

Many people's children benefit from their parents' motivation to give their offspring the happy childhood they wish they'd had. Others manage money diligently, spurred on by financial ruin in their earlier days. People who have benefited from counseling become excellent counselors. Men who watched their father's unfaithfulness are dedicated spouses. These few examples illustrate how a person's past need not take him or her out of the game.

When someone is rendered ineffective, his or her goal in life tends to be to *survive.* Have you been simply surviving for most of your life? Or, are you really living? We weren't meant to just make it through life, to get by until we are with Him in Heaven. If you have accepted Christ's sacrifice, and now look to God to be the Lord over your life, there are three realities that now characterize your life: (1) it is not your own, but to be surrendered to the Father for His work, (2) there is a spiritual battle around you and your life, and (3) what He terms the "abundant life" is for you. Surrender yourself to His purposes, engage in the battle back for your heart, and strip yourself of preconceptions about what the abundant life is. Then, from that vantage point, ask yourself, "What have I been through that now or someday is going to become the thing that God uses to make me more effective in His work?" Even more to the point – how will I be a better person because of what my past has handed me?

Made for More

Envisioning people with physical handicaps is instructive for us. What is something amazing about the person who is blind? Their sense of hearing overdevelops to compensate. For the person with no hands, feet become masterful instruments. The person with one arm can do the same work as someone with two. In other words, if you've been injured in one area, it is most likely that other capabilities have gotten stronger or become more developed. The wise person begins to look for the area of strength in him or herself instead of continually bemoaning the area of injury and subsequent weakness.

My friend Sandi was lost the other day, and saw a man coming towards her. Sure, he had a cane, she noted, but because he was walking in the area, she assumed she could ask him for directions. As she did, she was mortified to realize he was blind. This man, however, proceeded to give her very clear directions on how to get where she wanted to go. In their ensuing conversation, he revealed that he is a Christian, and shared with Sandi that his blindness gives him great opportunities to share the love and provision of Christ with others. Will you allow your weakness to come forward, that others might see God's hand? Do you embrace the strengths you undoubtedly now possess because of previous harm? Is it possible you could even get excited about this picture?

What Other Choice?

Please let me tell you about Brianna. A baby sitter sexually abused her when she was young. She was incredibly sick as a child, constantly in and out of hospitals, having to handle medications, inhalers, and injections regularly. She was also legally deaf. Brianna wanted so much to be included with others, but it never seemed to happen. Her medical challenges, which meant having to juggle much responsibility as a young child, caused her to be more like an adult than an adolescent. I met her at that time, and helped her come to terms with a realistic picture of herself, why she was the way she was, and how Christ was her only answer for all that her heart desired. She accepted, grieved, battled, pressed in to Jesus, and changed to the point where she was doing well, even though her life was certainly not what she desired.

She was allowing her healing to sink deeper, and walked with a new freedom of true acceptance from her Maker. In this new state, she began dating a fine young man who eventually asked her to marry him. They did so, and soon after she was blessed with being pregnant. Her husband was then given an assignment from the military, which meant they would be apart for periods of time. The short story is that he began pursuing another lifestyle, and ended up divorcing Brianna and leaving her with a brand new baby girl.

I lost touch with Brianna for about six years, and so was pleased to have the chance to see her at a recent women's retreat at which I was speaking. She looked beautiful, and the pictures of her daughter were priceless. As we talked, she thanked me for helping lay a foundation of faith, maturity, and truth that changed her life and steadied her for whatever life threw her. I must honestly say that it is I who owe her the thanks. You see, the intervening years had shown her more of the same challenges. Brianna, at age 26, lives life with a colostomy. Complications of her many medical conditions resulted in a massive removal of her intestines. In addition, Brianna has an open wound in her backside area that doctors cannot heal. On Saturday afternoon of the retreat, I joined up with some women and asked where Brianna was. Her mother said, "She was here swimming a little while ago and just left to go horseback riding." Can you see why I feel indebted to her?

How does a young woman at age 26, who has to manage a colostomy and open wound, get to the place where she will go swimming and horseback riding?! Many twenty-something females are still fresh from adolescence, unwilling to go out in public wearing the wrong nail polish. The absolute beauty of a person who has faced tremendous adversity and embraces life as worth the living is stunning. Such strength and perspective comes only as one rises above wounds and lives a better life as a result. When I chatted with her later, I told her how amazed I was by her potency. This was not the same insecure, struggling little girl I once knew. She responded to my comments with the attitude of "What other choice do I have?" It's almost as if Brianna knows there are two distinct options for doing life post trauma – let it take you out or believe God for the best and move forward embracing the moment, the circumstance, and the challenge.

A picture of someone who clearly embraces whatever her life contains is my previous neighbor, Elizabeth. Her daughter is a dwarf, who is wheelchair-bound. Her youngest son is severely retarded and must have round-the-clock care. The home health aides are there 24 hours a day, to assure he gets fed, changed, and remains nonaggressive. She is a highly successful teacher who works with the highest risk population of dangerous students. In the midst of this, she also tries to maintain some sense of normal life for her unimpaired middle son, tries to take the family to church, and tries to hold together a marriage where her husband had "checked out" years ago from all the stress. She is clearly the glue, to any outside observer. If you would talk with her, you would be shocked at her positive, upbeat, uncomplaining nature.

Sometimes you think a life of such trials can't get any worse. One Christmas Eve, however, the family was driving south for the holidays. Elizabeth was driving the van, hauling the handicapped son, daughter, and her wheelchair, while the father and other son followed behind. When they hit a patch of black ice, father and son watched as the van spun out of control, flinging the wheelchair into Elizabeth's body. Everyone at the scene thought she was dead. Her body had been decimated by the impact of the wheelchair, and she was life-flighted to the nearest hospital.

Indeed, the damage was severe. Her pelvis was crushed, and many of her internal organs demolished. Elizabeth was in critical condition for a month, and did not return home for six months. She had to learn to walk again, in addition to having to make many other adjustments because of her extensive injuries. But, miraculously, come home she did, and I happened to be watching out the window on that first day as it took her ten minutes to walk from the car to her door. This was a previously spunky, spry woman. I wept again for that family and all that they had endured.

When we heard she was returning to work that fall, we were flabbergasted. I caught up with her a bit later, and was privileged to talk with her about her life. Her pain is constant, and on some days, unbearable. She verified something she had suspected for years; her husband was seeing other women. Her middle son had detached from her in his own protective stance, certainly from having almost lost her, and was angry with his father for the neglect he experienced while Elizabeth was in the hospital. Her husband had not been working for the majority of time she was gone from the house. I asked her the question I'm certain you have… "How do you do it? How do you even get out of bed in the morning?"

It was then I learned how deep and unyielding the faith of this woman is. Elizabeth told me that God sustains her every moment. She talks with Him constantly, and will even ask, "Are you sure?" when He leads her to do what seems impossible. She hears His answers, and obeys in faith. As an example, she told me about one instance in the hospital. Doctors told her that in addition to the many other wounds, she would lose her bladder. You can imagine the far-reaching implications of not having a bladder. Elizabeth looked at all the hospital staff and said,

"Absolutely not. In the name of Jesus, I will *not* lose my bladder. No way." She said that she knew God would do this for her, and indeed He did. When I asked about her support system, she told me forthrightly something she admittedly doesn't tell many people. "Even Christians don't want to get close to us. They're afraid they'll catch it somehow. It's as if our weirdness is just too much." Her support is the living Lord. She prays constantly, and says it is the Lord who enables her to keep going. He is her joy, her companion, her strength, and her sustainer.

There are many lessons from Elizabeth's example. Her life certainly didn't look the way she preferred it to because of all the handicapped people around her. Instead of complaining about how she was suffering due to others, she became the joy for the handicapped. She didn't let their inabilities steal her spirit. As well, very literally the outworkings of someone else's handicap about killed her. Are you letting someone else's baggage steal your joy? Are you permitting a result of someone else's hurt to decimate you? Or, are you more connected to Jesus, more committed to prayer, more diligent to pursue healing because of life's challenges? Elizabeth has just been promoted to principal, moved her family to a different home, and is taking life without her husband head-on. Will you and I apply the force of our will to faith; a faith that grabs hold of hurtful times and squeezes them until the good starts to drip out?

Larry Crabb offers a quote that captures the lessons of Elizabeth: "People who embrace their hurt are able to pursue God more passionately. And their passion is contagious. Less passionate people can *instruct* others in biblical living, but only people filled with passion can *draw* others into biblical relationships."[5] Elizabeth's life draws me to a firmer faith. Your life and mine is meant to be just like hers in that we are designed to be billboards of belief, declaring by word and deed that Almighty God is real, involved, and reigning in power. We draw others to behold His power by walking in that power in our own lives. Doing so means we resolve not to be bound in graveclothes from some hurt. It means we determine to stay on the healing journey. It means we believe we are powerful because of our position. It means we embrace all that our lives have contained as for our refinement and betterment. It means holding fast to Jesus *no matter what*.

13

You Go!

Our deepest fear is not that we are inadequate. Our deepest fear is that we are powerful beyond measure. It is our light, not our darkness, that most frightens us. We ask ourselves, "Who am I to be brilliant, gorgeous, talented and famous?" Actually, who are you not to be? You are a child of God.
NELSON MANDELA

For you died, and your life is now hidden with Christ in God.
COLOSSIANS 3:3

People who have walked with Jesus on the journey to healing are identifiable by a number of intangibles. They have an aura of quiet confidence, accept struggles as part of the journey, infuse truth into their daily lives, give abundant grace to others, invest their energies in kingdom work, and rest squarely on God's opinion of them. When encountering these saints, we wonder how they got there. Most assuredly, their journeys have involved some level of trauma, brokenness, submission, or surrender.

I have often said the three things that grow us up are marriage, having children, and trauma. Ones who exude a sense of peace and purpose have wrestled with God in their relationships, circumstances, and pain, and found Him faithful. They have retrained their eyes to focus on the spiritual as opposed to the temporal, and have chosen self-denial as a way of life. While the "feeling" we get around them is indeed intangible, if we look closely, people serious about soul healing in Christ do have some observable traits. This chapter explicates some of those characteristics. In other words, if you wonder what you might be like if you are able to ingest what this book is about, here's a general idea!

Squarely Secure

People who have overcome their struggles and found healing in Jesus are people who live in God's truth, not their own. Because they do, they *live from a foundation of security, not insecurity.* God's promises are the "anchor for their soul," so they don't need to scurry about looking for other anchors (Hebrews 6:19). If you don't stand on God's Word as the final arbiter of truth for yourself, you will live insecurely, ever wondering what others are thinking, anxiety-ridden about things out of your control, and often taking too personally what others say. If you do stand squarely on God's Word, you "get it" that you are meant for eternal purposes. You believe you are chosen by God, for God, and grasp that you are meant to impact those around you with love. Secure people aren't guarded, defensive, or performance-driven. They smile more, listen more, and give more. Why? Because their security isn't derived from any earthly formula.

Fill it Up, Pour it Out

In like manner, mature people *look to give instead of look to get.* At the outset of the book, I described how very generally people fall into one of those two categories. If you have not explored damage from your wounds and pursued healing in Christ, most likely you will be a person who is still "trying to get." Exactly what each person is searching for is different, but the very fact that they continue to grope for satisfaction, grasp for meaning, and grovel for affirmation exudes a fundamental insecurity. The "trying to get" people are the ones whose hunger drives them to spend life trying to be filled up. In each situation, with every person, they exude "fill me up," "make me less hungry," "make me feel good," "be what takes away this longing or pain," "make right what was wrong in my past." It's easy to see that usually the people spending their lives trying to get filled up are the ones who have been wounded and haven't looked at the consequences, or don't really know what the wound has done. Their empty vats, internal vows, implanted lies, and numbing practices hold them hostage, and they don't even know it.

Such people often put others in the place only God can be. It can be safely said that every dysfunctional relationship involves putting others in the place where only God can be. A book title captures this essence. It reads, *When People are Big and God is Small.*[1] The secure soul accepts that people will always disappoint. They're *people.* However, after one is able to embrace the fallibility of others, then he or she can begin to really rejoice in the beauty and tremendous uniqueness of each person. When one stops inadvertently manipulating others to mold them into some God-like figure, then true love and healing can commence.

In contrast, the restored soul seeks to give. Give what? Love, time, resources, affection, deference. To whom? God and others. Their primary life's pursuit is not to wrench happiness from those surrounding them, but instead to pour out self at the feet of Christ, who, although being God, "made himself nothing, taking the very nature of a servant" (Philippians 2:7). A person who looks to give understands that life – being alive – is a blessing, and that *we are always blessed in order to then be a blessing.* The adage that if you want to make your dreams come true, spend your life making other people's dreams come true is apropos here. Jesus was certainly clear on this point, "For whoever wants to save his life will lose it, but whoever loses his life for me will save it. What good is it for a man to gain the whole world, and yet lose his very self?" (Luke 9:24-25). The secure soul has built his or her life on this truth.

Resultantly, God is the source of their significance and affirmation, not others. If we have engaged in the healing path, we can then freely give to others because we don't look toward them to "get." We take seriously 1 John 3:16 that we "ought to lay down our lives for our brothers" and John 15:13 that "greater love has no one than this; that one lay down his life for his friends." Instead of laying down one's life, if we don't know what is going on inside us, we will often reach to others to fill us up *and* reach to God to fill us up. We gaze vertically and cry, "fill me up," and then horizontally and beg, "fill me up." This is the wrong equation. Instead, true healing happens when our perspective is an upward cry to "fill me up" and an outward perspective of "pour me out." "You, Lord Jesus, fill me up, and I'll pour it all out for others." Hands are open to receive from the Lord, and open to give to others. We understand that true filling can only come from God alone, and then obey Jesus' admonitions in 1 John 4 to love others freely and completely.

Self-centeredness versus other-centeredness is a clear indication of life in the flesh versus life in the Spirit. Crabb says:

> There is one source of energy behind every interpersonal act: either a priority interest in ourself or a priority interest in others. The mark of the Christian is a quality of love that directs more energy towards others' concerns than towards one's own well-being.[2]

He also purports, "My love for you (not yours for me) determines in large measure my experience of joy and my sense of intactness. I can love because I am loved perfectly and fully by God."[3] Healed, mature people know that only God can supply what our souls most desire, and therefore give to others without looking to get something in return.

Prideless Power

Another indication of soul healing is when one is able to *move about in power*. Such a perspective has nothing to do with pride, but instead is based solely upon the revealed word of God. Chapter one addressed this truth in detail, but it is appropriate at this juncture. We have come full circle. By opening ourselves to examination, and doing the work of healing in Christ, now we can live freely in His truths. I said in the Introduction that this is my hope – you are freed up from the schemes of evil to liberally live in the lavishness of His love. It is a powerful position.

One who lives in this powerful position takes God at His Word and believes Him rather than his or her own self-evaluation. Such people choose God over the accusatory lies Satan daily throws. One's position in Christ is what defines him or her, not outward success or failure, not financial gain or ruin, not bad or good grades, not popularity or rejection, not attractiveness or unattractiveness. Mature people keep constantly in their minds that their lives are hidden with Christ in God and that Christ is now their life (Colossians 3:3-4). They move about in security, seeking to bless, and trusting that God is working through them according to His promises in Matthew 5 and Ephesians 2:9-10. The restored soul lives life from the inside out.

Counter to this is the fundamentally insecure person who lives life from the outside in. Whereas the mature Christian holds fast to the truth within him or her instead of others' opinions or circumstantial occurrences, those who have not journeyed toward soul healing believe life happens *to* them. They feel powerless to impact situations, much less to make changes. They often blame others for failures and dissatisfaction, and are defined by externals. The practice of living life from the outside in means if things are going well, they are doing well. If things are going poorly, they feel badly. If others like them, they like them. If others don't, they don't. Such is a true picture of codependency, which is a clear indication that dependence is not on God. One who moves in the quiet confidence of being chosen by the Lord *lives life from the inside out and not the outside in.*

Keys, Please

Comparison is arguably one of the most common hellish tactics, and is a primary reason we don't experience the power we have in Christ. It happens when we take the eyes of our hearts off the goodness of God and His activity in our lives and begin to look around at what others are doing, experiencing, looking like, etc. Comparison kills. It will zap our power in seconds. You know it – think about how you feel when thoughts like "I wish I could sing like her," "Why can't I look like she does?" or "I wish I had his job" come rushing in. At that point, we'll likely forget that we're having impact in our particular life situation because God made us for His specific purposes through us. The minute we are enticed to compare ourselves with others, we are bombarded with lies.

The unhealed soul looks at what others have, what they are doing, what they are wearing, reading, eating, you name it. In other words, the culture significantly shapes his or her perspective. Because comparison causes one's focus to be external, he or she always has an eye as to who's watching. We've all talked to them in the lobby at church; they're speaking to us, but are more in tune with the person in the corner than with our conversation. Comparison in the church is especially dangerous. Instead of giving us an appreciation for our own and other people's roles in the body of Christ, the practice of evaluating gifts, talents, and blessings can generate competition and spiritual pride. Comparison of any sort is a tool of Satan and must be duly rebuked. Remind the Enemy of his defeat and remember again God has given to each one whatever material substance, social standing, physical attributes, talents, and personality traits He needs to accomplish His purposes. Who are we to question Him?

Refusing to take the comparison bait makes one wise. Second Corinthians 10:12 plainly states, "When they measure themselves by themselves and compare themselves with themselves, they are not wise." Instead of comparing, a Christian can be absolutely freed up by a "keys" understanding. The spiritually mature person ***understands that the gifts, talents, appearance, and resources one has are all simply keys God has given to open specific doors for the advancement of His purposes***. Think of a key chain. Typically there will be something like a larger key for your car, a square key for your home, a round key for your office, a key with a black protector on it for your second car, a small key for your safe deposit box, etc. Each key has a specific purpose, and cannot do what the other keys were designed to do, and vice versa. Everything that makes us uniquely us (including our past experiences) is precisely the same. Only one key can unlock the door. Only one can start the car. A handful of other keys will do no good unless they fit what is in our lives. If you had another person's gifts and talents (keys), they would do you no good, because they will not work to fulfill God's specific design for you.

There is much time lost from people pining over keys they don't have. Women especially can become channel-locked on cultural adulation of one key in particular. What comes to mind when you think of what "beauty" is in America in the twenty-first century in the particular month of the particular year at which you are reading this? It's probably some variation of the thin, blond, white-toothed, tan, long-legged model. Now think of what beauty is in Zimbabwe or Taiwan, or even what was beautiful five hundred years ago. (By those standards, I was a goddess!!) The point is that beauty is culturally bound, fleeting and only one key. Yet, countless women spend hours in self-loathing that they don't match that standard. Myriad females are suppressed, oppressed, and even depressed all because they don't happen to fit the very narrow picture of beauty in this culture at this time in history.

I'll say it again – beauty is just one key. If you are skinny and gorgeous according to the standards of our culture, great. Use it for the purposes of God. How, you say? Well, people might be more apt to talk to you or look up to you because of what you look like. Use it for kingdom furthering, just like any other gift you have. If, however, you don't happen to fit into that thin window (pun intended), find peace with your other keys, realizing that if that particular trait was necessary to complete the work God has given for you to do, *you would have it*! Every gift and experience you have is to be used for the betterment of others for the Kingdom of God. Think, what are some of your keys?

Whatever you do, though, stop wasting your time and energy fantasizing about having another person's looks, life, car, teaching ability, money, parents, spouse, blue eyes…whatever! If you can teach, you do so for the glory of God. If you can baby sit, use it for Him. If you are an accomplished athlete, lean into His purposes for your success. Are you an intellectual? Skilled at finance? Exemplary in purity? Whatever the gift, it has been given to you to serve and honor the Lord. I have jumped through enough hoops to have some initials behind my name. They are just keys, though, to open certain doors that are for my purpose on earth.

Do they define me? No. Are they *my* gifts? No. They are His, and I know full well that if I seek to use them for my own ends, He could very well strip me of them instantly.

A soul finding rest in God alone knows He is the author of our differences. Such a person appreciates not only his or her own gifts, but others as well. When you look around and see her immaculate home, thank God for giving her that gift and ask Him to help her use it for His glory. When you are taken with his public speaking ability, pray for favor that he might be a vessel of the Holy Spirit. When you behold her beauty, pray for her protection, discernment, and wisdom for how to handle all the different ways people will treat her. Her personality, his striking features, and her talents – it's all about *Him*, not them. Our heavenly Father has given each of us "everything we need for life and godliness" and ordered our steps from the beginning of time (1 Peter 1:3, Psalm 139:16). Comparison moves us away from this truth every time.

The bottom line is to rejoice in each other's uniqueness. We've got to remember that any fruit hanging off the tree of another's life came from the vine. It is the vine's responsibility to do the producing, so let's be sure to give credit where credit is due. First Corinthians 3:7 instructs, "So neither he who plants nor he who waters is anything, but only God, who makes things grow." Appreciating differences and refusing to compare are marks of a mature, strong Christian. With such a perspective, we can experience deep oneness, which is heartening.

When we have the unity of the church in Acts, we'll have the power of the church in Acts. Comparison compromises such unity. It's like trying to tune and adjust piano keys to one another. Nothing will ever be in tune. Instead, if you tune them all to the same tuning fork, they will automatically be in tune with each other. Let's vehemently refuse to measure ourselves with each other, and instead spend our time getting in perfect tune with our Maker.

Comparison also leads to the danger of distinguishing between small and big assignments from God. In other words, we think Billy Graham's latest crusade is more important than inviting your neighbor to church or that singing in the choir on Sunday is more important than sacrificially taxiing your children to their activities. These formulations are worldly, not Biblical. It's precarious ground to distinguish between what we think are big and small assignments from God. If God has moved in you to pray for someone, to take a meal to a friend, or care for someone sick, embrace it wholeheartedly as part of His amazing plan for using you. It might not be preaching for thousands, but it's equally important.

The Green, Green Grass

In chapter nine, a spiritual practice to promote healing was described that also characterizes the life of a restored person. It is the ability to *focus on what is versus what is not*. An immature person concentrates on other's shortcomings, is never satisfied, and constantly zeroes in on imperfections. As opposed to the healed soul, he or she is often tired, grumpy, and blames others or even hormones. Conversely, a mature believer practices dwelling on Philippians 4:8, has learned to be content (Philippians 4:11, 12), and cultivates thankfulness. Focusing on what is good, perfect, lovely, beautiful, and blessed in our lives is a skill that comes when we find rest in God alone, and live above the damage intended us through all of life's blows.

It's challenging, however, in a world where advertisers spend massive amounts of money trying to get us to be discontent by focusing on what is wrong with us and others, and to convince us of how we should be different. From breath mint to beer commercials, the message is simple – who you are and what you are doing would be better *if...* you used this mint, drank this beer, whitened your awful yellow teeth, lost that terrible midriff, or colored that heinous gray. It's ingrained in us to search for flaws and ways to fix them. Focusing on what is not perfect may seem more natural to us, but we must train ourselves otherwise if we want to stay walking in the truth of God's peace and promise.

I had an opportunity to practice this myself. When we first moved up north after living in San Antonio for years, our dog had some adjusting to do, just like us. Champ was a 90-pound outdoor dog that had roamed freely in our gated yard all of his life. Winter weather and fenceless yards precluded such an arrangement in our new life, which did not bode well for the off-white carpet in our family room. At the time, the two other boys in our house were 2 ½ and nine months old. We were all getting adjusted to fighting cabin fever, as winter brought many challenges we hadn't faced before.

One day, Champ was whining and pacing, but so were the boys. It was naptime, juice cups needed filled, and crankiness was in full swing. I kept thinking I would get to Champ as soon as I got the boys down. Well, although he tried to warn me, Champ couldn't hold his potty needs at bay any longer, and had an accident on our off-white carpet. A large accident. I guess large dogs being patient for large amounts of time yield large and messy feces. Not to mention smelly. So, I picked up the phone and began to dial. No, not animal control or the carpeting store, but my angelic husband. Why did I call Mike, you ask? He was the one who originally wanted Champ; so I had made a deal with him that I would never, ever, under any occasion have to clean up the dog's excrement. He shook on it, and was completely faithful to his promise...until he was at his new job trying to make a good impression on his new boss and learn all his new responsibilities.

The high fever pitch of the children had only worsened; so I left the mess behind, still steaming, and ushered them upstairs. As I sat rocking my adorable baby, my mind was racing. "I can't believe it. The carpet will be ruined. I can smell it even up here. I think I'm going to gag. No, I'm going to throw up. I can't stand it. This putrid aroma will never leave the house." And on and on. Then, in only the gracious and kind way our Heavenly Father does, He figuratively tapped me on the shoulder and whispered in my ear. "Tammy, there will always be dung of some sort in life. You are missing out on the beautiful thing I have placed in your hands, right before your eyes, and instead allowing your mind to focus on what stinks." Obsessing in my mind over the problem at hand kept me from fully enjoying and embracing the healthy, amazing, gorgeous baby gazing at me. How often do we fail to notice something beautiful that we have in our hands or directly in front of our face because our minds are focusing on some troublesome, messy, or imperfect thing elsewhere? Focusing on what is instead of what isn't will characterize the life of all who pursue God's will for their thought life. (Oh, and Mike came home and cleaned up the mess. My eldest son assured me you would want to know this.)

In for the Long Haul

Another identifiable characteristic of a person who has trodden the painful and wonderful path to healing is *perseverance*. Such a person keeps the big picture, understands delayed gratification, and has trained him or herself to read the Word of God and pray consistently. A person who has not explored inner healing is often impatient, easily discouraged, lacking in discipline, and greatly feelings based. Such people always want immediate results, which attests to their shallow awareness of problem solving. The person experiencing God's restoration understands that life is both long and short, the passage of time permits for mature thinking, and problems will come and they will go. In effect, they have a *"long haul" perspective, which understands that victory is in the small steps.*

Dialed In

A peaceful person almost always has the characteristic of *listening for God's voice above the voices of other humans.* Often, it's because of a bittersweet formula: other's voices have hurt me; God's voice has healed me. The result, however, is someone who is a joy to be around because he or she is not always striving for attention, looking to dazzle others with their scintillating conversation, or relying entirely on other's opinions for getting through life. This person understands that God is always speaking, just like radio waves are constantly being sent through the air, but that we only discover what God is saying when we are "dialed in" to Him. When faced with a decision or situation that requires direction, the person seeking healing to the core concentrates on God's voice through His Word and leading of His Holy Spirit in prayer. When you need help, do you seek until you find God's channel?

Intentionally Involved

In chapter ten, being connected to other Christians is described as indispensable for authentic healing. Obviously, then, the life of a spiritually mature person will reflect the value that *being intentionally involved with others is vital to one's spiritual and emotional health.* In contrast, an indication that we are still living out of our wounds is that we isolate and withdraw from others. The wounded person lives self-protectively, is inauthentic, and closed with others. The healed person does not give up on people, confesses needs and sins to others, weeps with those who weep, and rejoices with those who rejoice (Hebrews 10:24-25, James 5:16, Romans 12:15).

What Speck?

A restored heart will reflect the heart of God by ***refusing to judge others, but instead offering deep, healing grace for them***. God's Word is forthright on this. Matthew 7:1 says, "Do not judge, or you too will be judged. For in the same way you judge others, you will be judged, and with the measure you use, it will be measured you." Maturity in Christ involves the ability to see your sin, at any given moment, and as a result to grasp the immense forgiveness of God. One who is aware of his or her own humanity is not appalled when the senior pastor speaks unkindly, a long-time Christian friend curses when a cement block falls on her foot, or a brother in a Bible study admits to viewing online pornography. He or she realizes there is not one without sin. Everyone is a sinner. So, when it "pops out" for us to see, we stand not in judgment, but prayer and partnership in the gospel, spurring one another on towards love and good deeds (Hebrews 10:25). We should be no more shocked or dismayed when a Bible study teacher commits an indiscretion than we are over our own ugly, hidden thought toward our spouse.

Do you honestly think there is one individual walking this earth who doesn't have at least one "issue?" I'm sure your answer is "no," but why then are you surprised when a sinner saved by grace sins? One of the benefits of my job is that I have counseled a wide spectrum of people, including doctors, lawyers, accountants, pastors, pastor's wives, corporate executives, and Lexus-driving Christians. I only mention these categories because our culture can tend to elevate such folks. There simply is no one who doesn't have a "thing" or two. Because of having been exposed to such a wide range of people and their tightly held struggles, I'm never surprised when their "thing" appears. In fact, more of an "I wondered when it would show itself" posture is actually helpful. Everyone's "thing" comes forward sooner or later. So, you need not be surprised when the CEO goes to the Emergency Room with a panic attack, the pastor becomes jealous of a well-liked elder, or the lawyer starts crying when startled. A person who is honest with his or her own issues before the Lord realizes that everyone has their "stuff" and has nothing but grace when it appears.

One reason for extending such healing acceptance is because we never know another's whole story. By beholding them in the present, we have no idea what they've been through in the past. We usually don't know if a person has been near death or never been sick a day in their life. We can't see how it was in their home growing up. We don't know what obstacles they've already overcome, what hidden talents they possess, or what they have to deal with in their home life on a regular basis. Someone may be eloquent in poetry though bumble through live conversation. A stroke victim may have a quicker mind than yours, though they have a cane, slow speech, and a slurred face. When we make judgments on what we perceive, it is an erroneous thing to do. The amount of information we have on a person is in actuality quite limited, considering the vast number of thoughts, interactions, and experiences a person can have even in a given day. The mature believer staunchly refuses to judge, and is committed to looking at a person's heart instead of their physical, behavioral, or personality presentation.

Not only does such a perspective free you up from the idea that certain others are "better" Christians, it also helps expose the lie that "you're the only one." In other words, how many times do Christians bear silent pain, battle inward shame, or feel intense loneliness because they believe they are the only one who has struggles to the degree they do? "If anyone ever knew how much I drink, or struggle with body image, or lust…they'd never want to be around me." Instead, if we understand that all Christians have sinned and will fight the flesh until we see Jesus face to face, then we are freed from the lie that we alone have issues. We're not the only ones to cry for deliverance and relief. Instead of giving Satan all sorts of room to romp on your soul, imprison you, and cause you shame, the knowledge that this side of heaven believers are flesh and righteous side by side can bring liberty and reprieve (see Romans 7). A Christian, some have said, can be described as God and garbage in a bag. However the conceptualization, grabbing hold of grace for self and others permits us to enter deeper regions of healing.

Big or Little?

The life of a person who has committed to the process of soul healing will indeed be distinguished from others in a number of indefinable yet discernable ways. Some of the ones mentioned here are that they will live from a foundation of security, not insecurity; look to give instead of looking to get; move about in power; live life from the inside out instead of the outside in; understand that the gifts, talents, appearance, resources one has are all simply keys God has given for His specific purposes; focus on what *is* versus what *is not*; persevere through a "long haul" perspective, which understands that victory is in the small steps; listen for God's voice above the voices of other humans; live the value that being intentionally involved with others is vital to one's spiritual and emotional health; and refuse to judge others, but instead offer deep, healing grace for them. While this list of characteristics is by no means exhaustive, crossing the threshold from being defeated to overcoming will definitely involve what I like to refer to as being the big person instead of the little person.

Said differently, a bottom-line question we can ask ourselves about our stance, attitude, and behavior at any given time is, "Am I being the big girl or the little girl?" or "Am I being the big boy or the little boy?" I'm sure you catch the sentiment, but being the big person involves such things as giving grace, refusing to personalize, believing the best about another, choosing to listen more than speak, being nondefensive, etc. When we are the little girl or boy, we want to argue our point, defend our actions, demand our way, speak until we are heard, and react over small details. The point is that choices we make have distinct consequences.

The idea of being the big boy or big girl is that we behave in the manner called for by the situation, relationship and context, rather than react according to our feelings. For instance, if I feel desperate for so-and-so to call me, I step back and think that she might need a phone call from me. Or if I find myself obsessing about why so-and-so didn't engage me personally at our small group, I'll check in with him next time I see him at church. Being a little girl when a friend passes you by without greeting in the lobby would go something like this: "I can't believe she ignored me. What did I do to deserve that? Is she mad at me? Is she upset that I didn't call her yesterday? What was her problem, anyway?" Being the big girl in that situation would sound more like, "Wow. That's really unusual that she didn't say 'hi' to me. I wonder if everything's okay with her. She might have had a bad morning, or maybe isn't even feeling well. Lord, I pray for my friend…"

I have a friend with whom I share leadership responsibilities for a large event. As such, it requires excellent communication and sometimes involves difficult decisions. Sometimes when faced with a larger issue, she will remind us that this is the time to "put on our big girl panties and deal with it." It's a great perspective with which to question ourselves. At any given time, we can ask, "Am I having the demands, expectations, or desires of the thirty, forty, or fifty-something person I am, or those of a self-concerned, limited-perspective child?" Moving from immaturity to maturity, spiritual failure to godliness, weakness to strength, self-centeredness to God-centeredness will most certainly involve choosing to be the big boy or girl time and again.

Victory is in the Process

The final hurdle in anyone's journey of healing is to have the correct and healthy picture of what "victory" is. As much as we might deny it, many times our hope is the absence of some challenge in our life or the complete nonexistence of a previous problem we had. We unconsciously think, "I'm going to get to a place where I have it all together" and imagine ourselves in some sinless state. While that is an exciting picture to think about, it is not a realistic goal (this side of Heaven), nor is it a good conception of victory. Victory is actually in the small steps. It is knowing that while the scars from our wounds won't ever entirely go away, we are less bound by them today than we were yesterday.

God was gracious to show me this when I was perusing my old journals awhile back. I was growing increasingly disheartened when, much to my chagrin, I realized that my journals from five and ten years ago contained the same struggles as my present-day ones. I began to wonder if all my work had changed me at all. Then God corrected my perspective to remind me that sanctification is His work and only His. I don't produce change by my effort. Growth comes only as we abide in Christ (John 15:4,5). Then, I continued reading those journals, and had eyes to see something different. Yes, while the *content* of my struggles is similar to years ago, the outcome is drastically different. What used to take me months to work through now takes me hours. What used to take me down and out for a week now disturbs me for a just a few minutes. Lies previously wreaking havoc are now identified and rejected. I could see how anxious ruminating had turned to prayerful petition, and emotional turmoil was now an opportunity to pour myself out to the Lord. The way in which God has changed me does not result in the absence of my issues, but in the meager-to-no impact they have to pull me off course in my communion with Christ.

Running to Jesus within two hours of feeling insecure instead of two weeks is victory. Catching your anger coming before you explode is victory. Sensing rousing anxiety as you head to a party and girding yourself with truth and faith is victory. Viewing pornography five times this year instead of the 55 times last year is victory. Celia's perspective on true victory needed this adjustment. She would become combative with her new husband when she was hurt. As she pressed into God's perspective and truth in her situation, she realized that she needed to stay in the realistic hurt she felt instead of rush to anger. Shortly after coming to this realization, they had a typical argument about something that hurt her feelings. She did not yell, lecture, or shame her husband, as was usually the case, but instead remained quiet. She even felt physically exhausted after the conversation from holding all her anger at bay and refusing to engage it. However, when we processed it, she expressed disappointment in herself because she didn't openly convey her hurt to her husband. In actuality, much ground had been gained by the excellent progress of holding her tongue, and being able to actually stay hurt instead of mask it with fury. Her faulty picture of victory was quick and immediate perfection in handling the situation. She thought, "Now that I know what to do, that is what I need to do from now on, and every time afterward."

Change Takes Time

If we do not celebrate the small steps, and recognize gradations of change, we will be putty in evil's hands, which so wants to tell us we'll never change, nothing is working to make a difference, God isn't coming through for us, and we might as well give up because we're just not making it. No one is transformed overnight unless he or she receives a direct, overturning, reversal from an encounter with Christ (like Saul in Acts 9). When we even start *catching* our thinking per 2 Corinthians 10:5 instruction to make every thought obedient to Christ, that is progress, even if our actions don't immediately change. Most true change is in the little modifications to behavior or adjustments in thinking. As a matter of fact, I tell my clients that true change only comes through two steps forward, one step back, five steps forward, two steps back, and so on. I don't trust it when someone's growth pattern is two steps forward, one step forward, three steps forward. That change doesn't stick. The problem is that hell wants us to believe a very specific lie when we take the backward step. It is that we are right back to square one, and nothing has done any good. That's simply not true. Growth that we have to fight for over time will take hold.

Noticing and celebrating small changes is necessary to combat our culture of immediacy. Being inundated with fast foods, instant messaging, instant lottery, thirty-second pregnancy tests, microwave dinners, and convenience stores has affected us. We become so quickly discouraged when something takes time, not realizing that long-term growth comes from the application of one's will to an issue consistently over time. It happens when we come, day in and day out, time and again, over and over to our Jesus, whose primary call is just that – to *come*. He says if anyone is thirsty – come, if anyone is burdened – come, if anyone is weary – come, if anyone can hear – come, and if anyone is hungry – come (John 7:37, Isaiah 55:1, Matthew 11:28, Revelation 22:17, Psalm 107:9, Revelation 7:16; 21:6). As has been said many times in a variety of ways throughout this work, if you are serious about becoming a more whole, mature, strong, healed person, it will not happen without a wholehearted commitment to making your lifestyle one of turning to Jesus.

If I could offer a practical equation for how to keep coming to Christ in hopes of transformation to His will and way, it would be: consistent engagement over time equals dependence, freedom, peace, purpose and maturity. "Consistency over time" is a phrase worth repeating over and over to yourself when you are zeroing in on some of your unhealthy ways. I liken it to dropping a nickel in a huge aluminum garbage can. Any time you identify a lie, read a verse, try on a new behavior, renounce a vow, forgive someone, grieve a hurt, reach out to someone new, it's like dropping a nickel in that can. It will frankly seem like nothing, and kind of jangle around noisily. Envision peering over it thinking, "Well, now, that's just hardly anything." However, if you just consistently keep dropping those nickels in there, focusing on continuing to do what God is prompting you, before you know it, you'll actually have quite an investment!

So, while the small thing you do or think differently about today may not seem like much, keep going. Focus on the next nickel. "What does God have for me now? Okay, I'll draw that boundary, choose that truth, drop that mask, pray instead of fret, choose to be thankful, tell evil to flee, stay in today…" Eventually, it won't be long until you wake up and realize you're not depressed, bitter, angry, isolated, anxious, or fraught with insecurity anymore. What mercy!!

Stay the Course

Since you have finished this book, it is clear you are committed to growing. You are on the right path, so *stay the course*!! Feelings will come and they will go. Some days you will seem quite healed and others you will wonder if your "stuff" will ever go away. No matter. You want to be wholly the Lord's, freed up from bondage to anything that encumbers His way in you, and He *will* honor this. This is the path to life – staying on the road to freedom, clarity, and just plain wide-open living no matter what befalls you. Being thankful in and for all things. Turning quickly to Jesus. Supping daily on His Word. Walking in freedom. Holding fast to peace. Such choices over time are like yeast, which works through the whole batch. All that your life has contained can make you stronger, even the darkest times. All aspects of your personality can be used in Kingdom work. All of your effort will pay off. Any smidge of drawing near to Him will be met with His presence (James 4:7). I will stand united with you in faith, hope, and belief in these truths. God bless you.

"The one who calls you is faithful, and He will do it" (1 Thessalonians 5:24).

"To Him who is able to keep you from falling and
to present you before his glorious presence without fault and
with great joy – to the only God our Savior be glory, majesty, power
and authority, through Jesus Christ our Lord, before all ages,
now and forevermore! Amen." Jude 24

NOTES

Chapter 1
1. David Silver, *The Meaning of Shalom*. Retrieved July 1, 2005, from http://www.therefinersfire.org/meaning_of_shalom.htm
2. DiAnna Paulk, *Yahweh, Part II*. (2002). Retrieved July 1, 2005, from http://www.path-light.com/IAM08.htm
3. Donald Miller, *Blue Like Jazz*. (Nashville: Thomas Nelson, 2003), p. 146.
4. Charles Spurgeon, *Morning and Evening*. (New Jersey: Hendrickson, 1991), p. 460.
5. The General Assembly of the Presbyterian Church, *The Book of Confessions*. (New York: The Office of the General Assembly), 7.001.
6. Rick Warren, *Purpose Driven Life*. (Grand Rapids: Zondervan, 2002).

Chapter 2
1. John Eldredge, *Waking the Dead*. (Nashville: Thomas Nelson, 2003).
2. The stronghold discussion and "out of joint" discussion preceding it were informed by Eldredge's *Waking the Dead*.
3. Eugene Peterson, *The Message*. (Colorado Springs: Navpress, 2002).
4. Beth Moore, "The Divine Healing of Full Redemption," plenary session at the 2003 American Association for Christian Counselors World Conference: Nashville: TN
5. Ibid.
6. Erwin McManus, *Seizing Your Divine Moment*. (Nashville: Thomas Nelson, 2002), p. 9.
7. Ibid., p. 15.

Chapter 3
1. *Random House Webster's College Dictionary*. (New York: Random House, 1997), p. 672.
2. John Townsend, *Hiding From Love*. (Colorado Springs: Navpress, 1991), p. 151.

3. Editors of Baby Center. (2006, January). Developmental Milestone: Separation and Independence. *Baby Center.* Retrieved February 13, 2006, from http://www.babycenter.com/refcap/baby/babydevelopment/6577.html.
4. John Townsend, *Hiding From Love.* (Colorado Springs: Navpress, 1991), p. 64-65.
5. Ibid.; Tim Clinton & Gary Sibcy, *Attachments* (Brentwood, TN: Integrity Publishers, 2002); John Bowlby, The influence of early environment in the development of neuroses and neurotic character. *International Journal of Psychoanalysis*, 21:1-25; M. Ainsworth, M.D. Blehar, E Waters, & S. Wall, *Patterns of Attachment.* (Hillsdale, NJ: Erlbaum).
6. John & Stasi Eldredge, *Captivating.* (Nashville: Nelson Books, 2005), p. 10.
7. Tim Clinton & Gary Sibcy, *Attachments.* (Brentwood, TN: Integrity Publishers, 2002), p. 36.
8. Ibid.
9. John Townsend, *Hiding From Love.* (Colorado Springs: Navpress, 1991), p. 71.
10. Tim Clinton & Gary Sibcy, *Attachments.* (Brentwood, TN: Integrity Publishers, 2002), p. 5.
11. Reda W. Bassali & John Benjamin, *Failure to Thrive.* Retrieved February 13, 2006, from www.emedicine.com/PED/topic738.htm.
12. John Townsend, *Hiding From Love.* (Colorado Springs: Navpress, 1991), p. 66.
13. Child Development Institute, *Stages of Social-Emotional Development in Children and Teenagers.* Retrieved February 13, 2006, from www.childdevelopment.info.com/development/erickson.shtml.
14. Tim Clinton & Gary Sibcy, *Attachments.* (Brentwood, TN: Integrity Publishers, 2002), p. 37.
15. Ibid., pp. 15-16.
16. Anne Lamott, *Traveling Mercies.* (New York: Pantheon Books, 1999), p. 222.
17. John & Stasi Eldredge, *Captivating.* (Nashville: Nelson Books, 2005), p. 153.
18. Ibid., p. 75.
19. Ibid., p. 10.
20. Anne Lamott, *Traveling Mercies.* (New York: Pantheon Books, 1999), p. 223.

298

Chapter 4
1. Tim Clinton & Gary Sibcy, *Attachments*. (Brentwood, TN: Integrity Publishers, 2002), p. 111.
2. Basal van der Kolk, "The Compulsion to Repeat the Trauma: Re-enactment, revictimization, and Masochism," *Psychiatric Clinics of North America*, 12 (1989), pp. 389-411.
3. Tim Clinton & Gary Sibcy, *Attachments*. (Brentwood, TN: Integrity Publishers, 2002), p. 58.
4. John & Stasi Eldredge, *Captivating*. (Nashville: Nelson Books, 2005), p. 73.

Chapter 5
1. Dallas Willard, *The Divine Conspiracy*. (San Francisco: Harper, 1998), p. 38
2. Dallas Willard, *Divine Conspiracy*. (San Francisco: Harper, 1998).
3. Tim Clinton & Gary Sibcy, *Attachments*. (Brentwood, TN: Integrity Publishers, 2002), p. 150.
4. Larry Crabb, *Inside Out*. (Colorado Springs: Navpress, 1988), p. 18.
5. Stephen Neill, *The Difference in Being a Christian*. (New York: Association Press, 1955), pp. 6, 11.
6. Larry Crabb, *Inside Out*. (Colorado Springs: Navpress, 1988), pp. 104-105.

Chapter 6
1. *Grief*. Retrieved October 13, 2005, from www.wordreference.com and www.Brainydictionary.com.
2. Wikipedia: The Free Encyclopedia, *Grief*. Retrieved October 3, 2005, from www.en.wikipedia.org/wiki/Grief.
3. James Pennebaker, *Opening Up*. (New York: The Guilford Press, 1990).
4. John Townsend, *Hiding From Love*. (Colorado Springs: Navpress, 1991), p. 195.
5. Frank B. Minirth & Paul D. Meier, *Happiness is a Choice*. (Grand Rapids: Baker Book House, 1978), p. 38.
6. Anne Lamott, *Traveling Mercies*. (New York: Pantheon Books, 1999), pp. 226-227.
7. Edward M. Hallowell, *Connect*. (New York: Pantheon Books, 1999), p. 29.
8. Larry Crabb, *Inside Out*. (Colorado Springs: Navpress, 1988), p. 82.

9. John & Stasi Eldredge, *Captivating*. (Nashville: Nelson Books, 2005), p. 102.
10. Ibid.
11. Anne Lamott, *Traveling Mercies*. (New York: Pantheon Books, 1999), pp. 70-73.
12. TLC group, *Beware the 5 Stages of "Grief."* Retrieved November 5, 2005, from www.counselingforloss.com/article 8.htm.
13. Larry Crabb, *Inside Out*. (Colorado Springs: Navpress, 1988), p. 13.
14. Ibid., p. 81.
15. Ibid., p. 86.

Chapter 7
1. *Miriam Webster Dictionary*. Retrieved October 2, 2005, from www.m-w.com/cgi-bin/dictionary?book=Dictionary&va=vow.
2. John & Stasi Eldredge, *Captivating*. (Nashville: Nelson Books, 2005), p. 75.
3. Ibid., p. 70.
4. Ibid.
5. Chuck Swindoll, *Dropping Your Guard*. (Waco: Word Books, 1983), preface.
6. John & Stasi Eldredge, *Captivating*. (Nashville: Nelson Books, 2005), p. 57.
7. Ernest Becker, *The Denial of Death*. (New York: Free Press, 1973), p. 284.
8. Larry Crabb, *Inside Out*. (Colorado Springs: Navpress, 1988), p. 82.
9. Ibid., p. 54.
10. St. Augustin, *The Confessions of St. Augustin*. Translated and Annotated by J. G. Pilkington, M. A., Vicar of St. Mark's, West Hackney; and sometime clerical secretary of the Bishop of London's Fund. Confessions i. 1. Retrieved February 15, 2006 from, www.cce.org/fathers2/NPNF1-01/npnf1-01-07.htm.
11. C.S. Lewis, *God in the Dock: Essays on Theology and Ethics*, Ed., Walter Hooper. (Grand Rapids: Eerdmans, 1970).
12. John Eldredge, *Waking the Dead*. (Nashville: Nelson Books, 2003), pp. 129-130.
13. John Townsend, *Hiding From Love*. (Colorado Springs: Navpress, 1991).

Chapter 8
1. Dallas Willard, *Divine Conspiracy*. (San Francisco: Harper, 1998), p. 80.
2. John Eldredge, *Waking the Dead*. (Nashville: Nelson Books, 2003).
3. John Eldredge, *Waking the Dead*. (Nashville: Nelson Books, 2003), p. 154.
4. Larry Crabb, Inside Out. (Colorado Springs: Navpress, 1988), p. 222.
5. Dallas Willard, *Divine Conspiracy*. (San Francisco: Harper, 1998), p. 297.
6. Robert Enright, *Forgiveness is a Choice*; Lewis Smedes, *The Art of Forgiving*; Everett Worthington, *Forgiving and Reconciling: Bridges to Wholeness and Hope*; Charles Stanley, *The Gift of Forgiveness*; Ken Sande, *The Peacemaker: A Biblical Guide to Resolving Personal Conflict*; Joyce Meyer, *The Power of Forgiveness: Keep Your Heart Free*.
7. John & Stasi Eldredge, *Captivating*. (Nashville: Nelson Books, 2005), p. 103. (They reference an uncited quotation from Neil Anderson, who has done excellent work on the topic of forgiveness.)
8. Tim Clinton & Gary Sibcy, *Attachments*. (Brentwood, TN: Integrity Publishers, 2002), p. 279.
9. Viktor Frankl, *Man's Search for Meaning*. (Boston: Beacon Press, 1963).
10. Dallas Willard, *Divine Conspiracy*. (San Francisco: Harper, 1998), p. 323.
11. Tim Clinton & Gary Sibcy, *Attachments*. (Brentwood, TN: Integrity Publishers, 2002).

Chapter 9
1. Larry Crabb, *Inside Out*. (Colorado Springs: Navpress, 1988).
2. Dallas Willard, *Divine Conspiracy*. (San Francisco: Harper, 1998), p. 341.
3. John Eldredge, *Waking the Dead*. (Nashville: Nelson Books, 2003), p. 152.
4. Ibid., p. 151.
5. Ibid., p. 172.
6. John & Stasi Eldredge, *Captivating*. (Nashville: Nelson Books, 2005), p. 154. (They reference an uncited quotation from A. W. Tozer's *Renewed Day by Day: A Daily Devotional*.)

7. Dallas Willard, *The Divine Conspiracy*. (San Francisco: Harper, 1998).

Chapter 10

1. Diane Langberg, *On the Threshold of Hope*. (Wheaton: Tyndale House Publishers, 1999).
2. Ibid., p. 126.
3. Frank B. Minirth & Paul D. Meier, *Happiness is a Choice*. (Grand Rapids: Baker Book House, 1978), p. 53. (Harry Stack Sullivan)
4. Edward M. Hallowell, *Connect*. (New York: Pantheon Books, 1999).
5. Larry Crabb, *The Safest Place on Earth*. (W Publishing Group, 1999), pp. 19-20.
6. Dietrich Bonhoeffer, *Life Together: The Classic Exploration of Faith in Community*. (San Francisco: Harper, 1978), chapter entitled "Community." Dallas Willard, *Divine Conspiracy*. (San Francisco: Harper, 1998).

Chapter 11

1. Tim Clinton & Gary Sibcy, *Attachments*. (Brentwood, TN: Integrity Publishers, 2002), p. 179, referencing Dallas Willard, *The Spirit of the Disciplines: Understanding How God Changes Lives*. (San Francisco: Harper & Row, 1980).
2. Ed Smith, *Healing Life's Deepest Hurts*. (Ann Arbor: Vine Books & Campbellsville: New Creation, 2002).
3. Dan Allender & Tremper Longman III, *Cry of the Soul*. (Colorado Springs: Navpress, 1999).
4. Dan Allender, "Psalms and Emotions," session given at an American Association of Christian Counselors Regional Conference.
5. Ibid.
6. Roy Hession, *The Calvary Road*. (Fort Washington, PA: CLC Publications). Also retrieved from www.worldinvisible.com/library/hession/calvary/%20road/chapter%204.htm.
7. Jim Petersen, *Lifestyle Discipleship*. (Colorado Springs: Navpress, 1993), p. 24.
8. John Eldredge, *Waking the Dead*; Ed Smith, *Healing Life's Deepest Hurts* and Theophostic trainings materials; Charles Kraft, *Deep Wounds, Deep Healing*; Terry Wardle, *Healing Care, Healing Prayer*

Chapter 12
1. Beth Moore, "The Divine Healing of Full Redemption," plenary
   session at the 2003 American Association for Christian
   Counselors World Conference: Nashville: TN
2. Ibid.
3. Cynthia Leal Massey, "What Happened to Misty Dawn?" *Scene in
   SA Monthly*, 2005, 6 (9), pp. 50-54.
4. Edward M. Hallowell, *Connect*. (New York: Pantheon Books,
   1999), p. 35.
5. Larry Crabb, *Inside Out*. (Colorado Springs: Navpress, 1988), p.
   103.

Chapter 13
1. Edward T. Welch, *When People are Big and God is Small*.
   (Philipsburg, NJ: P & R Publishing, 1997).
2. Larry Crabb, *Inside Out*. (Colorado Springs: Navpress, 1988), p.
   98.
3. Ibid., p. 188.

Once you start *living beyond the pain of your past…*
…you can begin *relating beyond the surface!*

ORDER FORM

Name: _____

Address: _____

City: _____ State: _____ Zip: _____

Phone: _____ Email: _____

Please include check or money order for $11.99 for each book ordered, and mail to:

Threshold
1115 Bethel Road, Suite 204
Columbus, OH 43220
For more information, check out: www.onthethreshold.org